3'

365 WAYS
TO COOK PASTA

365 WAYS
TO COOK
PASTA

JACQUES HARVEY
With the collaboration of Alfredo
of the world-famous restaurant
Alfredo l'Originale of Rome
Recipes translated by Rose G. Formiconi
Illustrations by Bill Goldsmith

1974
DOUBLEDAY & COMPANY, INC.
GARDEN CITY, NEW YORK

I would like to express my appreciation to Alitalia Airlines, who gave me such fine service in Italy as well as delicious pasta dishes for my meals, thus making my recipe collecting that much more pleasurable.

ISBN: 0-385-07079-9
Library of Congress Catalog Card Number 72–89314

To my mother-in-law with love

Contents

365 WAYS
TO COOK PASTA

Introduction

To gather all the recipes existing in Italy to write an "anthology" of Italian pasta is anything but a simple task, without comparing it to the labors of Hercules. The reason for this is that little more than a century ago Italy was still divided into independent states governed by kings and princes who were more concerned with fighting each other than exchanging their culinary specialities. Today these states comprise the regions of Italy and still cherish their own recipes.

Because of these regional variations I had to hunt for authentic recipes in their native habitats. During my long sojourn in Italy I learned many things about pasta, some of which I am happy to share with you here. If you are particularly anxious to fix a good dish of pasta and you glance through the ensuing pages, you may think the introduction is too long, that it takes too much time to reach the recipes. Patience! This prelude is essential, and I can assure you that after having studied its contents you will know not only as much about pasta as any Italian, but perhaps even more. You will also gain a clear idea of the way to succeed every time with every pasta from macaroni to cannelloni.

A WORD ABOUT THE HISTORY OF PASTA

Let's start with the history of pasta through the centuries.

The famous French poet Alfred de Musset wrote these verses to his friend, Count Antonio Savignano:

> Tu t'es bercé dans les flots purs
> Où Naples embrasse dans l'azur
> Son mosaïque, oreiller des lazzaroni
> Où sont nés les macaroni et la musique.

You were cradled in the pure waves
Where Naples embraces in the azur skies
Its mosaic, pillow of the urchins
Where macaroni and music were born.

If M. de Musset has honored the Neapolitans in writing this quatrain, we had better not mention it in Northern Italy. For, contrary to belief, neither spaghetti, macaroni, nor pasta in general was invented by the Neapolitans, although they proudly claim the invention today; nor did pasta even originate in Southern Italy. The birthplace of pasta lies to the north, in Lombardy, whose principal city is Milan. To be diplomatic, we should refrain from mentioning this fact in Southern Italy; for, not only does the cherished regional variety of pasta flourish throughout the nation, and for this we are thankful since it enriches our book, but regional rivalry still flourishes as well, over a century after Italian unification, and there is no sign that it is abating.

In my search for genuine recipes I have found irrefutable proof concerning the origins of pasta. We know, for example, that the good Neapolitans of the eighteenth century were nicknamed "the salad eaters" but naturally they prefer to ignore this designation. Even earlier than this, we know that in 1279, on February 4 to be precise, a notary of Genoa, Agolino Scarpa, announced to his client, Signor Ponzio, that, included in the legacy from one of his relatives was a large saucepan of macaroni.

The unusual inheritance of Signor Ponzio also destroys another legend, the one crediting Marco Polo with having imported and popularized spaghetti in Italy on his return from Asia. According to tradition, the Italian navigator saw the Chinese in Nankin eating spaghetti. But Marco Polo returned from China in 1279, long after Signor Ponzio had consumed his inheritance, hopefully with gusto. There are recipes for pasta in an old Chinese cookbook, the *Hon-zo*, so it is a strong possibility that the Chinese also invented pasta; but because there was little communication between the two countries, the Italians remain innocent of any charge of plagiarism.

Another valuable document from the Middle Ages is the book *De onesta voluptate*. This tract on Lombard cuisine honors a certain Meluzza of Como, a little town on Lake Como near Milan, as the inventor of spaghetti. The otherwise unknown Meluzza prepared it with oil and garlic, later to be the style preferred by the famous Genoese Admiral Andrea Doria. *De onesta voluptate* can be seen in the Museum of Pasta in the small town of Pontedassio on the Ligurian Sea. In addition there are other books and drawings in the museum which prove that pasta did indeed originate in the north of Italy.

The fame of pasta spread through Europe at an early date. The French became familiar with the pleasures of Italian cuisine in the sixteenth century: when Catherine de Medici married Henri II, she brought to the French court her indispensable Florentine chefs. In 1772 pasta was exported commercially from Europe for the first time on a boat sailing from Genoa to England.

As we have seen, pasta was invented by either the Northern Italians or the Chinese, or perhaps by both; but, to honor Southern Italy, I discovered in an old manual belonging to the Vatican Library how pasta was once made in Naples. Wheat was crushed into flour in a colossal mortar. The wheat was then pulverized by a long bar of wood fixed at one end of the mortar with a hinge. On the other end sat the men, working to the rhythm of songs and mandolins, transforming the wheat into flour. The ensuing operation was somewhat less than poetic: the flour was mixed with hot water and barefoot workers then stamped on it, keeping time to the music, to make a dough that was left in the sun to dry.

This technique, the hygiene of which left much to be desired, ended in 1833 when King Ferdinand II of Naples had the opportunity to see how his favorite dish was prepared. Stupefied and disgusted, Ferdinand asked a famous engineer of the time, Cavaliere Spadaccini, to devise a less primitive way to mix flour and water. After one year of research the clever Spadaccini presented a picturesque scheme that was immediately adopted. After the flour was mixed with boiling water, it was no longer mashed by the feet of singing Neapolitans, but by the feet of a puppet or, more precisely, of a bronze statue that was used like an enormous pestle to mash the dough.

The first pasta was imported to the United States in 1890, and today you can find fifty to sixty varieties in any Italian market, and perhaps almost as many in a well-stocked supermarket in a large American city.

Pasta varies from the provincial derivations such as "pizzocheri," which are eaten in the northern region of the Valtellina near Venice and "tacconelle," a speciality of the Abruzzi region, to the more celebrated prototypes, "gnocchi" and "fettuccine."

There are many varieties of pasta that resemble each other like sisters but carry different names. In Bologna, for example, people eat "cappelletti," but in Rome this same pasta is called "tortellini." Because our aim is not to discuss every pasta but mainly the ones that are universally known and enjoyed I shall say very little about soup pasta. This group includes about twenty shapes, all closely related. A good portion of them seems to have been invented for the delight of children. There are "alfabeto" (alphabet), "anezzi" (little rings), the star-shaped "astri," "crocette" (little crosses), and even "elefanti" (elephants) to amuse whomever partakes. Because it cooks so quickly, this family is called "minute pasta" in Italy. It can be used in soups or bouillons. You will find further examples of "minute pasta" in the recipes included in the chapter "Soups and Minestrone."

Now we begin the discussion of "real pasta," the type that makes the Italians so justifiably proud and our subject clearly becomes more interesting. When Italians go out to eat spaghetti or fettuccine they do not say, *"Andiamo a mangiare gli spaghetti o le fettuccine."* They say, "Let's go eat pastasciutta." Asciutta means "dry" and *pastasciutta* (pronounced: pas-ta-shoó-tah) refers to all types that are cooked with a sauce or baked in the oven, excluding the ones cooked with soup or minestrone: the minute pasta or "pasta in brodo" ("in broth"). Cuisine is an art and pastasciutta must be cooked and seasoned according to precise rules; to make spaghetti with a sauce created for lasagne and to choose a flat pasta when pierced or fluted pasta is needed are errors that must be avoided.

The Italians eat pasta at least once and often twice a day. For them it is not a secondary dish, as it is in some European countries; in France, England, and Germany, for example, pasta is often served instead of a vegetable. Italians, however, begin the meal with pasta;

it is their first course and they may deem rude a foreigner's attempts, however well meaning, to compare their national dish with, let us say, french fries.

In addition, never tell an Italian that pasta is fattening; he may become very angry. If you eat it instead of meat, or a starchy dish such as buttered potatoes or a dessert, you will have consumed approximately the same number of calories.

For those of you who are interested in dietetics you should note that three ounces of pasta with its sauce contains 250 calories, almost the equivalent of three ounces of meat (beef with 10 per cent of fat or lamb contains 200 calories, veal 160 calories). If you add to these sums the calories in the butter or oil used to cook the meat, the total will reach 250 calories.

As I mentioned earlier, there are dozens of types of pasta from which you can choose, but it would be impossible to discuss them all in these pages. Briefly, therefore, I want to describe only the kinds most often used in Italy and in the United States. For certain types of pasta you will find an abundance of recipes in this book, while for others there are considerably fewer. This imbalance is not due to my personal preference but instead reflects the popularity of certain pasta with the Italians.

Spaghetti, fettuccine, and macaroni are the most popular choices in Italy and throughout the world, and this book presents almost all the existing recipes for them. Everywhere in Italy and particularly in the south, spaghetti is eaten more frequently at home; other pastas are considered luxuries and are eaten on special occasions: on Sundays or when dining out. You can therefore understand why there are about seventy ways to prepare spaghetti, all of which you can find in the following pages, but about five recipes for agnolotti.

After spaghetti, fettuccine is undoubtedly the most celebrated pasta of the international gourmets. Called *nouilles* in France, *nudeln* in Germany, and noodles in England and America, this pasta has two designations in Italy, depending on the region where it is prepared. In Bologna, where legend has it that in the fifteenth century Zeffirino invented these noodles drawing his inspiration from the golden curls of Lucrezia Borgia, they are called tagliatelle; Romans, however, call them fettuccine. One small difference does distinguish them: while fettuccine dough may or may not contain

eggs, tagliatelle are invariably prepared with them. I have used both
names, respecting the regional recipes.

Macaroni is the most famous pasta after spaghetti and fettuccine,
and it is often amusing to watch the confusion people have in
identifying it. This error probably stems from the fact that in Genoa
and the surrounding Ligurian countryside, and in Naples, people use
the name "macaroni" to refer to every type of pasta. In Liguria, for
example, cannelloni are called Macaroni No. 1, camonciotti and
penne, Macaroni No. 2; but true macaroni: wide, long, and hollow—
cannot be taken for anything else. This distinctive pasta is a special
favorite in Southern Italy, particularly in Naples and its surround-
ings. The Four Cheeses Macaroni, which you can find in Chapter
III, comes from this region.

Penne enjoy a special place in the shell family. This pasta, wide,
short, and hollow, is cut in feather edge and may have either a
smooth surface or a grooved one (similar to the flutes on a classical
Greek column).

"Penne all'arrabiata" is one of the most famous recipes for this
pasta, and you can find it in Chapter IV.

Another pasta from the shell family that is very well known is
rigatoni. Rigatoni is highly esteemed in Central Italy. Rigatoni's
shape is similar to that of penne in that it is wide and hollow and is
cut in feather edge but it is twice the size of penne and has only a
smooth surface. At the restaurant Da Gino in Trastevere, one of the
oldest and certainly the proudest quarter of Rome, "rigatoni a modo
mio" is the speciality. When Elizabeth Taylor was filming *Cleopatra*
in Rome she discovered this dish, and before leaving asked Gino for
the recipe so that her personal chef could prepare it for her. For-
tunately Gino has been as generous with us as he was with her, and
you can find the recipe in Chapter IV. Maniche, so named because
they resemble the sleeves of a man's shirt, is another type of shell
pasta closely related to rigatoni.

Another variety of pasta, bucatini, can be classified between
spaghetti and macaroni; bucatini are long and thin like the latter. A
classic Neapolitan speciality, this pasta is often served with elaborate
sauces such as the "Bucatini Amatriciana" in Chapter II. The spiral-
shaped fusilli are also related to both spaghetti and macaroni and
are characteristic specialities of Calabria in the south.

Other varieties of pasta, perhaps less famous but just as pleasing to the palate and the eye, are farfallini (bow ties or butterflies), conchiglie (sea shells), elbow macaroni, and ditali, a Genoese specialty. Individual chapters are dedicated to these families.

I want to continue this brief survey by mentioning the oven pasta and the stuffed pasta.

Of course, practically all types of pasta may be baked in the oven, that is why you will find recipes for baked rigatoni, ditali, farfalle, and macaroni. But they cannot take the place of lasagne, for lasagne is the oven pasta whose unique virtues are praised in Italy and a host of other nations. It is wide and flat and must be baked in the oven (although there are a few exceptions to this rule and you will find them listed in Chapter III, along with an explanation), with tomatoes or meat sauce, and often with mushrooms, vegetables, and cheese. "To swim in the lasagne" (*Nuotare nelle lasagne*) is one of the proverbs this pasta has inspired, and it means "to be well off." Italians also say that, to prepare lasagne, you have to spend a bride's dowry, not because the pasta itself is so expensive, but because the sauce consists of expensive ingredients. You may find that it does cost more to prepare lasagne with asparagus than spaghetti with rosemary, but you should remember that Italians often save these dishes for special festivities such as weddings and baptisms.

The stuffed pastas also enjoy excellent reputations in and out of Italy, and like spaghetti, macaroni, and fettuccine, are eaten at the beginning of the meal. The meat-filled agnolotti (ravioli) are appreciated throughout the world and many have originated outside of Italy.

The Japanese version of pasta is cooked in salt water with raw fish, and in China pasta is seasoned with soy sauce; both of these recipes are centuries old. Many students of gastronomy believe this Far Eastern pasta to be an invention of the Jews. Some fifteenth-century Italian books state that the name *agnolotti* is derived from *agnello,* or lamb, because this pasta was stuffed with lamb, and was a main dish of the Jews in the century before Christ, when the Jews were under the jurisdiction of the Roman Empire. When the Roman soldiers returned to Italy they carried this recipe with them. In Italy today, agnolotti are prepared in a variety of tempting ways such as Agnolotti alla Piemontese.

Tortellini, a characteristic Bolognese specialty, is a third type of stuffed pasta, usually filled but sometimes empty, the origin of which is told in a suggestive legend. Once a famous chef had the opportunity to gaze upon the navel of a statue of Venus, goddess of love; obviously inspired by the sight, he preserved the image by modeling it in dough.

To conclude this survey, I must mention a pasta so unique that it remains in a class apart. Italians say, that gnocchi are the ancestors of all pastas. Round, oval, or fluted, they may be eaten with sauce, in bouillon, or baked in the oven. Because they are made with potato flour or sometimes with the potato itself, rather than with a wheat-based dough, they are distinguished from all other varieties. In Rome, tradition requires that gnocchi be eaten on Thursday.

SPECIAL TRICKS FOR PREPARING, COOKING, EATING PASTA

Before you prepare these recipes, I want to share with you advice given to me by some of the best chefs, particularly my collaborator on this book, Alfredo, owner of the internationally famous restaurant Alfredo l'Originale, located at Piazza Augusto Imperatore in Rome. These tricks are quite simple yet remain unknown to a majority of people, for chefs are often reluctant to divulge the secrets of their art.

Oil and Butter:

The Italians use olive oil in almost everything, especially in tomato sauce. It is preferred because it has the best taste and because it heats more slowly than other oils. Using olive oil, you have less worry about burning the onions or tomatoes. Peanut oil is used when the pasta has to be roasted or fried (see Skillet Spaghetti in Chapter I). Butter is used in Bolognese cuisine to cook the fatty ingredients such as sausages or bacon (see Spaghetti alla Carbonara). Butter and oil may be mixed, if preferred, but oil retains its flavor far better during cooking than butter and should really be used by itself.

The Herbs:

To make pasta truly *all'italiana,* you should always have certain herbs in your kitchen: basil, parsley, thyme, and bay leaves. Fresh ones are always preferable, but you can also use the dried or ground brands that are readily available in any supermarket.

If you select the dried brands you will have to use a large

quantity of them to get the same bouquet that fresh ones give. Some fresh herbs, such as thyme and bay leaves, which are removed from the sauce before serving, can be sewn into a small cheesecloth pouch (similar to a tea bag) that can be easily discarded after cooking.

The Tomatoes:

Sauces with a tomato base are frequently used to complement pasta. Depending on the season or the amount of time at your disposal, you may vary the preparation of the sauce, using either fresh tomatoes, their canned counterpart, or canned tomato sauce. Fresh tomatoes from the garden are the most savory and should be used when in season. Following is a simple procedure that will enable you to peel tomatoes and remove the seeds without difficulty.

Put a pot of cold unsalted water on the stove to boil, and wash the tomatoes under the tap. When the water comes to boil, add the tomatoes, leaving them in the boiling water for one minute. After taking the tomatoes out of the pot, peel them, reserving the skin. Next, cut each tomato into two pieces and scoop out the seeds. Put the seeds and the skin in a bowl or a blender and mash or blend them, then add this mixture to the tomatoes and cook them together, following the directions in the recipes.

If you cannot find really good fresh tomatoes in the market or have limited time to cook, canned tomatoes have an advantage, being already peeled and seedless. Because they have less flavor than garden fresh tomatoes (although more flavor than ordinary market tomatoes) and reduce a great deal in cooking, you should be prepared to add a tablespoon of concentrated tomato paste to restore the zest.

Concentrated tomato paste is packaged in a can and is used to give substance to liquid tomato sauce. Chef Ovidio Scocchera counsels that, in all recipes calling for fresh or canned peeled tomatoes, one or two tablespoons of tomato paste be added. Tomato paste can also be used by itself as a sauce if you are in a hurry, because it is already half cooked. For some very thick sauces, such as the sauce for Fiuggi Spaghetti, tomato paste is essential.

Preparation of the Garlic:

Garlic gives all its flavor to the sauce when it is cut so finely that it is almost mashed. It should be cooked alone, very slowly, in olive oil over a very low heat until it turns slightly golden, then the other ingredients should be added immediately.

If you object to the strong smell of garlic you should remove the tiny green germ at the center of the clove before cooking.

Preparation of the Onion:

As with the garlic, the onion should be cooked alone in a clean pot in the olive oil over a very low flame until it turns slightly golden (about 20–25 minutes), then the other ingredients should be added.

Preparation of the Parsley:

Remove all the stems and use only the tiny leaves, cutting them very finely with a chopping knife. Wrap the parsley in a towel and run cold water over it. Then, after you have strained it, removing all the water, the parsley is ready for cooking or for storing, covered, in the refrigerator. Prepared in this way, the parsley will keep for weeks without turning yellow.

Removing the Vegetables from the Pot:

Vegetables should always be lifted from the cooking water with a skimmer, rather than poured into a strainer. With the skimmer, any residue of dirt remains at the bottom of the pot instead of mixing with and ruining the vegetables.

Removing the Sand from the Clams:

First, clean the clams under running water, then put them in a saucepan with one half cup of cold tap water; cover the saucepan, and cook over a medium flame. When the water boils, stir the clams and re-cover the saucepan; repeat this two or three times. After four minutes, the clams will open and should be removed from the heat. Pour the water that is in the saucepan into one or two bowls you have ready, then take the clams out of their shells and put them in this water. Clean each clam well by hand by rinsing several times in this water. Put back in the water, and wait five minutes. Now remove the clams one by one, putting them in the second bowl; pour the water from the first bowl very slowly over the clams so that the sand remains at the bottom of the first bowl. Repeat this operation two or three times, going from bowl to bowl, and you will have removed all the sand.

Pasta al Dente:

To be eaten correctly, pasta must be served *al dente* or slightly undercooked. This Italian term means "to the touch of the teeth" and refers to the method of taking a tiny sample of pasta from the pot when the cooking time is about to expire and biting it to test its firmness. Beyond Italian borders pasta is usually overcooked, and chefs in restaurants and cooks at home are equally guilty.

There are two reasons why it is illogical to eat overcooked pasta. Because Italians invented pasta, and have certainly made it popular throughout the world, it should be eaten their way. Even more significant, pasta *al dente* is digested more easily than soft, overcooked pasta. Be sure to adhere to the cooking time indicated in each recipe.

Party Tip for Pasta:

When you give a party, it is easier to cook a large quantity of spaghetti than any other pasta because you can handle it more easily. Essential advice concerning the proper care and handling of spaghetti comes from Signor Marino, owner of the renowned Roman restaurant Piccolo Mondo: "You should never break spaghetti, even if you find it long. This pasta, which was born in the thirteenth century, keeps all its dignity and its good taste if you cook it according to the original recipe."

Cheeses:

Another tradition that must be observed to succeed with pasta concerns the correct use of cheeses. The most famous cheeses for pasta are: Parmesan, pecorino, mozzarella, ricotta, Gorgonzola, and Holland (Gouda). Parmesan is a mild cheese that accompanies all mild sauces. After the pasta has been mixed with its sauce, grated Parmesan is sprinkled on it using one tablespoon for two persons. Whenever you prepare a sauce with parsley, as in all seafood sauces, cheese is never added because it would kill the taste of the parsley.

The other cheeses mentioned above are seldom used, but some recipes for oven pasta or the special Four Cheeses Macaroni are exceptions. Precise instructions governing their use are given with all appropriate recipes.

I have described all the tricks you need to know about pasta. Now all you have to do is exercise your culinary talents and add a dash of imagination. This book has been prepared in collaboration with the best Italian restaurants and chefs, who have been very generous in sharing some of their hitherto secret recipes. Thanks to them and to this book you will be able to dream that you are dining in Rome, Florence, Naples, or Genoa. *Buon Appetito!*

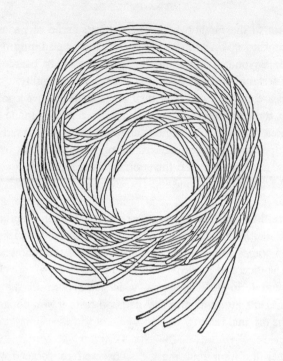

CHAPTER I
Spaghetti

One subject about which the Italians are very touchy is the way to cook pasta. If you can imagine that in 1966 a newly wed Neapolitan threw his wife out the window from the third floor of their house because she overcooked the spaghetti prepared for lunch, you can understand why all Italian housewives want to succeed when they make pasta: not because they fear being thrown out the window (the above is a unique example), but because for this it is a matter of honor. The ideal and classic way to make every pasta is *al dente,* slightly undercooked, so that it will be firm, rather than soft or pasty, as we have already mentioned in the Introduction.

There are three types of spaghetti, distinguished by width, not by length. Vermicelli, or Spaghetti No. 1, is the thinnest of the trio, and its cooking time *al dente* is 2 minutes. Because it is wider, spaghettini (Spaghetti No. 2) is cooked for 5 minutes. Of this trio, Spaghetti No. 3 is the most commonly used in Italy and requires approximately 8 minutes in boiling water to become *al dente.* You may select any of the three types, as you prefer, but always remember that the wider, regular spaghetti (No. 3) is the most frequent choice of the Italians.

The best way to cook regular spaghetti is as follows. Fill a large pot with cold water, adding 3 tablespoons of salt for every gallon of water. The more water you use, the better the result. As soon as the water comes to a boil, add the spaghetti; one pound suffices for 4 people. Let it cook for 8 to 10 minutes (the cooking time changes from pasta to pasta and sometimes from brand to brand, so note carefully the instructions on the package). From the eighth minute, and then every 30 seconds thereafter, take a tiny sample of pasta from the pot to taste it and to test it.

When you are sure the pasta is *al dente,* you must turn off the heat immediately and pour a pot of cold water that you have waiting into the boiling water. The cold water stops the cooking at once. Then you strain the spaghetti and season it with one of the sauces that we offer you in the following pages.

As you can see, you need not be a magician to cook spaghetti as the Italians do. You just have to follow these simple rules very carefully, because an additional minute in the cooking of pasta means that it is no longer cooked *all'italiana,* but merely boiled. Follow with care our advice and you will be sure to cook and season properly the 70 spaghetti recipes that we found for you and that are for us and for the chefs who collaborated on this book the only ones existing.

SPAGHETTI ALLA CARBONARA
(*Spaghetti alla Carbonara*)

This recipe, which is one of the great classics of Italian cooking, was given to me while I was having dinner at the Taverna Flavia, one of Rome's most famous restaurants. Signor Mimo, the proprietor, told me that this is a favorite dish of President Nixon. Apropos of Nixon, Signor Mimo said, "Mr. Nixon gave us here a good lesson in democracy when he was vice president. He had his secretary call to reserve a table, but I thought it was a joke. At eight-thirty, when he arrived, I didn't have a single table to offer him. He didn't get at all angry; he simply waited until a table was free." Herewith the recipe that keeps chiefs of state waiting.

Cooking time: 20 minutes

6 slices lean bacon	Pepper to taste
4 tablespoons oil	⅓ cup grated pecorino cheese
1 pound spaghetti	¾ cup grated Parmesan cheese
4 eggs	¼ cup reserved spaghetti water

Cut each slice of bacon into julienne strips. Put into a skillet with the oil and sauté slowly until almost golden. Now put the spaghetti in abundant boiling salted water and cook for 8 minutes. In the meantime, break the eggs into a small bowl, add 2 generous pinches of pepper and 2 tablespoons of pecorino and Parmesan mixed together. Beat together well. Remove the skillet with the bacon from the fire. Just before the spaghetti is cooked take ¼ cup of the water in which it is cooking and add to the bacon in the skillet. Drain the spaghetti and put into a preheated salad bowl (the bowl must be very hot). Add the contents of the skillet (which must also be very hot) and half of the remaining grated cheeses. Toss until well mixed. Now add the beaten eggs and cheeses and toss energetically until very well mixed. Serve in preheated dishes with the rest of the cheese sprinkled on top. Serves 4.

SPAGHETTI ALL'AMATRICIANA
(*Spaghetti all'Amatriciana*)

This recipe—as is the recipe for Spaghetti alla Carbonara—is one of the ten most famous ways of seasoning pasta. The actress Gina Lollobrigida confessed to me that she loves to prepare this herself. In Rome this is especially done at Restaurant Il Galeone. The décor of this restaurant, where pasta lovers gather, reminds one of a fifteenth-century Spanish galleon.

Cooking time: 15 minutes

¼ pound lean unsliced bacon	1 pound spaghetti
1 pound tomatoes (3 medium)	3 tablespoons grated pecorino
3 tablespoons oil	cheese
¼ teaspoon ground red pepper	Pepper
¼ teaspoon salt	

Cut the bacon into small cubes. Wash the tomatoes, peel them, and remove the seeds. Cut them into small pieces. Brown the bacon in a small saucepan with the oil. Add the tomatoes, the red pepper, and salt. Cook on a high flame for about 12 minutes, stirring from time to time. Pour mixture over freshly cooked, drained spaghetti. Add the pecorino cheese, mixed with a pinch of pepper, toss until well mixed and serve immediately. Serves 4.

GONDOLIERS' SPAGHETTI
(*Spaghetti alla Barcarola*)

"*La Barcarola*" is a chant, sung by the Venetian gondoliers, whose rhythm reminds one of the rocking of a boat on the waves. This recipe is particularly appreciated in Veneto Province and dates back to the romantic era.

Cooking time: 30 minutes

2 ounces shelled clams	½ cup white wine
2 ounces shelled shrimp	Salt and pepper to taste
3 ounces baby squid	1 pound spaghetti
2 cloves garlic	4 tablespoons butter
5 tablespoons oil	3 tablespoons finely chopped
¼ teaspoon crushed red pepper	parsley
1 tablespoon flour (heaping)	

First of all, prepare the seafood: wash the clams and cut the shrimp in half unless they are especially small. Clean and wash the squid and cut into spaghetti-like strips. Pass the garlic through a garlic press and sauté in a saucepan with the oil until it is almost golden in color. Add the squid and the red pepper and cook over a high flame for 5 minutes, stirring continuously. Now lower the flame and add the clams. Stir. Add the shrimp and sauté for 2 more minutes. Add the flour and stir until the contents of the saucepan are well mixed. Pour in the white wine and when half of it has evaporated pour in 1 cup of hot water, salt, and pepper. Stir and allow to simmer slowly for about 15 minutes. When the sauce is almost done, cook the spaghetti in abundant boiling salted water for 8 minutes. While the spaghetti is cooking, put the butter, the finely chopped parsley, and a pinch of pepper on a chopping board.

With a small spatula or the blade of a table knife make a paste of
the mixture and add to the sauce. When the spaghetti is cooked,
drain it and put it into a large serving bowl. Pour the sauce into the
bowl and toss until well mixed. Serve, making sure that each portion
has its share of the different types of seafood. Serves 4.

SPAGHETTI BERSAGLIERE
(Spaghetti alla Bersagliere)

This recipe dates back to 1836 and was dedicated, by an unknown cook, to the famous regiment of the Bersaglieri, in which
the handsomest and the strongest young men in Italy are enrolled,
which explains the presence of the rich and nourishing ingredients
of this succulent dish.

Cooking time: 27 minutes
1 medium onion	2 heaping tablespoons diced
4 tablespoons oil	provolone cheese
¼ pound salami	1 pound spaghetti
½ cup white wine	2 tablespoons grated Parmesan
1½ pounds ripe tomatoes (5	cheese
medium)	

Slice the onion very thinly and soften in the oil over a low flame.
Add the thinly sliced salami and brown slightly. Pour in the white
wine and allow to evaporate (about 5 minutes). Now add the
tomatoes, which have been peeled and passed through a food mill
or a blender. Cook very slowly for 15 minutes. Now add the diced
provolone to the sauce and cook for 2 minutes more. Pour the
sauce over freshly cooked, drained spaghetti and toss until well
mixed. Sprinkle with Parmesan and serve immediately. Serves 4.

SPAGHETTI PILAFF
(Spaghetti alla Pilaff)

This recipe was given to me by a cheerful great-grandmother who
is ninety years old. She lives in Opi, a tiny village of three hundred
inhabitants tucked into an Abruzzi mountainside. She assured me

that she owes her longevity to the following method of seasoning spaghetti. Be it true or not, it is truly delicious.

Cooking time: 60 minutes

1 medium onion	½ cup red wine
4 tablespoons oil	4 ounces tomato paste (½ cup)
⅓ cup diced beef	1 bouillon cube
⅓ cup diced pork	1 pound spaghetti
½ cup diced lamb	6 tablespoons grated Parmesan
1 clove garlic, crushed	cheese
Salt and pepper to taste	

Finely chop the onion and soften in the oil over a slow fire until almost golden in color. Cut up the meat in small pieces and brown well. Add the clove of garlic, crushed, and the salt and pepper. Stir for about a minute. Pour in the red wine and allow to evaporate. Dilute the tomato paste in a cup of bouillon made with the bouillon cube, then add it to the other ingredients in the saucepan. Cover the saucepan and simmer for about 50 minutes. Pour this sauce over freshly cooked, drained spaghetti, toss until well mixed, and serve with the Parmesan sprinkled on top. Serves 4.

COUNTESS CASTIGLIONE'S SPAGHETTI
(Spaghetti della Contessa Castiglione)

This recipe, which dates back to the nineteenth century, was invented by the Contessa Virginia Castiglione for her friend Napoleon III. They say in Italy, and particularly in Tuscany, that the countess herself cultivated rosemary even while she was in the emperor's court from 1856 to 1859.

Cooking time: 50 minutes

1 pound ripe tomatoes (3 medium)	2 cloves garlic
1 bouillon cube	1 tablespoon flour
8 rosemary leaves (or ½ teaspoon dried)	Salt and pepper to taste
½ pound slightly fatty pork	10 to 12 green olives
3 tablespoons oil	1 pound spaghetti
	6 tablespoons grated Parmesan cheese

Cut the tomatoes into pieces and put into a saucepan with the bouillon cube, half of the rosemary, and ½ cup of hot water. Cook over a high flame for 10 minutes. In the meantime put the pork through a meat grinder and sauté it in the oil in another saucepan. Put the garlic through a garlic press (or crush and finely chop) and add to the meat together with the finely chopped rosemary leaves that remain. Continue to sauté until brown. Add the flour and mix well. Remove the saucepan from the fire. Add salt and pepper. Put the tomato sauce through the fine blade of a food mill (or blend in a blender) and pour into the saucepan in which you have sautéed the meat. Return to the fire, stir well, and bring to a boil again. Lower the flame and simmer for 40 minutes more. Remove the pits from the olives and cut the olives into julienne-like strips. Add to the simmering sauce. The sauce should be fairly thick. When it is almost ready, cook the spaghetti in abundant boiling salted water. Drain and put in a large serving bowl. Add the sauce and half of the grated cheese. Toss until well mixed. Serve with the rest of the grated cheese sprinkled on top.
Serves 4.

NEAPOLITAN SPAGHETTI
(*Spaghetti del Napoletano*)

Cooking time: 40 minutes

1 small onion	Salt and pepper to taste
5 tablespoons oil	¼ dried red pepper
1 clove garlic	2 tablespoons chopped parsley
2 basil leaves (or ⅛ teaspoon dried)	1 pound spaghetti
⅓ cup white wine	4 tablespoons grated Parmesan cheese
1½ pounds ripe tomatoes (5 medium)	

Finely chop the onion and sauté in the oil in a saucepan. Crush the garlic on a wooden bread board and chop finely together with the basil. Put in saucepan and continue to sauté. Add the white wine and when half of it has evaporated, add the tomatoes, cut up in pieces, and salt and pepper to taste. Cook over a moderate flame for 35 minutes. Also add the red pepper and the chopped parsley.

Stir often. The sauce should be fairly concentrated. When the sauce is almost done, cook the spaghetti in abundant boiling salted water from 8 to 10 minutes, as desired. Drain and mix with the sauce and half of the grated Parmesan. Serve with the rest of the cheese sprinkled on top. Serves 4.

HOME-STYLE SPAGHETTI
(*Spaghetti all'Uso di Casa*)

Cooking time: 80 minutes

2 slices lean bacon
1 clove garlic
5 rosemary leaves (or ¼ teaspoon dried)
¼ teaspoon salt and pepper
2 pounds leg of lamb
4 tablespoons oil
2 tablespoons flour
1 medium onion
1 medium carrot
1 stalk celery

½ cup red wine
1½ pounds tomatoes (5 medium)
2 basil leaves (⅛ teaspoon dried)
Salt and pepper to taste
1 bouillon cube
1 pound spaghetti
6 tablespoons grated Parmesan cheese

Finely chop the bacon on a wooden bread board. Peel the clove of garlic, crush it, and chop it very finely together with the rosemary leaves. Mix with the chopped bacon and continue to chop until well mixed. Add salt and pepper and mix. With a pointed knife, make a series of holes in the piece of lamb and fill with the chopped mixture. Do this until you have used up all of the mixture. Put the oil in a large saucepan and heat it over a high flame. Dredge the piece of meat with flour and brown in the hot oil, turning the meat often in order to brown it uniformly. Cut the onion in pieces, add to the saucepan, and sauté. Slice the carrot and the celery and add. Stir for 1 minute. Add the red wine and allow half of it to evaporate. Add the tomatoes, peeled and cut in pieces, the basil, and salt and pepper to taste. Stir. Turn the piece of meat and cook for 5 minutes. Dissolve the bouillon cube in 1½ cups of hot water and add to the saucepan. Bring to a boil over a high flame, then lower the flame and simmer for 65 minutes. Stir from time to time, turning the meat often so that the sauce will not stick to the bottom of the saucepan. When the sauce is almost done, cook the spaghetti in boiling salted water. While it is cooking, remove the piece of meat from the sauce. Pass the sauce through the medium blade of a food mill (or blender). Drain the cooked spaghetti and put into a large serving bowl. Add ⅔ of the sauce and half of the grated cheese. Toss until well mixed. Serve with the rest of the cheese sprinkled on top.

Cut the meat into slices and serve with the rest of the sauce. Serve as a second course accompanied by whatever vegetable you desire. Serves 4.

AROMATIC SPAGHETTI
(*Spaghetti ai Molti Odori*)

Cooking time: 30 minutes

3 slices lean bacon	Salt and pepper to taste
1 medium onion	1 bouillon cube
4 tablespoons oil	1 small clove garlic
1 tablespoon flour	2 basil leaves (or ⅛ teaspoon
6 rosemary leaves (or ¼	dried)
teaspoon dried)	2 tablespoons chopped parsley
2 sage leaves	Sprinkling of nutmeg
2 bay leaves	2 tablespoons butter
2 whole cloves	¾ cup grated Parmesan cheese
1½ pounds tomatoes (5	1 pound spaghetti
medium), peeled	

Dice the bacon and the onion, put into a saucepan with the oil, and sauté until golden. Add the flour, the rosemary, the sage, bay leaves, the whole cloves, and mix well. Add the tomatoes cut in pieces, salt and pepper, and the bouillon cube dissolved in ½ cup of hot water. Stir and allow to simmer for 25 minutes more. In the meantime, crush the garlic on a wooden chopping board and finely chop it together with the basil, the parsley, and the nutmeg. To this mixture add the butter, a generous pinch of pepper, and 1 tablespoon of grated cheese. Make a paste out of these ingredients by mixing with a spatula or the flat side of the blade of a knife. When the 25 minutes are almost up, pass the sauce through the fine blade of a food mill (or blend in a blender), return it to the fire in its original saucepan, add the paste you have made, and bring to a boil again. Cook the spaghetti until it is done, drain it, and put it into a large serving bowl. Add the sauce and half of the remaining grated cheese. Toss until well mixed. Serve with the rest of the cheese sprinkled on top. Serves 4.

N.B. This advice is valid for all types of pasta: after mixing the pasta with the sauce and making the individual portions, often some sauce remains in the bottom of the serving bowl, together with pieces of meat or whatever other ingredients the sauce contains. This is particularly true of long pastas. Care should be taken to spoon this sauce over each portion so that every bit of it is used up.

SPAGHETTI WITH SAGE
(*Spaghetti alla Salvia*)

Cooking time: 40 minutes

1 small onion	1 bouillon cube
3 tablespoons oil	Salt and pepper to taste
1 stalk celery, chopped finely	3 slices lean bacon
2 cloves garlic	1 tablespoon oil
1 tablespoon flour	1 pound spaghetti
8 leaves fresh sage (or 1 tablespoon dried)	¾ cup grated Cheddar cheese
1 pound ripe tomatoes (3 medium)	

Cut the onion into pieces, put into a saucepan with 3 tablespoons of the oil, and sauté until almost golden. Add the celery and the unpeeled garlic and continue to sauté. Add the flour and stir. Add 6 sage leaves and the tomatoes, cut up and peeled. Cook over a moderate flame. Dissolve the bouillon cube in ½ cup of hot water and add, together with salt and pepper. Simmer for 35 minutes. When the sauce is almost done, cut the bacon into julienne strips and sauté it in a small skillet with 1 tablespoon of oil until it is golden. Finely chop 2 sage leaves and add to the bacon after you have removed it from the fire. Cook the spaghetti in abundant boiling salted water. While it is cooking, pass the sauce through the fine blade of a food mill (or blender). Drain the cooked spaghetti and put into a large serving bowl. Add the sautéed bacon with the oil and sage. Mix well. Add the sauce and half of the grated cheese. Toss until very well mixed. Serve with the rest of the cheese sprinkled on top. Serves 4.

SPAGHETTI WITH PLAIN SAUCE
(*Spaghetti alla Salsa Semplice*)

Cooking time: 40 minutes

1 medium onion	Salt and pepper to taste
1 medium carrot	4 leaves fresh basil (or ¼
1 stalk celery	teaspoon dried)
3 tablespoons oil	1 bouillon cube
2 tablespoons flour	1 pound spaghetti
6 tablespoons butter	¾ cup grated Parmesan cheese
1 pound ripe tomatoes (3 medium)	

Cut up the onion, carrot, and celery in pieces. Sauté the onion in the oil for a minute or so and add the carrot and celery. Stir and sauté for another minute. Add the flour and the butter and stir until just mixed. Add the tomatoes, cut in pieces, salt and pepper, and the basil leaves. Stir. Dissolve the bouillon cube in ½ cup of hot water and add. Simmer for 35 minutes, stirring from time to time. Just before the sauce is done, cook the spaghetti in abundant boiling salted water. While it is cooking, put the sauce through the medium blade of a food mill and allow it to come to a boil again. The sauce should be fairly concentrated. Drain the cooked spaghetti and put in a preheated serving bowl. Add all the sauce and half of the grated cheese. Toss until well mixed. Serve with the rest of the cheese sprinkled on top. Serves 4.

SPAGHETTI WITH GARLIC AND OIL
(*Spaghetti Aglio ed Olio*)

This extremely simple recipe is a favorite with most Italians, and particularly with Marcello Mastroianni, who told me he knows how to prepare this dish as well as the finest of chefs.

Don't forget that there is a little secret about cooking garlic . . . a secret that you will find in the Introduction.

Cooking time: 20 minutes

1 pound spaghetti	½ cup spaghetti water (see
3 cloves garlic	below)
3 tablespoons oil	1 teaspoon pepper
½ dried red pepper	3 tablespoons finely chopped
Salt to taste	parsley

Put the spaghetti in abundant boiling salted water. While it is cooking (10 minutes), peel the garlic and slice thinly. Put in a skillet or a shallow pan with the oil and the red pepper sliced into wheels. Add salt. Sauté slowly over a low fire. Just as the garlic begins to get golden in color, add ½ cup of the water in which the spaghetti is cooking, pepper, and the parsley. When the spaghetti is cooked, drain it and put in the pan in which you have prepared the garlic, etc. Toss until well mixed and serve immediately.
Serves 4.

SPAGHETTI WITH WHITE CLAM SAUCE
(*Spaghetti alle Vongole in Bianco*)

This recipe originated in Naples, as did many recipes with a fish base. Naples is on the Mediterranean coast and is Italy's third largest city after Rome and Milan. Spaghetti with white clam sauce is a specialty of the famous Neapolitan restaurant Zi Teresa.

Cooking time: 30 minutes

2 cloves garlic	1 tablespoon flour
5 tablespoons oil	½ cup white wine
¼ dried red pepper	1 pound spaghetti
½ pint or 1 (8-ounce) can	4 tablespoons butter
chopped shelled clams	2 tablespoons chopped parsley
Salt and pepper to taste	

Peel the garlic and put it through a garlic press (or mash it and chop it very finely). Put it into a fairly small saucepan with the oil and the piece of red pepper and sauté over a low flame. When the garlic is almost golden in color, add the clams and salt and pepper and continue to sauté for a few minutes. Add the flour and stir well. Add the white wine, stir, and allow half of it to evaporate. Pour in ½ cup of hot water (more if needed) and continue to cook over a low fire for 15 minutes. In the meantime, the water for the spaghetti will have come to a boil. Cook the spaghetti for 8 minutes. While the spaghetti is cooking, add the butter and the chopped parsley to the sauce. Add a little more hot water if necessary and continue to cook until the spaghetti is ready. Drain the cooked spaghetti and put into a serving bowl. Add all of the sauce and toss until well mixed. Serve, dividing the clams equally among the portions. Serves 4.

SPAGHETTI WITH BASIL
(*Spaghetti al Basilico*)

This recipe was one of King Farouk's favorites while he was living in Rome. A great eater, he was mad about spaghetti, but he also had a great liking for meat and particularly for birds. In 1956, during a dinner to which I also had been invited, I saw the ex-king eat 12 dozen ortolans, and he told me that in his younger days it was not unusual for him to eat twelve chickens at one sitting!

Cooking time: 40 minutes

2 slices bacon	1 bouillon cube
¼ cup chopped onion	Salt and pepper to taste
1 stalk celery	6 leaves basil (or ¼ teaspoon
5 tablespoons oil	dried)
1 tablespoon flour	1 pound spaghetti
1 pound ripe tomatoes	2 tablespoons butter
(3 medium)	¾ cup grated Parmesan cheese

Sauté the bacon and the onion and celery, cut in pieces, in a saucepan in the oil. When golden, add the flour and mix well. Add the tomatoes, cut up in pieces, and cook over a high flame. Dissolve the bouillon cube in ½ cup of hot water and add to the saucepan together with salt and pepper and the basil. Simmer for 30 minutes. When the sauce is almost done, cook the spaghetti in abundant boiling water for 8 minutes. In the meantime, put the sauce through the fine blade of a food mill (or blender), return to the saucepan in which it has cooked, add the butter, and bring to a boil again. By this time the spaghetti is cooked. Drain and put in a serving bowl. Add the sauce and half of the grated cheese. Toss until well mixed. Serve with a sprinkling of grated Parmesan over each portion. Serves 4.

SPAGHETTI WITH SARDINES
(*Spaghetti alle Sardine*)

Cooking time: 40 minutes

¾ pound fresh sardines	1 pound ripe tomatoes (3
2 cloves garlic	medium)
6 tablespoons oil	Salt and pepper to taste
¼ dried red pepper	3 tablespoons chopped parsley
2 tablespoons flour	1 pound spaghetti
⅓ cup white wine	

Wash the sardines after cleaning them carefully by removing the heads and interiors. Put them into a roomy saucepan and pour in enough water to cover them. Cook over a moderate flame until they come to a boil. Quickly remove the saucepan from the fire and allow the sardines to cool in the water. Now begin the sauce: crush and finely chop the garlic (or put it through a garlic press) and put it in a saucepan with 4 tablespoons of the oil and the red pepper. Sauté until almost golden. Add the flour and stir well. Pour in the wine and allow half of it to evaporate, stirring continuously. Finely chop the tomatoes and add together with salt and pepper. Cook for 35 minutes. As soon as the sardines have cooled, bone them very carefully, making sure that the tiny bones along the sides are also removed. Put the remaining 2 tablespoons of oil in a small skillet and heat. Add the boned sardines, including even the broken pieces, just so long as they are completely boned. Sauté together with 1½ tablespoons of the chopped parsley and additional salt and pepper to taste. Add all the contents of the skillet to the sauce and mix well. The sauce should be quite thick and slightly oily. Cook the spaghetti in abundant boiling salted water for 8 minutes. Drain and put into a serving bowl. Add the sauce and the rest of the chopped parsley, mix well, and serve. Serves 4.

BÉCHAMEL SAUCE (WHITE SAUCE)
(*Salsa Besciamella*)

Cooking time: 15 minutes

5 tablespoons butter
5 tablespoons flour
4 cups milk, scalded

Salt to taste
Sprinkling of nutmeg (optional)

Melt the butter in a small saucepan over a low flame. Add the flour and stir with a wooden spoon—or, better still, with a wire whisk—for about 4 minutes, until the flour and butter are well blended. Now add the scalded milk a little at a time, stirring continuously until a delicate, homogeneous cream results. Add salt and, if you like, a little freshly grated nutmeg. Cook slowly for 10 more minutes. Serves 4.

POPE'S SPAGHETTI
(*Spaghetti del Papa*)

This recipe was given to me by one of the Vatican cooks who assured me that this was one of Pope John XXIII's favorite dishes.

Cooking time: 25 minutes

4 slices lean bacon
4 tablespoons oil
1 small onion
¼ pound boiled ham
2 tablespoons flour
½ cup white wine

1 chicken bouillon cube
Salt and white pepper to taste
1 pound spaghetti
1 whole egg plus 2 egg yolks
¾ cup grated Cheddar cheese
4 tablespoons butter   ?

Slice the bacon into julienne strips. Put into a saucepan with the oil and the onion finely chopped. Sauté until almost golden over a moderate flame. The ham, also, is to be julienne-sliced and added to the saucepan, but care must be taken not to brown it too much. Now add the flour and stir for a while. Pour in the white wine and allow half of it to evaporate, stirring continuously. Dissolve the bouillon cube in ¾ cup of hot water and add to the saucepan with salt and white pepper to taste. Simmer for 15 minutes. Cook the spaghetti in boiling salted water for 8 minutes. In the meanwhile put the whole egg and the 2 yolks into a small bowl together with a pinch of pepper and ½ tablespoon of the grated cheese and beat well. When the spaghetti is cooked, put it into a preheated serving bowl with the butter cut in pieces. Mix. Add all the sauce and half of the remaining grated cheese. Toss. Add the egg mixture and toss energetically until very well mixed. Serve with the rest of the cheese sprinkled on top. Serves 4.

SPAGHETTI COUNTRY STYLE
(*Spaghetti alla Paesana*)

This recipe dates back to the nineteenth century. It was invented by Napoleon's sister, Maria Paola Borghese Bonaparte, while she was living in Rome. The recipe has become a specialty of the Roman restaurant Il Piccolo Mondo where a great many stars and international personalities are to be found each evening.

Cooking time: 20 minutes

1 clove garlic	Salt and pepper to taste
4 tablespoons oil	2 tablespoons finely chopped
½ dried red pepper	parsley
½ pound fresh "porcini" (flat)	1 pound spaghetti
mushrooms	4 tablespoons butter

Put the garlic through a garlic press (or mash it first with a spatula and chop very finely) and put in a large skillet with the oil and the red pepper, cut in 2 pieces. Wash the mushrooms well and slice them. Sauté the garlic and red pepper over a low flame until the garlic is just beginning to get golden in color. Add the mushrooms, salt and pepper, and half the parsley and cook over a moderate flame for 20 minutes, stirring from time to time. Cook the spaghetti in abundant boiling salted water for 8 minutes, stirring every so often with a large wooden fork. Drain it and put it in the skillet with the mushrooms. Also add the butter cut in small pieces. Toss until well mixed. Serve in large bowl with the rest of the parsley sprinkled on top. If desired, you may remove the red pepper. Serves 4.

SPAGHETTI WITH GOLDEN SAUCE
(*Spaghetti in Salsa Doré*)

Cooking time: 40 minutes

1 small onion
3 tablespoons oil
2 medium-size ripe tomatoes
2 basil leaves (or ¼ teaspoon dried)
Salt and pepper to taste
4 tablespoons butter

2 tablespoons flour
½ cup milk
1 chicken bouillon cube
1 pound spaghetti
½ cup grated Parmesan cheese (or grated Cheddar cheese)

Cut the onion into pieces and sauté until almost golden in the oil. Add the tomatoes, also cut up in pieces, the basil, and salt and pepper. Cook over a moderate flame for 20 minutes. In the meantime, melt the butter in a small saucepan. Add the flour, stirring continuously with a wooden spoon or a wire whisk until creamy. Add the milk a little at a time, stirring continuously. Dissolve the bouillon cube in ½ cup of hot water and add this gradually to the béchamel sauce (or white sauce) you have just made. Cook the spaghetti in abundant boiling salted water for 8 minutes. While the spaghetti is cooking, put the tomato sauce through the fine blade of a food mill (or blend in the blender). Add the white sauce to the tomato sauce and mix well. Pour over the cooked, drained spaghetti, add half the grated cheese, and toss until well mixed. Serve with the rest of the cheese sprinkled on top. Serves 4.

SPAGHETTI WITH SQUID
(*Spaghetti alle Seppie*)

Cooking time: 60 minutes

1 medium onion
6 tablespoons oil
3 cloves garlic
¼ dried red pepper
1 pound ripe tomatoes (3 medium)
3 basil leaves (or ¼ teaspoon dried)

¼ teaspoon salt and pepper
2 pounds squid
1½ tablespoons flour
½ cup white wine
1¼ cups shelled green peas
Salt and pepper to taste
1 pound spaghetti
2 tablespoons chopped parsley

Cut the onion into pieces and put into a saucepan with 3 table-spoons of oil, 1 unpeeled clove garlic, and the ¼ red pepper. Sauté for a minute or so. Add the tomatoes cut up in pieces, the basil, and ⅛ teaspoon salt and pepper. Cook for 20 minutes over a moderately high flame. Meanwhile, cut the squid into long, narrow slices. Put the 2 cloves of garlic through a garlic press and put into another saucepan with the remaining 3 tablespoons of oil. Sauté until the garlic is barely golden in color. Now add the squid and stir over a fairly high flame. You will find that squid make their own liquid. Cook until this liquid has evaporated, then add the flour, ⅛ teaspoon salt and pepper and mix well. Pour in the white wine. When half the wine has evaporated, add ½ cup of hot water, cover the saucepan, and simmer for 45 minutes, stirring often. In the meantime, boil the peas (if you are using fresh ones). In order to keep fresh peas green they should be cooked in rapidly boiling water. By this time the tomato sauce is done. Pass it through the medium blade of the food mill (or blender) and add to the saucepan in which the squid are cooking. Stir and continue to cook, tasting to test for salt. When the sauce is almost done, cook the spaghetti in rapidly boiling salted water for 8 minutes, drain, and put into a serving bowl. Ladle the sauce over the spaghetti, making sure to leave a little with the squid in the saucepan. Sprinkle with the chopped parsley and toss until well mixed. Add the cooked peas to the saucepan with the squid and allow to simmer slowly while you are eating the spaghetti. Serve the squid with the peas as a second course. Serves 4.

SPAGHETTI WITH PORK CHOPS
(*Spaghetti alla Lombatina di Maiale*)

Cooking time: 50 minutes

1 pound ripe tomatoes (3 medium)	½ cup white wine
1 medium onion	Salt and pepper to taste
1 small sprig rosemary (or ⅛ teaspoon dried)	1 small clove garlic
1 bouillon cube	14 to 15 pitted green olives
4 tablespoons oil	3 basil leaves (or ¼ teaspoon dried)
4 tablespoons flour	1 pound spaghetti
4 large pork chops	1 cup grated Parmesan cheese (or grated Cheddar cheese)

Put into a saucepan the tomatoes cut in pieces, half of the onion chopped coarsely, the rosemary, ½ cup of water, and the bouillon cube. Cook over a high flame for 10 minutes. In the meantime, put the oil in a saucepan large enough to hold the 4 chops. (Make sure that the pork chops are well cut so that there will be no danger of bone splinters in the sauce.) Flour the chops and brown in the hot oil on both sides. Chop the rest of the onion finely and allow it to sauté with the chops, being careful not to burn it (it should be golden, not brown). Now add the white wine. Lower the flame and allow half the wine to evaporate. In the meantime, put the tomato mixture through the fine blade of a food mill (or blend in a blender) and add to the saucepan in which the chops are cooking. Add salt and pepper, stir well until all the ingredients are well mixed, and bring the sauce to a boil again. Now lower the flame and allow the sauce to simmer slowly. Put the garlic through a garlic press so that it becomes a paste. Chop the olives very finely together with the basil. Mix with the garlic and add to the sauce. Stir. Simmer for 30 minutes more (by this time the chops will have been cooking for 20 minutes). Cook the spaghetti in abundant boiling salted water. Drain. Pour most of the sauce on the spaghetti and add half the grated cheese. Toss until well mixed. Serve with the rest of the cheese sprinkled on top.

The pork chops may be served as the second course, served with potatoes cooked as follows: cut the potatoes in pieces and cook in water in which you have added 3 tablespoons of the sauce, a bouillon cube, and salt and pepper to taste. Serves 4.

SPAGHETTI ROSEMARY
(*Spaghetti al Rosmarino*)

Cooking time: 30 minutes

3 slices bacon	⅓ cup white wine
4 tablespoons oil	1¼ pounds ripe tomatoes (4 medium)
1 tablespoon chopped onion	
2 cloves garlic	1 pound spaghetti
1 sprig rosemary (¼ teaspoon)	1 tablespoon butter
⅛ teaspoon each salt and pepper	¾ cup grated Parmesan cheese (or Cheddar cheese)
2 teaspoons flour	

Thinly slice the bacon and put into a saucepan with the oil, the onion and the unpeeled cloves of garlic. Sauté until golden but not brown. Add the rosemary and salt and pepper. Stir. Add the flour and stir well. Pour in the white wine and when half of it has evaporated add the tomatoes cut in pieces. Stir until well mixed and cook over a moderate flame for 25 minutes. Ten minutes before the sauce is done, put the spaghetti in abundant boiling salted water and cook for 8 minutes. In the meantime, put the sauce through the finest blade of a food mill (or blend in a blender). Put the drained spaghetti into a serving bowl with the butter cut in pieces, the sauce, and half the grated cheese. Toss until well mixed. Serve with the rest of the cheese sprinkled on top. Serves 4.

COOK'S SPAGHETTI
(*Spaghetti della Cuoca*)

Cooking time: 40 minutes

1¼ pounds lamb chops (4)	Salt and pepper to taste
Flour	½ cup white wine
5 tablespoons oil	1¼ pound ripe tomatoes
1 medium onion	(4 medium)
1 small stalk celery	1 pound spaghetti
1 small carrot	¾ cup grated Parmesan cheese
1 clove garlic	
6 rosemary leaves (or ¼ teaspoon dried)	

Prepare the lamb chops by cutting the membrane around each one every inch or so with a sharp knife or some scissors. This will keep the chops from getting out of shape during the cooking. Flour the chops and brown in a roomy saucepan in the hot oil. When browned on both sides add the onion, the celery, and the carrot, cut in pieces, the clove of garlic and the rosemary. Sauté over a low flame. Add salt and pepper to taste and pour in the white wine. Raise the flame and allow half the wine to evaporate. Now add the tomatoes cut in pieces and ⅓ cup of hot water. Bring to a boil again, then lower the flame and simmer for 25 minutes more. When the sauce is almost done, cook the spaghetti in abundant boiling salted water. While it is cooking, remove the chops from the sauce and put the sauce through a blender or the fine blade of a food mill. Put aside about 5 tablespoons of the sauce and pour the rest of it over the cooked, drained spaghetti together with half of the grated cheese. Toss until well mixed. Serve with the rest of the cheese sprinkled on top.

Serve the lamb chops as a second course with the sauce you have set aside spooned over them, and accompanied by baked beans. Serves 4.

PARSLEY SPAGHETTI
(*Spaghetti con Burro e Prezzemolo*)

Cooking time: 30 minutes

10 tablespoons butter	4 tablespoons mild cheese
1 tablespoon flour	spread
1 bouillon cube	3 tablespoons finely chopped
Salt and pepper	parsley
1 pound spaghetti	½ cup grated Cheddar cheese

Into a small saucepan put 4 tablespoons of the butter and the flour. Mix together over a low flame. Pour in, a little at a time, 1 cup of hot water in which the bouillon cube has been dissolved, stirring rapidly. Add a little salt and some pepper and continue to cook over a low flame for 15 minutes. When the sauce is almost done, put the spaghetti in abundant boiling salted water and cook for 8 minutes. While it is cooking add the cheese spread and 2 tablespoons of the parsley to the saucepan. Mix well and continue to cook slowly. When the spaghetti is cooked and drained, transfer it to a pre-heated serving bowl and add the rest of the butter cut in pieces, and toss well. Now add the cream sauce, half of the grated cheese, and the remaining tablespoon of parsley. Toss until all the ingredients are well mixed. Serve with the rest of the grated cheese sprinkled on top. Serves 4.

SKILLET SPAGHETTI
(*Spaghetti in Padella*)

Cooking time: 40 minutes

4 slices bacon	3 basil leaves (or ¼ teaspoon
1 medium onion	dried)
3 tablespoons oil	Salt and pepper to taste
1 pound ripe tomatoes (3	1 pound spaghetti
medium)	¾ cup grated Parmesan cheese

Cut the bacon and the onion into julienne strips and sauté in a saucepan with the oil until golden. Now add the peeled tomatoes (either fresh or canned), finely chopped, the chopped basil, and the salt and pepper. Stir well. Simmer for 30 minutes, stirring from time to time and mashing the larger pieces of tomato with a wooden spoon so that they become completely disintegrated. When the sauce is almost done, cook the spaghetti in abundant boiling salted water. Drain and put into a large ovenproof serving dish. Add all the sauce and half of the grated cheese. Mix well and spread evenly. Sprinkle with the rest of the grated cheese. Put in a preheated hot (425° F.) oven for about 10 minutes or until golden on top and along the sides. Serves 4.

SPAGHETTI WITH HOT SAUCE
(*Spaghetti Salsa Piccante*)

Cooking time: 40 minutes

3 slices bacon

1 medium onion

3 tablespoons oil

1 clove garlic

½ dried red pepper

1 stalk celery

1½ tablespoons flour

1 pound ripe tomatoes (3 medium)

¼ teaspoon paprika

2 basil leaves (or ⅛ teaspoon dried)

Salt and pepper to taste

1 bouillon cube

1 pound spaghetti

¾ cup grated pecorino cheese (or any local sharp cheese)

Thinly slice the bacon and the onion and put into a saucepan with the oil, the unpeeled clove of garlic, and the red pepper, chopped. Sauté over a moderate flame. Slice the celery and add. When all is golden, add the flour, stir well, and add the tomatoes, chopped, the paprika, the basil, salt, and pepper. Stir and cook over a high flame for 2 minutes. Dissolve the bouillon cube in ⅔ cup of hot water and pour into the saucepan. Allow the sauce to come to a boil again and then lower the flame. Simmer for 35 minutes more. When the sauce is almost done, cook the spaghetti in abundant boiling salted water for 8 minutes. Drain and put into serving bowl. Pour on all the sauce and half the grated cheese. Toss until well mixed. Serve with the rest of the cheese sprinkled on top. Serves 4.

SPAGHETTI WITH CLAMS AND TOMATOES
(*Spaghetti alle Vongole e Pomodoro*)

Cooking time: 40 minutes

2 cloves garlic
5 tablespoons oil
¼ dried red pepper
½ cup shelled clams
Salt and pepper to taste
1 tablespoon flour
⅓ cup white wine

1 pound ripe tomatoes (3 medium) (or canned peeled tomatoes)
2 basil leaves (or ⅛ teaspoon dried)
1 pound spaghetti
2 tablespoons chopped parsley

Peel the garlic and put it through a garlic press. Put into a saucepan with the oil and the red pepper and sauté over a low flame. When the garlic begins to get golden in color, add the clams, salt, and pepper. Sauté for 1 minute, stirring constantly. Now add the flour. Stir. Pour in the white wine and allow half of it to evaporate, stirring all the time. Add the tomatoes, chopped and peeled (if canned, also add the juice in the can), stir well, add the chopped basil, and simmer for 30 minutes. When the sauce is almost done, cook the spaghetti in abundant boiling salted water for 8 minutes. Drain and put into serving bowl. Pour on all the sauce and the chopped parsley. Toss until well mixed. Serve, making sure that each portion has its share of the clams left in the bottom of the bowl. Serves 4.

SPAGHETTI WITH SMOKED SALMON
(*Spaghetti al Salmone Affumicato*)

Cooking time: 40 minutes

½ pound smoked salmon
2 cloves garlic
5 tablespoons oil
¼ dried red pepper
2 teaspoons flour
⅓ cup white wine
1½ pounds ripe tomatoes (5 medium)

Salt and pepper to taste
3 basil leaves (or ¼ teaspoon

1 pound spaghetti
  dried)
1 chicken bouillon cube
2 tablespoons chopped parsley

First, soak the smoked salmon in cold water for about 10 minutes. Remove from water and dry with paper towel. Put the garlic through a garlic press and sauté in the oil until almost golden. Add the red pepper and continue to sauté. Cut the salmon into small pieces and add. Sauté for 1 minute, stirring continuously. Add the flour and stir. Pour in the white wine and stir until half the wine has evaporated. Now add the tomatoes (if you use canned tomatoes, chop them finely and add them to the saucepan with all their juice. If you use fresh tomatoes, peel them, remove the seeds, and chop them before adding to the saucepan). Add the salt and pepper and the basil. Dissolve the bouillon cube in ½ cup of hot water and pour into the sauce. Stir and allow to come to a boil again over a high flame. Now lower the flame and simmer for 35 minutes. The sauce should not be too liquid. Before the sauce is done, cook the spaghetti in abundant boiling salted water for 8 minutes. Put the cooked, drained spaghetti into a serving bowl with the sauce and half the chopped parsley. Toss until well mixed. Be sure to divide the pieces of salmon equally among the individual portions. Serve with the rest of the parsley sprinkled on top. Serves 4.

THE AUTHOR'S SPAGHETTI
(*Spaghetti dell'Autore*)

Cooking time: 40 minutes

1 pound ripe tomatoes (3 medium)	1 small onion
	3 tablespoons oil
1 clove garlic	Salt and pepper to taste
2 basil leaves (or ⅛ teaspoon dricd)	1 tablespoon flour
	1 bouillon cube
2½ tablespoons dried mushrooms	1 pound spaghetti
	2 tablespoons butter
½ pound pork (including fat)	¾ cup grated Parmesan cheese
¼ pound breast of chicken	

Peel tomatoes and then cut into pieces and put into a small saucepan together with the unpeeled clove of garlic and the basil leaves. Boil for 5 minutes. In the meantime put the mushrooms to soak in 1 cup of hot water. Chop the pork (with the fat) and the chicken breast together. Chop the onion finely. Put into a saucepan with the oil and sauté until almost golden in color. Add the chopped meat, salt and pepper, and then brown. Sprinkle the flour over the meat mixture and add the chopped mushrooms. Stir. Add the tomatoes, which have been passed through the fine blade of a food mill or in electric blender (until you have a purée). Stir again and pour into the mixture the bouillon cube dissolved in ½ cup of hot water. Cook over a moderate flame for 30 minutes. When the sauce is about done, put a large pot of salted water on to boil. When the water is boiling briskly, add the spaghetti. Cook for 8 minutes. Drain. Put onto serving platter. Place dabs of butter here and there on the spaghetti and pour the sauce over all with half of the Parmesan. Mix well and serve with the rest of the Parmesan sprinkled on top. Serves 4.

GOURMET SPAGHETTI
(Spaghetti del Buongustaio)

Cooking time: 50 minutes

3 slices bacon	1 bay leaf
¼ pound veal (stew meat)	1¼ pounds ripe tomatoes
1 medium large onion	(4 medium)
5 tablespoons oil	1 bouillon cube
2 cloves garlic	1 pound spaghetti
1 tablespoon flour	6 tablespoons grated Parmesan
½ cup white wine	cheese
Salt and pepper to taste	
4 basil leaves (or ¼ teaspoon dried)	

Slice the bacon, the veal, and the onion very thinly and put all into a saucepan with the oil and the unpeeled cloves of garlic. Brown over a high flame for 5 minutes. Add the flour and mix. Pour in the white wine and cook until half of it has evaporated. Stir. Add salt and pepper, the basil and bay leaf, and the tomatoes, which have been washed and cut up in pieces. Dissolve the bouillon cube in ¾ cup of hot water and add. Stir. Cover the saucepan and simmer over a moderate flame for 40 minutes. When the sauce is almost done, cook the spaghetti in abundant boiling salted water for 8 minutes. While it is cooking, put the sauce through the fine blade of a food mill, making sure that all the meat passes through until no pieces remain. If you have difficulty in doing this, you will find that, by returning some of the sauce to the food mill, the last traces of meat will disappear. When the spaghetti is cooked, drain and turn into a large serving bowl. Add the sauce and half the Parmesan and toss until well mixed. Serve with the rest of the Parmesan sprinkled over the individual servings. Serves 4.

SPRINGTIME SPAGHETTI
(Spaghetti Primavera)

This recipe was given to me by the hotel Le Dune, in Sabaudia, 50 miles from Rome. Its restaurant is considered the best in the area.

Cooking time: 30 minutes

1 medium onion	3 small ripe tomatoes
4 tablespoons oil	¾ cup shelled fresh peas
⅛ pound fresh mushrooms	2 thin slices cooked ham
1 medium carrot	Salt and pepper to taste
1 stalk celery	1 pound spaghetti
2 basil leaves (or ⅛ teaspoon dried)	¾ cup grated Parmesan cheese

Cut the onion into very thin strips and allow to soften—do not brown—in the oil. Wash the mushrooms and cut into very thin slices. Add to the onion mixture and cook for 2 minutes on low flame. In the meantime, cut up the carrot, the celery, the basil leaves, and the tomatoes into very thin strips and add all at once. Add the peas, which have been boiled in salted water and drained. Next add the ham, also cut up into very thin strips, and the salt and pepper. Simmer slowly for 15 minutes. Cook the spaghetti in abundant boiling salted water for 8 minutes and drain. Turn onto a large preheated serving dish. Pour the above sauce over the spaghetti, add the Parmesan, mix well, and serve.
Serves 4.

SPAGHETTI WITH BUTTER AND PARMESAN CHEESE
(*Spaghetti al Burro e Parmigiano*)

Cooking time: 15 minutes

1 pound spaghetti	1 cup grated Parmesan cheese
½ cup reserved spaghetti water	Salt and white pepper to taste
¾ cup butter	

Cook the spaghetti for 8 minutes in a large pot containing about a gallon of boiling salted water. Drain, being careful to reserve ½ cup of the water. Return the drained spaghetti to the pot in which it has been cooked (and which should still be hot). Add the ½ cup of water and the butter in pieces here and there. Mix well. Add the grated Parmesan a tablespoon at a time, tossing energetically after each addition. Continue tossing until creamy. Serve in heated plates with a sprinkling of Parmesan on top. Serves 4.

SPAGHETTI WITH CHICKEN LIVERS
(*Spaghetti con Fegatini di Pollo*)

This dish is a specialty of Maria di Michele, an expert cook and charming old lady who lives in Pescara, in Abruzzi. For seven years Signora di Michele served as cook to Queen Marie José di Savoia.

Cooking time: 25 minutes

1 small onion, chopped	3 basil leaves (or ¼ teaspoon
3 tablespoons oil	dried)
2 tablespoons butter	Salt and pepper to taste
6 chicken livers	1 pound spaghetti
1 pound tomatoes (3 medium)	¼ cup grated Parmesan cheese

Sauté the onion in the oil and butter until golden. Add the chicken livers, cut into small cubes. While they are cooking, peel the tomatoes and cut into pieces. Put into the saucepan with the chicken livers and add the basil leaves, salt, and pepper. Cook for 15 minutes more over a moderate flame or until the tomatoes are completely disintegrated. Cook the spaghetti in abundant boiling salted water for 8 minutes and drain. Pour the sauce over the spaghetti. Sprinkle with grated Parmesan, mix well, and serve immediately. Serves 4.

DUCAL SPAGHETTI
(*Spaghetti Ducale*)

Cooking time: 50 minutes

½ pound lamb	1 bouillon cube
¼ pound pork (with fat)	¼ cup seedless raisins
1 stalk celery	6 to 8 green olives
1 medium onion	2 basil leaves (or ⅛ teaspoon
5 tablespoons oil	dried)
Salt and pepper to taste	1 pound spaghetti
½ cup red wine	¾ cup grated Parmesan cheese
½ cup tomato paste	

Put the meat and the celery through the finest blade of the meat grinder. Chop the onion finely and put into a saucepan with the oil. When the onion is almost golden in color, add the ground meat mixture and salt and pepper to taste. Mix and brown over a high flame for 5 minutes. Pour in the red wine and stir. When half the wine has evaporated, add the tomato paste. Stir for 1 minute. Dissolve the bouillon cube in 1½ cups of hot water, pour into the saucepan, and stir well. When the sauce comes to a boil again, lower the flame and simmer for 40 minutes. In the meantime, cut up the raisins (which have been previously washed) into pieces. Also cut up the olives, from which the pits have been removed. Add the raisins, the olives, and the cut-up basil leaves when the sauce is almost done. Cook the spaghetti in abundant boiling salted water for 8 minutes. Drain and turn into a large serving bowl. Pour all the sauce over the spaghetti together with half the Parmesan. Toss until well mixed. Serve with the rest of the Parmesan sprinkled over individual servings. Serves 4.

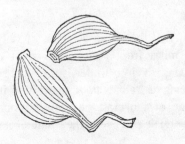

SPAGHETTI WITH PIGEON RAGÙ
(*Spaghetti con Ragù di Piccione*)

Cooking time: 55 minutes

1 young pigeon	Pinch of pepper
1 medium onion	2 bouillon cubes
2 tablespoons oil	1 pound spaghetti
½ cup white wine	1 cup grated Parmesan cheese
¼ cup butter	Salt and pepper to taste
1 tablespoon flour	5 slices American cheese
2 tablespoons tomato paste	(optional)

Clean the pigeon, debone it, and chop the meat. Finely chop the onion and sauté in the oil. Add the pigeon meat and sauté until golden. Add the white wine and allow it to evaporate. Add the butter, and when it has melted add the flour. Stir until well mixed over a low fire. Dilute the tomato paste in a little warm water and add. Now add some pepper and allow to simmer slowly. Make a broth by diluting the bouillon cubes in 1½ cups of hot water. When the sauce begins to thicken, add the broth a little at a time, whenever necessary. Simmer for 40 minutes. Cook the spaghetti in abundant boiling salted water for 8 minutes and drain. Put into serving bowl with the Parmesan. Mix well. Add salt and pepper to taste. Add the sauce and toss until well mixed. If desired, arrange slices of American cheese over all and cover in order to allow the cheese to melt. Keep covered for a few minutes. When cheese is melted, serve. Serves 4.

SPAGHETTI WITH TUNA FISH
(*Spaghetti al Tonno*)

This is a specialty of the Abruzzi region of Italy, an area that is about a hundred miles from Rome. The most important city of the region is l'Aquila, which in winter is the ideal spot for ski lovers. In summer thousands of Italians flock to Abruzzi in order to take in the beauties of one of the most beautiful national parks in Italy, where many wild animals still live in their natural state.

Cooking time: 43 minutes

2 cloves garlic

3 tablespoons oil

15 small pitted green olives
(black olives may also be
used)

1 (7-ounce) can tuna fish

1 tablespoon chopped parsley

1 pound tomatoes (3 medium)

Salt and pepper to taste

1 pound spaghetti

Sauté the finely chopped garlic in a saucepan with the oil. Now add
the olives, halved, the tuna fish, which you have previously crumbled
with a fork, and the finely chopped parsley. Cover the saucepan and
cook for 3 minutes. Add the tomatoes, peeled and mashed, the
salt and pepper. Simmer slowly for 40 minutes. Cook the spaghetti
in abundant boiling salted water for 8 minutes and drain. Pour
sauce over spaghetti and serve immediately.
Serves 4.

SERGEANT'S SPAGHETTI
(*Spaghetti del Sergente*)

Cooking time: 50 minutes

½ pound beef

7 tablespoons oil

1 medium large onion

1 clove garlic

1 stalk celery

3 basil leaves (or ¼ teaspoon
dried)

1 tablespoon flour

½ cup red wine

½ cup tomato paste

1 bouillon cube

Salt and pepper to taste

1 pound spaghetti

¾ cup grated Parmesan cheese

Cut the beef into very small pieces, put into a saucepan with the
oil, and start to brown. Finely chop the onion and add to the
saucepan. Sauté until the meat is nicely browned. Put the garlic
through a garlic press and finely chop the celery and the basil leaves.
Sauté for a minute or so. Add the flour, stirring until the ingredients
are well mixed. Add the wine, and when half of it has evaporated,
add the tomato paste. Stir. Dissolve the bouillon cube in 1½ cups of
hot water and pour into the saucepan. Add salt and pepper and
allow to come to a boil again. Lower the flame and allow the sauce
to cook slowly for 40 minutes. Cook the spaghetti in abundant
boiling salted water for 8 minutes. Drain and put onto a large

serving dish. Mix with all of the above sauce and half the Parmesan. Serve with a sprinkling of Parmesan over each individual serving. Serves 4.

OVEN-BAKED SPAGHETTI
(*Spaghetti Pasticciati*)

Cooking time: 25 minutes

¼ pound chicken livers
6 tablespoons butter
2 cups Ragù (see Index)
¼ cup sliced truffles

1 pound spaghetti
¾ cup grated Parmesan cheese
Salt and pepper to taste

Preheat oven to 350° F. Sauté the chicken livers in the butter until well browned. Mix together with the ragù and the thinly sliced truffles. Cook the spaghetti in abundant boiling salted water for 8 minutes and drain. Pour ragù over spaghetti. Add the Parmesan, add salt and pepper and toss until well mixed. Put into an ovenproof dish that has a tightly fitting cover. Cook covered in the oven for 15 minutes. Serve the spaghetti directly from the dish in which it has been cooked. This is an excellent picnic dish if care is taken to add a little extra ragù when mixing the spaghetti. Serves 4.

SPAGHETTI WITH ANCHOVIES AND MUSHROOMS
(*Spaghetti con Acciughe e Funghi*)

This sauce is a specialty of the Abruzzi area. It is also known by the name "woodcutters' spaghetti" (*spaghetti del boscaiuolo*), probably because woodcutters know where to look for and gather the excellent mushrooms that abound in the Abruzzi forests, one of the most beautiful national parks in Italy.

Cooking time: 20 minutes

1 pound fresh mushrooms
3 tablespoons oil
2 cloves garlic
1 (3-ounce) can anchovies

3 tablespoons finely chopped
   parsley
Salt to taste
1 pound spaghetti

Wash the mushrooms well and slice thinly. Boil for about 3 minutes in very little water. Drain. Put the oil and the cloves of garlic in a saucepan and fry over a low flame until the garlic is almost golden in color. Add the anchovies, cut up into small pieces. Brown slightly. Add the mushrooms and cook for 15 minutes. Two minutes before the sauce is done, add the parsley and the salt, being careful not to over-salt, since the anchovies are salty. Cook the spaghetti in abundant boiling salted water for 8 minutes and drain. Pour the sauce over very hot spaghetti and serve immediately. Serves 4.

SPAGHETTI ALLA PUTANESCA
(*Untranslatable*)

This spaghetti is a favorite dish at the Roman restaurant Il Caminetto, operating since 1959. This restaurant owes its excellent reputation to its good food and its famous customers, such as Katharine Hepburn, Stewart Granger, and Kirk Douglas.

Cooking time: approximately 20 minutes

10 to 15 black olives	3 anchovy fillets
1 pound very ripe tomatoes	4 tablespoons oil
(3 medium)	2 cloves garlic
1 tablespoon capers	3 tablespoons finely chopped
1 small dried red pepper (or	parsley
1 teaspoon crushed red	Salt to taste
pepper)	1 pound spaghetti

Remove the pits from the olives and cut olives into small pieces. Peel the tomatoes and cut them into very thin slices. Wash the capers and chop extremely finely. If you are using a whole red pepper, cut it into very small pieces. Mash the anchovies with a fork. Put the oil into a saucepan. Add the garlic, which has been finely chopped. When it begins to color, add the red pepper, anchovies, olives, capers, parsley, and tomatoes. Add salt to taste. Cook for 15 minutes. Cook the spaghetti in abundant salted water for 8 minutes. Pour the sauce over the drained spaghetti and serve. Serves 4.

SPAGHETTI WITH MOZZARELLA
(*Spaghetti con Mozzarella*)

The mozzarella cheese that is used in this recipe—and in numerous other Italian recipes—is an excellent cheese of Sicilian origin but widely used in all of Italy, particularly in the preparation of pizza. It is without doubt, together with Parmesan, the most popular cheese in this country.

Cooking time: 18 minutes

1 pound spaghetti	½ pound mozzarella cheese
¾ cup butter	2 cups milk
3 tablespoons grated Parmesan cheese	

Preheat oven to 450° F. Break the spaghetti in half and cook in abundant boiling salted water for about 8 minutes. Drain and season with the butter and 2 tablespoons of the Parmesan. Place the spaghetti in a buttered ovenproof dish, shallow enough so that the spaghetti is about 1½ inches deep. Thinly slice the mozzarella and arrange over the spaghetti. Pour the milk over all and sprinkle with the remaining grated Parmesan. Place in a hot oven for about 10 minutes or until the mozzarella is melted. Serve at once. Serves 4.

SPAGHETTI WITH TUNA AND ROSEMARY
(*Spaghetti con Tonno e Rosmarino*)

This easy-to-do dish comes to us from the city of Ancona, in the Marches region of Central Italy.

Cooking time: 12 minutes

1 pound spaghetti	1 piece fresh rosemary (or
3 tablespoons oil	1 teaspoon dried rosemary
2 cloves garlic, finely chopped	leaves)
1 (7-ounce) can of tuna	Pepper

Make the sauce while the spaghetti is cooking in abundant boiling salted water for 8 minutes. Put the oil and the garlic in a saucepan. Cook slowly until the garlic is almost golden in color. Mash up the tuna with a fork and add it to the saucepan. Now add the rosemary and 2 tablespoons of water. Cover the saucepan and cook for 10 minutes. Pour the sauce over the cooked, drained spaghetti, add 2 pinches of pepper, toss until well mixed, and serve. Serves 4.

SPAGHETTI MILANESE
(*Spaghetti Milanese*)

Cooking time: 25 minutes

½ pound asparagus	1 pound spaghetti
1 medium onion	2 eggs
4 slices lean bacon	¾ cup grated Parmesan cheese
3 tablespoons oil	Pepper
1 tablespoon flour	2 tablespoons butter
½ cup white wine	Salt and pepper to taste
1 chicken bouillon cube	

Remove the tough part of the asparagus stalks. Boil the tender tips and cut into 1-inch pieces. Slice and cut both the onion and the bacon into very thin julienne strips. Allow to brown slowly with the oil in a skillet. Add the flour. Stir. Pour the white wine into the mixture and allow to evaporate a little. Dissolve the chicken bouillon cube in 1 cup of hot water and add. Simmer over a moderate flame for 5 minutes. Add the asparagus tips and cook for 10 minutes more. In the meantime, cook the spaghetti in abundant boiling salted water for 8 minutes. While the spaghetti is cooking, break the eggs into a small bowl and beat with ½ tablespoon Parmesan and a pinch of pepper. Place the drained spaghetti in a preheated large serving bowl. Add butter, salt, and pepper, and mix well. Pour the sauce over the spaghetti with half the remaining Parmesan. Mix well. Add the beaten eggs. Toss until well mixed. Serve with a sprinkling of Parmesan over each serving. Serves 4.

SPAGHETTI WITH ANCHOVIES, TOMATOES, AND MUSHROOMS
(*Spaghetti con Acciughe, Pomodori, e Funghi*)

This dish is a specialty of the Abruzzi region of Italy.

Cooking time: 25 minutes

1 pound mushrooms	1 pound tomatoes (3 medium)
4 tablespoons oil	Salt and pepper to taste
2 cloves garlic	1 pound spaghetti
2 (2-ounce) cans anchovy fillets	2 tablespoons chopped parsley

Wash and thinly slice the mushrooms. Boil them for about 3 minutes in as little water as possible. Drain and set aside for use later. Put the oil and the garlic, very finely chopped, in a saucepan. Sauté gently for about 2 minutes. Mash the anchovies with a fork and add to saucepan. Add the mushrooms and the tomatoes, peeled and chopped. Stir. Add salt and pepper. Cook over a moderate flame for about 20 minutes. Cook the spaghetti in abundant boiling salted water for 8 minutes. Drain and put into a large serving bowl together with the sauce and the parsley. Toss until very well mixed. Serve immediately. Serves 4.

SPAGHETTI WITH UNCOOKED SAUCE
(*Spaghetti in Salsa Cruda*)

Cooking time: 10 minutes
Preparation time: 30 minutes

5 tablespoons oil
1 cup tomato juice (or prepared tomato sauce)
8 to 10 green olives
½ cup groviera (Swiss) cheese
4 ounces mozzarella cheese
1 tablespoon chopped parsley
2 fresh basil leaves (omit if you do not have fresh basil)
¼ teaspoon cayenne
Salt and pepper to taste
1 pound spaghetti
¼ cup heavy cream

Put into a bowl the following ingredients: the oil, the tomato juice (or sauce), the olives, pitted and cut in julienne strips, the groviera and mozzarella cheeses, also cut in julienne strips, and chopped parsley, the chopped basil, the cayenne, and salt and pepper to taste. Mix well and allow to stand at least 30 minutes. Cook the spaghetti in abundant boiling salted water for 8 minutes, drain, and put into a large serving bowl. Add the sauce and toss. Add the cream and toss again until well mixed. Serve immediately. Serves 4.

SPAGHETTI WITH VORACI CLAMS
(*Spaghetti alle Vongole Voraci*)

Voraci clams are a great delicacy in Italy. They are tiny triangular hard-shell clams with a firm, delicious flesh. A good substitute for the *voraci* clams in this recipe would probably be cherrystone clams as small as you can find them.

This recipe is a specialty of the Roman restaurant Piccolo Mondo. The proprietor, Signor Marino, told me that he prepared this dish while he was in Moscow on a trip to Russia. "It happened in a large hotel," he told me. "When the water began to boil, I threw the spaghetti into the pot. Naturally, instead of remaining vertical in the water, the spaghetti softened and the water covered it completely. The Russian cooks who were watching me, thinking that spaghetti should remain vertical in order to cook well and not stick together, hurried over with forks and knives in an effort to keep the spaghetti upright! As I didn't know how to speak Russian, I couldn't explain to them that their efforts were in vain!"

Signor Marino concluded from the above experience that in Russia pasta is not very well known.

Cooking time: 40 minutes

1 small onion	Salt and pepper to taste
6 tablespoons oil	2 cloves garlic
1 tablespoon flour	⅓ dried red pepper
1 pound ripe tomatoes (3 medium)	½ pound shelled voraci clams
	3 tablespoons chopped parsley
2 basil leaves (or ⅛ teaspoon dried)	½ cup white wine
	1 pound spaghetti
1 bouillon cube	

Thinly slice the onion and put into a saucepan with 2 tablespoons of oil. Sauté over a very low flame until the onion just begins to get golden. Add the flour and stir. Add the tomatoes, cut in pieces, and the basil leaves. Dissolve the bouillon cube in ½ cup of hot water and pour into the saucepan. Add salt and pepper, stir, and simmer for 20 minutes. In the meantime, put the garlic through a garlic press (or crush and finely chop) and put in a small skillet with 4 tablespoons of oil and the red pepper. Sauté gently until the garlic just begins to become golden in color. Add the clams and half the parsley. Continue to sauté until most of the moisture has evaporated. Add the white wine and allow half of it to evaporate. By this time the tomatoes in the saucepan should be done. Put the sauce through the medium blade of a food mill (or use a blender). Add the contents of the skillet to the sauce, stir, and continue to cook for 20 minutes. Stir every so often. The sauce should be fairly concentrated. Cook the spaghetti in abundant boiling salted water, for 8 minutes, drain, and put into a large serving bowl. Add the sauce and the rest of the parsley. Toss until well mixed. Serve immediately, making sure that each portion gets its share of the clams.

Serves 4.

SPANISH STEPS SPAGHETTI
(Spaghetti alla Piazza di Spagna)

The Piazza di Spagna, where the Spanish Steps are located, is without doubt the most famous piazza in Rome. In all of the neighboring streets one can find deluxe restaurants where one can eat marvelously well. Via Condotti, the most elegant street in Rome, leads into the Piazza di Spagna.

Cooking time: 50 minutes

½ ounce dried mushrooms	2 tablespoons flour
2 slices bacon	⅓ cup white wine
¼ pound stewing veal	⅓ cup tomato paste
1 stalk celery	1 bouillon cube
1 medium onion	1 bay leaf
3 tablespoons oil	1 pound spaghetti
Salt and pepper to taste	¾ cup grated Cheddar cheese

First of all, put the mushrooms to soak in ½ cup hot water. Put the bacon, the veal, and the celery through the fine blade of the meat chopper. Finely chop the onion, put it in a saucepan with the oil, and sauté. Add the ground meat mixture and salt and pepper to taste. Mix and sauté over a high flame. Add the flour and stir well. Pour in the white wine and allow half of it to evaporate while you stir. Add the tomato paste. Stir over a moderate flame. Dissolve the bouillon cube in 1½ cups of hot water and add. Remove the mushrooms from the water in which they have been soaking and add. Also add the bay leaf. Simmer over a moderate flame for 40 minutes, stirring often. When the sauce is almost done, cook the spaghetti in abundant boiling salted water for 8 minutes. Drain the spaghetti and put into a large serving bowl. Add the sauce and half of the grated cheese. Toss until well mixed. Serve with the rest of the cheese sprinkled on top. Serves 4.

SPAGHETTI WITH ONIONS
(*Spaghetti con Cipolle*)

Cooking time: 40 minutes
2 medium onions
4 tablespoons oil
1 tablespoon tomato paste
Salt and pepper to taste
1 pound spaghetti

Peel the onions and slice them very thinly. Put in a small saucepan with the olive oil and sauté over a *very low fire* for 30 minutes so that the onions become soft but not brown. Add the tomato paste, 4 tablespoons of water, and salt and pepper. Simmer over a low flame for 10 minutes. Cook the spaghetti in abundant boiling salted water for 8 minutes. Drain and put in large serving bowl. Add the sauce, toss until well mixed, and serve. Serves 4.

HERMIT'S SPAGHETTI
(*Spaghetti dell'Eremita*)

It is well known that hermits are poor, but that doesn't mean that they don't eat well, in Italy, at least. This recipe is very easy and is often prepared in Italian convents.

Cooking time: 30 minutes
3 slices lean bacon
4 tablespoons oil
2 cloves garlic
2 tablespoons flour
1 bouillon cube
½ pound fresh mushrooms
Salt and pepper to taste
2 eggs
Pepper
¾ cup grated pecorino cheese
1 pound spaghetti

Cut the bacon into julienne strips and put it in a saucepan with the oil and the garlic, very finely chopped. Sauté until golden over a low flame. Add the flour and stir. Dissolve the bouillon cube in

1 cup of hot water and add gradually, stirring continuously. Cut the mushrooms first into thin slices and then into julienne strips and add to the saucepan together with salt and pepper. Cook for 20 minutes over a moderate flame. In the meantime, break the 2 eggs into a bowl and beat together with a pinch of pepper and 1 tablespoon of the cheese. Cook the spaghetti in abundant boiling salted water for 8 minutes. Drain and put into a preheated serving bowl. Add the sauce and half of the remaining cheese. Toss. Add the beaten eggs and toss energetically. Serve with the rest of the cheese sprinkled on top. Serves 4.

SPAGHETTI TIVOLI STYLE
(*Spaghetti alla Tivolese*)

Tivoli, a marvelous city 17 miles from Rome, is famous for its fountains, which are situated in four different parks called: Villa Adriano, Villa d'Este, Villa Gregoriana, and in the street Viale delle Cento Fontane (Avenue of the Hundred Fountains). Naturally the beauty of this area draws thousands of tourists, and good restaurants are equally abundant. The following recipe comes from one of these, La Villa d'Este.

Cooking time: 50 minutes

¼ pound breast of chicken (or turkey)
3 tablespoons flour
4 tablespoons oil
3 slices lean bacon
1 medium onion
⅔ cup white wine
¼ pound fresh mushrooms

1 chicken bouillon cube
Salt and pepper to taste
¼ cup shelled green peas
2 eggs
¾ cup grated Parmesan cheese
Pepper
1 pound spaghetti

Cut the breast of chicken (or turkey) into slices. Pound the slices with a meat mallet so that they become uniformly thin, flour them, and brown them on both sides in a saucepan with the oil. When they are well browned, remove from the saucepan. Cut the bacon into julienne strips and put in the hot oil in the saucepan together with the onion, finely chopped. Sauté until almost golden in color. Add the rest of the flour and stir. Add the wine and the thinly sliced

mushrooms and cook over a moderate flame for 8 minutes. Dissolve
the bouillon cube in 1 cup of hot water and add to the saucepan
together with the salt and pepper. Bring to a boil again and add the
peas if fresh. If the peas are canned or if you have already cooked
them, first add the chicken breast sliced into julienne strips, cook for
10 minutes, and then add the peas. Continue to cook for 20 minutes
more over a low flame. In the meantime, break the eggs into a bowl
and beat, together with 1 tablespoon grated Parmesan and a pinch
of pepper. Cook the spaghetti in abundant boiling salted water for
8 minutes. Drain and put into a preheated serving bowl. Add all
of the sauce and half of the remaining grated cheese. Toss until very
well mixed. Add the beaten eggs and toss energetically. Serve, making
sure that each portion gets it share of the meat, the peas, and the
mushrooms and with the rest of the cheese sprinkled on top.
Serves 4.

SPAGHETTI WITH RAGÙ AND PEAS
(Spaghetti al Ragù con Piselli)

Cooking time: 80 minutes

Ragù (see Index)
2 slices lean bacon
1 tablespoon butter
1 tablespoon oil
2 tablespoons finely chopped
  onion

Salt and pepper to taste
1 pound green peas, shelled
  (2 cups)
1 pound spaghetti
¾ cup grated Parmesan cheese

Make the ragù as described in Chapter III. While it is cooking,
cut the bacon in julienne slices and put it in a saucepan with the
butter, the oil, and the onion. Sauté. If your peas are fresh add 1½
cups of hot water, salt and pepper, and the peas. If canned peas are
used, simply add ½ cup of water with the peas. Cook until the peas
are done. The mixture should not be too liquid. When the ragù is
almost done, cook the spaghetti in abundant boiling salted water.
Drain and put into a large serving bowl. Add ⅔ of the sauce and
half of the Parmesan. Toss. Serve with the rest of the cheese
sprinkled on top and with a spoonful of peas over each individual
portion. The meat may be sliced and served as a second course with
the rest of the sauce and the peas. Serves 4.

EMILIA-STYLE SPAGHETTI
(Spaghetti Emiliana)

Cooking time: 60 minutes

4 slices lean bacon	Salt and pepper to taste
1 medium onion	1 bouillon cube
4 tablespoons oil	⅓ cup tomato paste
¼ pound link sausage	2 slices mortadella sausage (or
1 stalk celery	bologna)
1 clove garlic	½ cup red wine
4 tablespoons flour	1 pound spaghetti
2 bay leaves	¾ cup grated Parmesan cheese

Cut the bacon into slices and then into julienne strips. Put in a saucepan with the onion also cut in julienne strips, and sauté in 2 tablespoons of oil until golden. In the meantime, boil the sausages in water in a small saucepan for 5 minutes. Finely chop the celery and the garlic, add to the saucepan with the bacon and the onion, and continue to sauté for 1 minute. Add the flour and stir. Add the bay leaves and salt and pepper. Dissolve the bouillon cube and the tomato paste in 1½ cups of hot water and add. Mix well and continue to cook for 50 minutes over a low flame. Remove the sausages from the water in which they have boiled and slice into coin-like slices. Brown these slices in the other 2 tablespoons of oil in a small skillet. Cut the mortadella into julienne slices and add to the skillet. Pour in the red wine and allow half of it to evaporate. Add the contents of the skillet to the sauce in the saucepan, stir and continue to cook. When the sauce is almost done, cook the spaghetti in abundant boiling salted water for 8 minutes, stirring often. When cooked, drain and put into a serving bowl. Add the sauce and half of the grated cheese. Toss until well mixed and serve with the rest of the cheese sprinkled on top. Serves 4.

FOUR SEASONS SPAGHETTI
(*Spaghetti Quattro Stagioni*)

Remember that in the Introduction of this book you will find several useful hints, such as how to keep parsley for several days.

Cooking time: 30 minutes

3 slices bacon	8 black olives
2 cloves garlic	2 eggs
2 tender artichokes	2 tablespoons chopped parsley
4 tablespoons oil	½ teaspoon salt
¼ pound fresh mushrooms	4 small ripe tomatoes
¼ pound fresh peas (½ cup shelled)	Salt and pepper to taste
	1 pound spaghetti

Slice the bacon into thin slices and brown slowly in a saucepan with the chopped garlic. Clean the artichokes and remove the leaves. Slice the artichoke hearts thinly. Add to saucepan with 3 tablespoons of the oil. Wash and thinly slice the mushrooms and add. Cook for 10 minutes. Next add the peas, which have been cooked previously, and the olives, pitted and thinly sliced. Beat the eggs together with the parsley and some salt. Grease a skillet with some oil and make a thin omelet. Slice this also and add to the contents of the saucepan, together with the tomatoes cut in slices, and salt and pepper. Simmer for 10 minutes. Cook the spaghetti in abundant boiling salted water for 8 minutes and drain. Pour the sauce over the spaghetti in a serving bowl. When making up the individual servings, make sure that each guest gets his share of the various ingredients of the sauce. Serves 4.

FIUGGI-STYLE SPAGHETTI
(*Spaghetti alla Fiuggi*)

This method of preparing spaghetti is characteristic of the Lazio province and particularly of the city of Fiuggi, an important Italian spa.

Cooking time: 50 minutes

1 medium onion	½ cup tomato paste
4 tablespoons oil	1 bouillon cube
½ pound lamb	2 fresh basil leaves (or ⅛
¼ pound pork (slightly fatty)	teaspoon dried)
1 stalk celery	1 pound spaghetti
Salt and pepper to taste	¾ cup grated Parmesan cheese
1 tablespoon flour	

Finely chop the onion and sauté in a saucepan with the oil over a low flame. In the meantime put the lamb, the pork, and the celery through the fine blade of a meat grinder. Add to the saucepan as soon as the onion begins to become golden in color. Brown over a high flame. Add salt and pepper and stir continuously for about 5 minutes. Add the flour and stir. Add the tomato paste and 1¼ cups of hot water in which the bouillon cube has been dissolved. Stir. Add the basil, chopped, stir, and continue to cook over a moderate flame for 35 minutes. Stir from time to time. When the sauce is almost done, cook the spaghetti in abundant boiling salted water, drain, and put in serving bowl with all the sauce and half the grated Parmesan. Toss until well mixed and serve with the rest of the cheese sprinkled on top. Serves 4.

SPAGHETTI PARTY
(*Spaghetti per una Festa*)

I thought that some of my readers who like to entertain might be pleased to know how to prepare a large quantity of pasta. Naturally, this recipe for 50 persons may be cut or increased according to your requirements.

Cooking time: 80 minutes

4 cups oil	½ cup flour
1 pound onions	1¼ cups tomato paste
5 cloves garlic	5 chicken bouillon cubes
8 pounds ripe tomatoes (24 medium)	1 pound fresh mushrooms
	¼ pound butter
Salt and pepper to taste	2 tablespoons lemon juice
10 leaves basil (or ¾ teaspoon dried)	1 pound cooked salami
	11 pounds spaghetti
2 pounds pork (slightly fatty)	2 pounds grated Cheddar cheese
1 pound breast of turkey	

Put half the oil in a large saucepan and add half the onions, cut up in pieces, and 2 unpeeled cloves of garlic. Sauté until golden. Add the tomatoes, cut in pieces, salt and pepper, and 5 leaves of basil. Cook for 10 minutes over a high flame. In the meantime, finely chop the rest of the onions and put into a large saucepan with the rest of the oil. Sauté until just golden. Grind the pork and add salt and pepper to taste. Sauté. Finely chop the breast of turkey and add. Stir and continue to sauté. Put the remaining cloves of garlic through a garlic press (or crush and finely chop) and chop the remaining basil leaves. When the meat is well browned, add the garlic and basil. Stir for 1 minute. Add the flour and stir until well mixed. Add the tomato paste and stir for about 2 minutes. Dissolve the bouillon cubes in 7 cups of hot water and add to the saucepan. Bring to a boil. Now take the tomato sauce in the other saucepan and pass it through a food mill or put in a blender. Add to the meat sauce, mix well, and simmer for 65 minutes. In the meantime, wash the mushrooms, slice them, and cut the slices into julienne strips. Put into a saucepan with the butter and lemon juice. Cook over a high flame. While the mushrooms are cooking, cut the cooked salami into slices and then into julienne strips. Add to the mushrooms together with salt and pepper to taste and cook over a low fire for 20 minutes. When the sauce has been cooking for about 60 minutes, add the mushroom-salami mixture. Cook the spaghetti in abundant boiling salted water for 8 minutes. It would probably be easier to divide the spaghetti in thirds and cook in three separate pots, figuring about 3 quarts of

water per pound of spaghetti. When the spaghetti has been cooked and drained, put into bowls or receptacles large enough to enable you to mix well with the sauce. Divide the sauce and grated cheese according to the number of batches of the spaghetti. Add the sauce and half the cheese allotted to each batch, toss and serve with the rest of the cheese sprinkled on top. Also have grated cheese on the table so each guest may help himself.
Serves 50.

PERUGIA-STYLE SPAGHETTI
(*Spaghetti alla Perugina*)

Perugia, the birthplace of this recipe, is in the province of Umbria, at an altitude of 1200 feet. In the thirteenth century Perugia was famous for her towers—70 in all! Later she was chosen as a papal residence. Perugia is one of the loveliest cities in Italy and has had the great fortune of being able to conserve throughout the centuries a great number of her historical monuments.

Cooking time: 80 minutes

½ pound pork	1 bouillon cube
6 tablespoons oil	2 eggs
1 medium onion	2 tablespoons milk
Salt and pepper to taste	2 tablespoons chopped parsley
1 tablespoon flour	¾ cup grated Parmesan cheese
1 pound ripe tomatoes	1 pound spaghetti
(3 medium)	

Thinly slice the pork and put it into a saucepan with 4 tablespoons of oil and the onion, also thinly sliced. Add salt and pepper to taste, and sauté until golden. Add the flour and stir. Add the tomatoes, coarsely chopped, and 1 cup of hot water in which you have dissolved the bouillon cube. Stir until well mixed and cook, covered, over a moderate flame for 70 minutes. Stir every once in a while. In the meantime, break the eggs into a small bowl and beat together with the milk, the parsley, ½ tablespoon of the grated Parmesan, salt and pepper. Heat the remaining 2 tablespoons of oil in a very large skillet (or use 2 small ones) and make a very thin crêpe-like omelet. Put the omelet on a wooden cutting board

to cool. When cool, cut into pieces about ½ inch square. Ten minutes before the sauce is done, cook the spaghetti in abundant boiling
salted water for 8 minutes. While it is cooking put the sauce through
the medium blade of a food mill (or in a blender). If you use a
food mill, make sure all the meat passes through. This will be easier
if you return some of the sauce already passed through to the food
mill. Put the blended sauce back into its original saucepan, add the
omelet squares, and bring to a boil again. By now the spaghetti has
cooked its required time. Drain and put into a large serving bowl.
Add all the sauce and half of the remaining Parmesan. Toss until
well mixed. Serve with the rest of the Parmesan sprinkled on top.
Serves 4.

LIGURE-STYLE SPAGHETTI
(*Spaghetti alla Ligure*)

A "Ligure" is an inhabitant of Liguria, a region of Northern Italy,
where pasta originated around the twelfth century (see the Introduction). Its most important cities are: La Spezia, Savona, Im-
peria, and, naturally, Genoa, which is one of the most important parts
of Europe.

Cooking time: 40 minutes

½ pound breast of turkey	Salt and pepper to taste
4 thin slices ham	1 clove garlic
2 tablespoons flour	5 leaves fresh basil (or ¼
5 tablespoons oil	teaspoon dried)
1 medium onion	1 tablespoon chopped parsley
½ cup white wine	2 tablespoons butter
1 pound ripe tomatoes (3	Pepper
medium)	1 pound spaghetti
1 chicken bouillon cube	¾ cup grated Parmesan cheese

Cut the turkey breast into fairly thick slices and then flatten each
slice with a meat mallet until quite thin. Spread the slices out on a
table top and put a slice of ham on each slice of turkey breast. Roll
each slice with care, making sure that the ham is on the inside
of each roll. Put the rolls on skewers, flour them on all sides, and
put them in a saucepan with the oil and the onion, cut in pieces.

Sauté until golden. Pour in the white wine and stir. When half the wine has evaporated, add the tomatoes, cut in pieces. Stir well and bring to a boil over a high flame. Dissolve the bouillon cube in ½ cup of hot water and add. Add salt and pepper to taste. Cook over a moderate flame for 30 minutes. In the meanwhile, make a paste out of the clove of garlic, crushed, the basil, very finely chopped, the parsley, the butter, and a generous pinch of pepper. Cook the spaghetti in abundant boiling salted water for 8 minutes. While the spaghetti is cooking, remove the turkey-ham rolls from the saucepan. Put the sauce through the fine blade of a food mill (or put in the blender) and return it to the saucepan in which it cooked originally. Add the paste you have prepared and allow to come to a boil again. Remove the rolls from the skewers and put into the sauce. When the spaghetti is cooked and drained, put in a large serving bowl with ¾ of the sauce and half of the Parmesan. Toss until well mixed. Serve with the rest of the Parmesan sprinkled on top. Serve the remaining sauce in a serving bowl along with the pasta. Serve the turkey-ham rolls as a second course accompanied by whatever vegetable you desire. Serves 4.

SPAGHETTI WITH ZUCCHINI
(*Spaghetti con Zucchini*)

Cooking time: 40 minutes

¾ pound small zucchini	1 bouillon cube
Salt	2 basil leaves (or ⅛ teaspoon
5 tablespoons oil	dried)
2 cloves garlic	2 tablespoons chopped parsley
4 anchovy fillets	Pepper
1 tablespoon flour	1 pound spaghetti
¼ cup white wine	½ cup grated Cheddar cheese

First of all prepare the zucchini. Slice the zucchini in very thin lengthwise slices, and then cut each slice into spaghetti-like strips about 3 inches long. Sprinkle with salt and put in a colander so that the water given off by the zucchini will drain off. Put the oil and the garlic, finely chopped, in a medium-size saucepan, and sauté until the garlic is almost golden in color. Cut up the anchovies into small pieces and add. Stir, mashing the anchovies with a wooden spoon

until they become a paste. Add the flour and stir well. Pour in the white wine and allow half of it to evaporate, stirring all the time. Now add the bouillon cube, dissolved in ½ cup of hot water, the basil leaves, cut in pieces, and the parsley. Do not add salt but add a generous pinch of pepper. Stir and simmer for 15 minutes. While the sauce is simmering, dry the zucchini with paper toweling, then flour. Fry them in a deep fat fryer or in a skillet with at least 4 inches of hot oil (corn, peanut, etc.). When the zucchini are nicely golden, remove with a slotted spoon and drain on paper toweling. Cook the spaghetti in abundant boiling salted water for 8 minutes, drain and put into a serving bowl. Add all of the sauce and the grated cheese. Toss until well mixed. Now add the zucchini. Mix, being careful to keep some of the zucchini aside to scatter on top of the spaghetti when it is brought to the table.
Serves 4.

MOLISE-STYLE SPAGHETTI
(*Spaghetti alla Molisana*)

Cooking time: 60 minutes

½ pound lamb	1 bay leaf
¼ pound hot Italian sausage	1 bouillon cube
1 medium onion	4 tablespoons mild cheese
4 tablespoons oil	spread
Salt and pepper to taste	1 pound spaghetti
1 small stalk celery	¾ cup grated Parmesan cheese
½ cup tomato paste	(or grated pecorino cheese)

Grind the lamb and the sausage, peeled. Finely chop the onion and sauté it in a saucepan with the oil until it is almost golden in color. Add the ground meat and sausage and the salt and pepper, and brown. Add the chopped celery. When all is well browned, add the tomato paste and the bay leaf. Dissolve the bouillon cube in 1½ cups of hot water and pour into the saucepan. Stir well. Simmer for 50 minutes, stirring from time to time. Ten minutes before the sauce is done, add the cheese spread and stir until it has melted, being very careful not to allow the sauce to come to a boil again after the addition of the cheese. Cook the spaghetti in abundant boiling salted water for 8 minutes, drain, and put in a serving dish.

Pour the sauce and half the grated cheese over spaghetti. Toss until well mixed. Spoon whatever sauce is left in the serving dish over each individual portion and sprinkle with the rest of the grated cheese. Serves 4.

GRAND HOTEL SPAGHETTI
(*Spaghetti alla Grand Hotel*)

While dining one evening at the Grand Hotel's restaurant The Rallye, one of the most elegant places in Rome, I enjoyed this dish so much I asked for the recipe so I could pass it on to you.

Cooking time: 50 minutes

¼ pound chicken breast	2 bouillon cubes
3 tablespoons oil	4 tablespoons butter
3 tablespoons flour	4 sprigs of parsley, chopped
1 medium onion	Pinch of pepper
3 thin slices cooked ham	¾ cup grated Parmesan cheese
2 tablespoons tomato paste	(or grated Cheddar cheese)
Salt and pepper	1 pound spaghetti

Slice the chicken breast into thin slices and pound them with a meat mallet to make them uniformly thin. Put the oil into a saucepan and heat. Flour the chicken breast slices and sauté in the hot oil until just golden. Remove from the saucepan. Finely chop the onion and put into the saucepan. Sauté over a low flame. In the meantime, cut the slices of chicken that you have already sautéed into julienne strips and return to the saucepan with the onion. Cut the ham also into julienne strips and add. Cook for 2 minutes. Add the remaining flour and mix well. Now add the tomato paste, the salt and pepper. Stir. Dissolve the bouillon cubes in 2 cups of hot water and pour into the saucepan. Allow to come to a boil again and then lower the flame and simmer for 40 minutes, stirring often. Meanwhile, make a paste by blending together the butter, the chopped parsley, a pinch of pepper, and 1 tablespoon of the grated cheese. Cook the spaghetti in abundant boiling salted water for 10 minutes. Just before it is done add the paste you have made out of the butter, etc. to the sauce. Bring it to a boil again and stir until well mixed. Drain the spaghetti and put into a preheated serving bowl with the sauce and half of the grated cheese. Toss until well mixed. Serve with the rest of the cheese sprinkled on top. Serves 4.

SPAGHETTI MARINO STYLE
(Spaghetti alla Marinese)

This recipe originated in Marino, a town about 25 miles from Rome, in what is known as the Castelli area.

Cooking time: 30 minutes

1 medium onion	Salt and pepper to taste
2 tablespoons butter	½ cup seedless raisins
½ pound ripe tomatoes (2 medium)	4 slices lean bacon
	3 tablespoons oil
2 basil leaves (or ⅛ teaspoon dried)	2 eggs
	¾ cup grated Parmesan cheese
1 bouillon cube	1 pound spaghetti

Cut the onion up in pieces and put into a saucepan with the butter. Cook until golden over a moderate flame. Next add the tomatoes, cut up in pieces, the basil leaves and the bouillon cube, dissolved in 1 cup of hot water. Salt and pepper. Cook for 20 minutes. In the meantime put the raisins to soak in a cup of water so that they will become plump. Cut the bacon in julienne strips and brown in a small skillet with the oil. Beat the eggs in a small bowl with a pinch of pepper and ½ tablespoon Parmesan and set aside for use later. When the tomatoes in the sauce are cooked, pass all the contents of the saucepan through the fine blade of a food mill. Return the sauce to the saucepan and add the raisins, which have been removed from the water and cut up into 2 or 3 pieces each. Bring sauce to a boil again and allow to simmer slowly. In the meantime, cook the spaghetti in abundant boiling salted water for 8 minutes. Drain. Place in a large serving bowl. Add the bacon and the oil in which it has been browned. Toss. Pour on the sauce, add half the Parmesan, and toss until well mixed. Now add the beaten eggs. Toss until well mixed. Serve with remaining Parmesan sprinkled over each serving. Serves 4.

ALFREDO'S SPAGHETTI
(*Spaghetti alla Alfredo*)

This is one of the recipes given to me by Alfredo, who collaborated with me on this book, on one hand by supervising the recipes
and on the other by revealing some of the secrets that he has picked
up during his 40 years as one of the best chefs in Italy.

Cooking time: 30 minutes

3 slices lean bacon	2 basil leaves (or ⅛ teaspoon
3 tablespoons oil	dried)
1 medium onion	1 pound spaghetti
1 clove garlic	4 tablespoons butter
¼ pound breast of chicken	¾ cup grated Parmesan cheese
Salt and pepper	
½ pound tomatoes (2 medium),	
peeled	

Cut the bacon into 2-inch julienne strips and sauté in the oil in a
saucepan. Add the *whole* onion and the *whole* clove of garlic and
brown slightly. Cut the chicken breast into julienne strips like the
bacon and add to the saucepan. Sauté slowly. Add salt and pepper
to taste. In the meantime you will have prepared the peeled tomatoes
(see Index). Cut the tomatoes also into julienne strips and add to
the saucepan. Stir for 1 minute until all the ingredients are well
mixed. Remove the onion and the garlic and allow the sauce to
simmer for about 20 minutes over a low flame, after having added
the basil. Cook the spaghetti in abundant boiling salted water for 8
minutes. Drain well and put into a serving bowl. Add the butter, cut
in pieces, the sauce, and half of the Parmesan. Toss until well
mixed. Serve with a sprinkling of Parmesan on each portion.
Serves 4.

SPAGHETTI LORENZA
(*Spaghetti Lorenza*)

The name of this recipe originally comes from *Lorenzaccio,* a five-
act drama by the French poet Alfred de Musset, a great lover of
Naples and of pasta. In our Introduction we quote a short passage

from one of his works which glorifies Italy. The Neapolitans made a recipe for *spaghetti alla Lorenzaccio,* which later was shortened to *alla Lorenza.* If this dish lost part of its name, it still maintains in its entirety its delicious flavor when it is prepared as indicated below.

Cooking time: 10 minutes

3 slices lean bacon	Salt to taste
3 tablespoons oil	1 cup sour cream
4 sage leaves (or ¼ teaspoon dried)	1 pound spaghetti
2 egg yolks	½ cup grated Parmesan cheese

Cut the bacon into small cubes and sauté it in the oil. Add the sage leaves. In a large serving bowl (the same in which you plan to serve the spaghetti) beat the egg yolks with a pinch of salt. Add the sour cream and mix. Cook the spaghetti in abundant boiling salted water for 8 minutes and drain, quickly add it to the bowl containing the egg-cream mixture, and toss very quickly and very thoroughly. Add the sautéed bacon cubes and the oil, mix well, sprinkle with the Parmesan, and serve. Serves 4.

SPAGHETTI SALAD NO. 1
(*Insalata di Spaghetti No. 1*)

This method of preparing pasta is more commonly used in summer, and particularly on the Italian Riviera, in San Remo among other places.

Cooking time: 5 minutes (for the sauce)
                10 minutes (for the spaghetti)

1 (5-ounce) can tuna	2 cloves garlic
¼ pound Swiss cheese	4 leaves basil (or ¼ teaspoon dried)
4 small pickles	
8 small pickled mushrooms	5 tablespoons oil
3 red peppers	1 pound spaghetti
6 green olives, pitted	

Cut up into small pieces the tuna, the Swiss cheese, pickles, mushrooms, red peppers, and the olives. Put all in the bowl in which

you plan to serve the spaghetti. Finely slice the garlic, chop the basil, and sauté in the oil in a small skillet. Cook the spaghetti in abundant boiling salted water for 8 minutes, drain, and add to the ingredients in the bowl. Mix well. Now pour the oil, the garlic, and the basil over all, toss until well mixed, and serve immediately.
Serves 4.

SEAFOOD SPAGHETTI
(*Spaghetti ai Frutti di Mare*)

A specialty from Pescara, in Abruzzi.

Cooking time: 20 to 25 minutes

½ pound frozen mussels	4 tablespoons oil
½ pound frozen clams	¼ cup brandy
½ pound frozen shrimp	1 tablespoon flour
½ teaspoon lemon juice	1 pound spaghetti
¼ pound mushrooms	2 tablespoons chopped parsley
1 medium onion	

First defrost the seafood. Now start the sauce. Put some lemon juice in the water you use for cleaning the mushrooms. Drain the mushrooms and slice very thinly. Thinly slice the onion, and sauté it in the oil in a saucepan. Add the mushrooms and cook for about 10 minutes. Pour in the brandy and allow to evaporate. Add the flour and stir well. Add a little of the clam water and stir until creamy. Add the defrosted mussels, clams, and shrimp, and cook for 5 minutes, always stirring gently. If the sauce becomes too thick, add a little of the clam water. Cook the spaghetti in abundant boiling salted water for 8 minutes, drain, add the sauce and the chopped parsley, toss until well mixed, and serve. Serves 4.

SPAGHETTI WITH RAGÙ, ITALIAN STYLE
(*Spaghetti al Ragù all'Italiana*)

Ragù is a sauce for spaghetti and macaroni which is widely used in Italian cuisine. There are several varieties of ragù. This sauce may be used with all types of spaghetti or macaroni and particularly with oven-baked pasta. This is Chef Scocchera's recipe for this delicious sauce, reference to which is made several times in this book, such as in Spaghetti Pasticciati.

Cooking time: 80 minutes

2 ounces dried mushrooms
3 slices bacon
1 medium onion
3 tablespoons oil
1 medium carrot
1 stalk celery
1 pound beef (the beef may be eye of the round, heel of the round, round, or pot roast)
1 bay leaf

Salt and pepper to taste
1 cup white wine
⅓ cup tomato paste
1 pound tomatoes (3 or 4 medium), peeled
2 basil leaves (⅛ teaspoon dried)
1 pound spaghetti
¾ cup grated Parmesan cheese

Put the dried mushrooms to soak in a cup of lukewarm water. Thinly slice the bacon and the onion, put into a saucepan with the oil, and sauté slowly. Finely chop the carrot and the celery and add. Cook for 2 minutes. Now add the beef, the bay leaf, and salt and pepper. Brown for about 10 minutes. Pour in the white wine. When the wine has evaporated, add the tomato paste and the tomatoes, which have been put through the fine blade of a food mill or puréed in a blender. Finely chop the mushrooms and the basil and add to the sauce. Cook over a moderate flame for 70 minutes. Cook the spaghetti (or macaroni) in abundant boiling salted water for 8 minutes, drain, put in serving dish. Add sauce and Parmesan. The meat may be sliced and served apart with its own sauce.
Serves 4.

SUMMERTIME SPAGHETTI
(Spaghetti per l'Estate)

Cooking time: 25 to 30 minutes

2 medium carrots
1 leek
1 large stalk celery
5 basil leaves (or ½ teaspoon dried)
5 tablespoons oil

1 tablespoon tomato paste
1¼ cups shelled peas
Salt to taste
5 anchovy fillets
1 pound spaghetti

Finely chop the carrots, the leek, the celery, and the basil. Put into a saucepan with the oil and cook very slowly over a very low fire until softened—about 10 or 15 minutes. Stir occasionally. Dilute the tomato paste in a cup of warm water and pour over the vegetables. Add the peas with a pinch of salt, cover, and simmer for about 15 minutes (depending on the size of the peas). Stir from time to time, adding a little boiling water when necessary. When the sauce is ready, add the anchovies, cut up into small pieces. Cook the spaghetti in abundant boiling salted water for 8 minutes, drain. Pour sauce over spaghetti and serve immediately.
Serves 4.

SPAGHETTI WITH PIZZA SAUCE
(*Spaghetti alla Pizzaiola*)

The Neapolitans created this sauce for pizza. Later, around the end of the nineteenth century, it was used for pasta . . . *ergo* the name *pizzaiola.*

Cooking time: 30 minutes

2 cloves garlic	1 pound ripe tomatoes (3 or
6 tablespoons oil	4 medium)
1 tablespoon flour	Salt and pepper to taste
1 teaspoon dried chopped	1 small bouillon cube
orégano leaves (or ½	1 pound spaghetti
teaspoon if in powder)	3 tablespoons chopped parsley

Put the garlic through a garlic press (or crush and finely chop). Put in a saucepan with the oil and sauté slowly until the garlic is almost golden. Add the flour and the orégano and stir. Add the tomatoes, which you have peeled and chopped finely, and add salt and pepper (be generous with the pepper). Mix well. Pour in ⅓ cup of water in which the bouillon cube has been dissolved. Stir and continue to cook for about 25 minutes. Stir every once in a while. When the sauce is almost done, cook the spaghetti in abundant boiling salted water for 8 minutes. Add the parsley to the sauce. The sauce should be fairly thick, not watery. Drain the cooked spaghetti and put into a large serving bowl. Add the sauce and toss until well mixed. Spoon the sauce left in the bottom of the bowl over each individual portion. Serves 4.

SPAGHETTI ALLA MARINARA
(*Spaghetti alla Marinara*)

There isn't a single restaurant along the Italian coast which does not serve spaghetti seasoned in the manner described below. *Spaghetti alla marinara* originated in Pescara, a city in Abruzzi on the Adriatic coast.

Cooking time: 40 minutes

2 cloves garlic	Salt and pepper to taste
6 tablespoons oil	2 leaves fresh basil (or ⅛
½ dried red pepper	teaspoon dried)
1 tablespoon flour	1 pound spaghetti
⅓ cup white wine	3 tablespoons chopped parsley
1¼ pounds ripe tomatoes (4 or	
5 medium), peeled, chopped	

Put the garlic through a garlic press (or crush and finely chop). Put into a saucepan with the oil and the red pepper, thinly sliced, and sauté until the garlic is almost golden in color. Add the flour and stir. Pour in the white wine and allow half of it to evaporate, stirring continuously. Add the tomatoes (either fresh or canned), salt and pepper, and the basil, chopped. Stir until all the ingredients are mixed and simmer for 35 minutes. When the sauce is almost done, cook the spaghetti in abundant boiling salted water for 8 minutes. The sauce has continued to simmer and has become fairly thick. Drain the spaghetti and put in a preheated serving bowl. Add all the sauce and the parsley. Toss until very well mixed. Serve immediately. Serves 4.

LIGHT CAVALRY SPAGHETTI
(*Spaghetti alla Cavalleggera*)

One must go back to the nineteenth century to find the source of this recipe, which owes its existence to a Neapolitan cook who dedicated it to a light cavalry regiment in which he was fulfilling his military duty. The name of the regiment, Cavalleggera, comes from *cavallo,* which means "horse."

Cooking time: 10 minutes

6 tablespoons butter	Salt and white pepper
4 egg yolks	1 cup shelled walnuts
1 cup grated Parmesan cheese	1 pound spaghetti

In the bowl in which you plan to serve the spaghetti beat together the butter, softened, the egg yolks, the grated Parmesan, and the salt and white pepper. Chop the walnuts and add to the bowl. Cook the spaghetti in abundant boiling salted water for 8 minutes, drain, toss with the walnut mixture until well mixed, and serve immediately. Serves 4.

SPAGHETTI NOVARA STYLE
(*Spaghetti alla Novarese*)

Cooking time: 60 minutes

3 slices bacon	2 tablespoons flour
1 medium onion	½ cup red wine
4 tablespoons oil	Salt and pepper to taste
½ pound lamb	¼ pound fresh mushrooms
1 clove garlic	1 pound spaghetti
6 rosemary leaves (or ¼ teaspoon dried)	¾ cup grated Parmesan cheese
½ pound ripe tomatoes (2 medium)	

Cut the bacon and the onion into julienne strips and sauté in a saucepan with the oil. Cut the lamb into julienne strips also and add to the saucepan. Allow to brown slowly. In the meantime put into a small saucepan the chopped garlic and rosemary and the tomatoes, cut in pieces. Boil for 8 minutes. Pass the tomatoes through the fine blade of a food mill (or blend in a blender). By this time the bacon, onion, and lamb are sufficiently browned. Add the flour and mix well. Pour in the red wine and stir. When half the wine has evaporated, add salt and pepper and the tomato mixture. Stir. Simmer slowly for 40 minutes. Twenty minutes before the sauce is done, add ½ cup of hot water and the mushrooms, which have been washed and thinly sliced. Ten minutes before the sauce is done, cook the spaghetti in abundant boiling salted water for 8 minutes. Drain and put in large serving bowl. Pour the sauce and sprinkle half the Parmesan over the spaghetti. Toss. Serve with the rest of the cheese sprinkled on top. Serves 4.

FUSILLI ROMAN STYLE
(Fusilli alla Romana)

Cooking time: 40 minutes

½ pound chicken giblets
5 tablespoons dried mushrooms
   (or ½ pound fresh)
3 slices bacon
4 tablespoons oil
1 medium onion
Salt and pepper to taste

1 bay leaf
½ cup white wine
1 pound peeled tomatoes (3 or
   4 medium)
1 pound fusilli
1 cup grated Parmesan cheese

Wash the giblets well and boil for 2 minutes. Put the dried mushrooms to soak in 1 cup warm water. Sauté the bacon, thinly sliced, in oil in a saucepan. Coarsely chop the giblets and sauté together with the bacon, the onion, finely chopped, salt and pepper, and the bay leaf for 5 minutes. Pour in the white wine and allow half of it to evaporate. Remove the mushrooms from the water and chop coarsely. Add and stir. Add the tomatoes, chopped (for peeling instructions see the Introduction), and stir. Simmer over a moderate flame for 30 minutes. Just before the sauce is ready, cook the fusilli in boiling salted water for 10 minutes. Drain and put in a serving bowl. Add all the sauce and half the grated cheese. Toss until well mixed. Serve with the rest of the cheese sprinkled on top. Serves 4.

FUSILLI WITH MUSHROOM SAUCE
(Fusilli in Salsa di Funghi)

Cooking time: 30 minutes

3 ounces dried mushrooms
½ pound ground pork (fatty)
3 tablespoons oil
2 cloves garlic
3 basil leaves (or ¼ teaspoon
   dried)
Salt and pepper to taste

2 tablespoons flour
½ cup white wine
¼ cup tomato paste
1 bouillon cube
1 pound fusilli
1 cup grated Parmesan cheese

Put the dried mushrooms to soak in 1½ cups warm water. Brown the ground pork in a saucepan with the oil. While it is browning, finely chop the garlic and the basil leaves. Add as soon as the meat is well browned. Add salt and pepper to taste. Add the flour and stir. Pour in the white wine and allow half of it to evaporate, stirring constantly. Remove the mushrooms from the water (reserve), chop finely, and add to the saucepan. Add the tomato paste, continuing to stir until it is well blended. Dissolve the bouillon cube in the mushroom water and add. Simmer over a moderate flame for 20 minutes. When the sauce is almost ready, cook the fusilli in abundant boiling salted water for 10 minutes. Drain and put in a serving bowl together with the sauce and half of the grated Parmesan. Mix well and serve with the rest of the cheese sprinkled on top.
Serves 4.

FUSILLI AURORA
(*Fusilli Aurora*)

Cooking time: 30 minutes

10 tablespoons butter	½ cup milk
1 medium onion	Salt and pepper to taste
2 tablespoons flour	1 pound fusilli
½ pound tomatoes (2 medium), peeled	1 cup grated Swiss cheese
	1 pinch cayenne

Melt half of the butter in a small saucepan. Add the onion, coarsely chopped, and sauté until softened but not colored. Add the flour and stir a minute or so. Add the tomatoes, cut up, milk, and salt and pepper. Simmer for 30 minutes over a low flame. When the sauce is almost ready, cook the fusilli in abundant boiling salted water for 10 minutes. Drain and put in a serving bowl. Add the sauce and half of the cheese. Mix well. Mix the rest of the cheese with a generous pinch of cayenne and sprinkle on top.
Serves 4.

FUSILLI VILLA D'ESTE
(*Fusilli alla Villa d'Este*)

This recipe was given me by the restaurant Villa d'Este, considered one of the best in Milan.

Cooking time: 40 minutes

⅓ pound pork (fatty)
¼ pound chicken breast
2 tablespoons oil
1 small onion
Salt and pepper to taste
2 tablespoons flour
1 chicken bouillon cube
¼ cup tomato paste

2 basil leaves, chopped (or ⅛ teaspoon dried)
½ cup heavy cream
⅓ cup shelled green peas
1 pound fusilli
4 tablespoons butter
1 cup grated Parmesan cheese

Grind together the pork and the chicken breast, and put in a saucepan with the oil and the onion, finely chopped. Add salt and pepper, and brown over a moderate flame for 10 minutes. Add the flour and stir. Dissolve the bouillon cube in 1½ cups hot water in which the tomato paste has also been diluted. Add to the saucepan and stir. Add the chopped basil, the cream, and cover and simmer for 30 minutes more. In the meantime, the water for cooking the fusilli shall have been heating. Also, in a small saucepan cook the peas in water until done. When the sauce is almost ready, cook the fusilli in boiling salted water for 10 minutes. Drain and put in a serving bowl. Add the sauce (to which the peas have been added), the butter in dabs, and half of the grated cheese. Mix well and serve with the rest of the cheese sprinkled on top.
Serves 4.

SPRINGTIME FUSILLI
(Fusilli Primavera)

Cooking time: 30 minutes

3 slices lean bacon
4 tablespoons oil
1 medium onion
1 stalk celery
1 small carrot
½ pound peas
Salt and pepper to taste
¾ pound ripe tomatoes (3 medium)

½ pound fresh mushrooms
¼ pound asparagus tips (⅓ cup)
2 basil leaves (or ⅛ teaspoon dried)
1 pound fusilli
2 tablespoons chopped parsley

Cut the bacon into julienne strips and brown in 2 tablespoons of the oil in a saucepan. Add the thinly sliced onion and sauté. Add the celery and the carrot, cut in strips. Cook for 2 minutes. Add 1 cup boiling water. Stir and bring to a boil again. Add the peas and the salt and pepper, allowing to boil over a high flame. While the peas are cooking, put the cut-up tomatoes in another saucepan. Boil for 2 minutes and pass through the fine blade of a food mill or put in a blender. In the same saucepan put the thinly sliced mushrooms and the rest of the oil. Cook for a minute or so, then add the puréed tomatoes. Boil for 5 minutes, then add the asparagus tips. Simmer for 10 minutes more. Add salt and pepper and the finely chopped basil leaves. The peas should be cooked by this time. Mix the contents of the 2 saucepans and cook for 5 minutes. Cook the fusilli in abundant boiling salted water for 10 minutes, drain, and put in serving bowl. Add the parsley to sauce just before mixing with the fusilli. Serves 4.

FUSILLI SICILIAN STYLE
(Fusilli alla Siciliana)

Cooking time: 40 minutes

2 cloves garlic
4 tablespoons oil
½ pound tomatoes (2 medium), peeled
⅓ pound eggplant
¼ pound yellow peppers
1 (2-ounce) can anchovy fillets
3 ounces (10 to 12) pitted olives

2½ tablespoons chopped capers
4 basil leaves (or ¼ teaspoon dried)
Salt and pepper to taste
1 pound fusilli
1 cup grated pecorino cheese

Cut the garlic cloves in half and sauté in the oil in a saucepan. When golden in color, remove the garlic and add the cut-up peeled tomatoes. Cook for a few minutes over a moderate flame. Dice the eggplant and add to the sauce. Cook for 5 minutes. Cut the yellow peppers into julienne strips and add, together with the cut-up anchovies and olives. Finely chop the capers and the basil and add also the salt and pepper. Stir and simmer for 30 minutes over a low flame. Cook the fusilli in abundant boiling salted water for 10 minutes. Drain. Add the sauce and the grated pecorino. Toss to mix well. Serves 4.

FUSILLI IN GOLDEN SAUCE
(*Fusilli in Salsa Dorè*)

Cooking time: 25 minutes

¼ cup tomato paste
1 chicken bouillon cube
Salt and pepper to taste
1 pound fusilli
8 tablespoons butter

1 cup grated Dutch cheese
  (Edam or Gouda)
⅔ cup grated Parmesan cheese
2 egg yolks
1 cup cream

Preheat oven to 325° F.

In a small saucepan put 1½ cups hot water, the tomato paste, the bouillon cube and salt and pepper. Simmer for 15 minutes. Cook the fusilli in abundant salted water for 10 minutes, drain and put in ovenproof dish. Add the butter in dabs, the sauce, and half of the 2 types of cheese mixed together. Mix well. Beat the 2 egg yolks with the cream and add to the pasta. Toss to mix well. Level off the pasta, sprinkle the rest of the cheese on top, and put in a moderately slow oven for 10 minutes. After removing from the oven allow to rest a few minutes before serving. Serves 4.

FUSILLI ITALIAN STYLE
(*Fusilli all'Italiana*)

Cooking time: 40 minutes

1 1½-pound spring chicken
2 tablespoons flour
5 tablespoons oil
1 large onion
1 clove garlic
Salt and pepper to taste
1 carrot
1 stalk celery

½ cup white wine
½ pound ripe tomatoes (2
  medium)
1 chicken bouillon cube
3 basil leaves (or ¼ teaspoon
  dried)
1 pound fusilli
1 cup grated Parmesan cheese

Cut the chicken into 8 pieces. Roll in flour and brown in the oil in a saucepan. Add the sliced onion and garlic, and sauté for 3 minutes. Add salt and pepper to taste. Add the sliced carrot and celery and the wine, and allow to evaporate for 2 minutes. Add the cut-up tomatoes and mix well. Dissolve the bouillon cube in ¾ cup hot water and pour into saucepan. Bring to a boil and add the basil leaves. Lower flame and simmer for 30 minutes. When the sauce is almost done cook the fusilli in abundant boiling salted water for 10 minutes. While it is cooking, remove the chicken from the saucepan and pass the sauce through the fine blade of a food mill or put in a blender. Drain the cooked fusilli and add all but 5 tablespoons of the sauce and half the grated cheese. Mix well and serve with the rest of the cheese sprinkled on top. Spoon the rest of the sauce over the chicken and serve as a second course. Serves 4.

FUSILLI ISLE OF CAPRI
(*Fusilli all'Uso di Capri*)

The isle of Capri is located in the Gulf of Naples and is a great tourist center. Every summer many members of the international jet set may be found there.

Cooking time: 40 minutes

1 pound ripe red tomatoes (3 medium)	3 basil leaves (or ¼ teaspoon dried)
1 medium onion	1 tablespoon chopped parsley
4 tablespoons oil	2 thin slices cooked ham
¾ pound lamb, finely ground	1 pound fusilli
Salt and pepper to taste	4 tablespoons butter
1 clove garlic	1 cup grated Parmesan cheese

Cut up the tomatoes and put in a saucepan. Bring to a boil and boil for 2 minutes. Pass the tomatoes through the fine blade of a food mill or put in a blender. Sauté the finely chopped onion in the oil. When golden add the lamb, salt, and pepper, and brown over a moderate flame for 6 minutes. In the meantime chop together *very* finely the crushed garlic, the basil, and the parsley, and add to the meat mixture. Stir for 1 minute, then add the sieved tomatoes. Stir, cover, and allow to simmer for 30 minutes. Stir from time to time. Cut the ham into julienne strips and have ready to add to the sauce 1 minute before seasoning the pasta. Cook the fusilli in abundant boiling salted water for 10 minutes. Drain and put in a serving bowl with the sauce (to which the ham has been added), the butter, and half of the grated cheese. Mix well and serve with the rest of the cheese sprinkled on top. Serves 4.

FUSILLI CALABRESE STYLE
(*Fusilli alla Calabrese*)

Calabria is a region with a particularly hot climate. It is in the extreme southern part of the Italian peninsula and its principal city is Reggio Calabria.

Cooking time: 40 minutes

½ pound pork, slightly fatty	35 to 38 pitted black olives
3 tablespoons oil	Salt and pepper to taste
2 cloves garlic	1 pound fusilli
½ teaspoon ground red pepper or paprika	1 cup grated pecorino cheese
½ cup plus 2 tablespoons tomato paste	

Put the pork through the fine blade of the meat grinder and sauté in the oil in a saucepan over a high flame until nicely browned. Add the crushed, finely chopped garlic and the hot pepper (or paprika), and sauté for 1 minute more. Add the tomato paste and stir continuously for 1 minute, then add 1½ cups hot water. Add the coarsely chopped olives, salt, and pepper. Stir and cover the saucepan. Simmer for 30 minutes. When the sauce is almost done, cook the fusilli in abundant salted boiling water for 10 minutes. Drain and put in a serving bowl. Add all the sauce and half of the grated cheese. Mix well and serve with the rest of the cheese sprinkled on top. Serves 4.

FUSILLI WITH CREAM
(*Fusilli in Salsa Panna*)

Cooking time: 20 minutes

1 small onion	Salt to taste
6 tablespoons butter	1 pound fusilli
1 tablespoon chopped parsley	½ cup heavy cream
Freshly grated nutmeg	1 cup grated Parmesan cheese

Chop the onion very finely and sauté in the butter in a saucepan until barely golden. Add the parsley, a little freshly grated nutmeg, and 2 tablespoons of water. Simmer for 12 minutes over a very low flame. Salt to taste. In the meantime cook the fusilli in rapidly boiling salted water for 10 minutes. Drain and put in a preheated serving bowl. Add the contents of the saucepan, the cream, and half the grated Parmesan. Mix well and serve with the rest of the grated cheese sprinkled on top. Serves 4.

FUSILLI WITH EGG SAUCE
(*Fusilli in Salsa di Uova*)

Cooking time: 20 minutes

4 slices lean bacon	1 pound fusilli
2 tablespoons oil	4 egg yolks
1 chicken bouillon cube	1 cup grated Parmesan cheese
Salt to taste	4 tablespoons butter
Pinch of white pepper	

While the water is heating for the fusilli, cut the bacon into julienne strips and brown in the oil in a saucepan. Dissolve the bouillon cube in ½ cup hot water and add to the saucepan with very little salt and a pinch of white pepper. Simmer over a low flame until the fusilli are cooked. The fusilli should cook in abundant boiling salted water for 10 minutes. In the meantime, beat together in a small bowl the egg yolks, a generous pinch of white pepper, and 1 tablespoon of the grated cheese. Drain the cooked fusilli and put in a serving bowl. Add the contents of the saucepan, the butter in dabs, and half of the remaining grated cheese. Mix well. Add the egg yolks and toss vigorously until very well mixed. Serve with the rest of the cheese sprinkled on top.

Variation: This recipe is delicious with ¼ pound sausage meat substituted for the bacon. Serves 4.

VERMICELLI WITH HAM
(*Vermicelli con Prosciutto*)

Cooking time: 5 minutes

½ cup butter	1 pound vermicelli
5 thin slices cooked ham	1 cup grated Parmesan cheese

Melt half of the butter in a skillet, add the ham cut in strips, and sauté for 5 minutes. Cook the vermicelli in abundant boiling salted water for 10 minutes, drain and put in a serving bowl. Add the rest of the butter in dabs, the sauce, and half of the grated Parmesan. Serve with the rest of the cheese sprinkled on top.

Variation: Sauté a small chopped onion with the ham and add ½ pound (1 cup shelled) peas. Serves 4.

VERMICELLI PICCOLO MONDO
(*Vermicelli alla Piccolo Mondo*)

Cooking time: 30 minutes

3 slices bacon	½ pound peeled tomatoes
3 tablespoons oil	(2 medium)
2 tablespoons butter	1 pound vermicelli
¼ pound (½ cup shelled) peas	1 cup Béchamel Sauce (see
Salt and pepper to taste	Index)
1 clove garlic	½ cup grated Parmesan cheese
¼ pound mushrooms	

Sauté the thinly sliced bacon in 1 tablespoon of the oil and 2 tablespoons of butter. When brown add ½ cup boiling water and the peas. Add salt and pepper. Cook over a high flame until the peas are cooked. In the meantime, in another saucepan, sauté the thinly sliced garlic in the rest of the oil until barely golden. Add the sliced mushrooms together with 2 tablespoons of juice from the tomatoes. Sauté until most of the liquid has evaporated. Pass the tomatoes through the fine blade of a food mill or put in a blender. Add to the first saucepan with the bacon and the peas and bring to a boil. Add the mushrooms, salt and pepper, and simmer slowly. In the meantime, cook the vermicelli in abundant boiling salted water for 10 minutes. Drain and put in a serving dish. Add the sauce, the béchamel, and half of the grated Parmesan. Mix well and serve with the rest of the cheese sprinkled on top. Serves 4.

VERMICELLI ALLA HELSA
(*Vermicelli alla Helsa*)

Cooking time: 30 minutes

¼ pound chicken breasts	2 basil leaves (or ⅛ teaspoon
2 tablespoons flour	dried)
4 tablespoons oil	1 pound vermicelli
2 slices bacon	1 whole egg
1 small onion	2 egg yolks
Salt and pepper to taste	White pepper
⅓ cup white wine	1 cup grated Cheddar cheese
1 chicken bouillon cube	

Have the chicken breasts sliced thinly, beat with a mallet to make them thin. Dust with flour and sauté in the oil until golden. Remove from the saucepan and set aside. Cut the bacon into julienne strips and add to the saucepan. Brown. Add the finely chopped onion and continue to sauté until softened. Cut the chicken breasts into julienne strips and add. Add salt and pepper. Add the white wine and stir until half of it has evaporated, then add the bouillon cube dissolved in 1 cup of hot water. Stir. Add the basil leaves. Simmer for 20 minutes over a low flame. When the sauce is almost ready, cook the vermicelli in abundant boiling salted water for 10 minutes. In the meantime, beat the whole egg and the egg yolks in a small bowl with a pinch of white pepper and 1 tablespoon of the grated cheese. When the vermicelli is cooked, drain and return to the pot in which it was cooked. Add the sauce and half of the remaining cheese. Mix well. Add the beaten egg mixture, toss again, and serve with the rest of the cheese sprinkled on top. Serves 4.

VERMICELLI WITH GARLIC AND ANCHOVIES
(*Vermicelli con Aglio e Acciughe*)

Cooking time: 20 minutes

2 cloves garlic	½ cup white wine
4 tablespoons oil	3 tablespoons chopped parsley
1 (2-ounce) can anchovy fillets	Salt and pepper to taste
¼ hot red pepper	1 pound vermicelli
1 tablespoon flour	4 tablespoons butter

Put the garlic through a garlic press (or chop very finely) and sauté in the oil in a saucepan. As soon as the garlic begins to color (it must not color too much) add the anchovies. Continue to sauté, pressing down on the anchovies with a spatula in order to disintegrate them. Add the red pepper. Continue to stir over a low flame. Add the flour and blend. Pour in the white wine and when half of it has evaporated add ½ cup hot water, the parsley, and salt and pepper. If the sauce seems too thin, raise the flame in order to thicken it. In the meantime the salted water for the vermicelli has been coming to a boil. Cook the vermicelli for 10 minutes, drain, and put in a serving bowl. Add the butter in dabs and the sauce. Mix well and serve immediately. Serves 4.

VERMICELLI WITH TUNA AND MUSHROOMS
(*Vermicelli al Tonno e Funghi*)

Cooking time: 20 minutes

½ pound mushrooms	½ hot red pepper
1 tablespoon lemon juice	2 tablespoons flour
2 cloves garlic	¾ cup canned tuna
5 tablespoons olive oil	2 tablespoons chopped parsley
Salt and pepper to taste	1 pound vermicelli

Clean and thinly slice the mushrooms and put them in a bowl with the lemon juice. Mix well and set aside for use later. Finely chop the garlic and sauté it in the oil in a saucepan. When almost golden, add the mushrooms and cook over a high flame until the liquid evaporates. Add salt and pepper. Add the hot red pepper and sauté. Add the flour. Stir. Add the coarsely chopped tuna and the parsley. Stir again. Pour in ½ cup hot water and simmer. At this point start cooking the vermicelli in abundant boiling salted water. Allow the sauce to simmer for the 10 minutes it takes the vermicelli to cook. Drain the vermicelli and put in a serving bowl together with the contents of the saucepan. Mix well and serve. This dish may also be served cold. Serves 4.

NOTE: Always leave pepper in ½ or ¼ as directed in recipes for sautéing.

VERMICELLI ELENA
(*Vermicelli Elena*)

Cooking time: 60 minutes

Generous ½ pound pork, slightly fatty	¼ cup tomato paste
4 tablespoons oil	1 bouillon cube
1 medium onion	4 tablespoons butter
1 small clove garlic	2 tablespoons flour
⅓ cup white wine	1 cup milk
Salt and pepper to taste	1 pound vermicelli
3 basil leaves (or ¼ teaspoon dried)	1 cup grated Cheddar cheese

Preheat oven to 450° F.

Slice the meat *very* thinly and sauté it in the oil in a saucepan. When almost golden, add chopped onion and garlic and continue to sauté until the onion and garlic begin to color. Pour in the white wine and allow to evaporate, stirring constantly. Add salt and pepper, basil leaves, and the tomato paste. Stir well. Add 1½ cups hot water in which the bouillon cube has been dissolved. Stir and cover the saucepan. Simmer for 50 minutes, stirring from time to time. While the sauce is simmering, melt the butter in a small saucepan. Add the flour and stir. Gradually add the milk, stirring all the time with a wooden spoon or whisk in order to prevent lumping. Add salt and pepper. Cook over low flame for 10 minutes. When the sauce is almost done, cook the vermicelli in abundant boiling salted water for 10 minutes. While it is cooking, pass the sauce (including the meat) through the fine blade of a food mill or blend in a blender.

If you have trouble passing the meat through the food mill, simply return some of the liquid sauce to the food mill to help the meat pass through. Add the white sauce to this and simmer slowly over a low fire. Drain the vermicelli, add sauce, and half of the cheese. Mix well and put in an ovenproof dish. Sprinkle the rest of the cheese on top. Put in a 450° oven for 4 minutes. Allow to rest 2 or 3 minutes before serving. Serves 4.

VERMICELLI WITH WHITE SAUCE
(Vermicelli in Salsa Bianca)

Cooking time: 20 minutes

¼ pound butter	Salt and pepper to taste
½ cup potato flour	1 pound vermicelli
1 chicken bouillon cube	⅔ cup grated Swiss cheese
½ cup cream	⅓ cup grated Parmesan cheese

Put the water for the vermicelli on to boil. Melt the butter in a small saucepan and add the potato flour. Dissolve the bouillon cube in a cup of hot water. Note: Add this broth and the cream, to the saucepan a little at a time, stirring constantly with a wooden spoon. A very delicate cream will result. Add a little salt and some pepper. Continue to cook slowly, if possible in a double boiler. Cook the vermicelli in abundant boiling salted water for 10 minutes. Drain and put in a serving bowl. Add the sauce and half of the grated cheese. Mix well and serve with the rest of the cheese sprinkled on top.
Variation: If desired, a pinch of sugar may be added to this recipe. Serves 4.

VERMICELLI GALLANT
(Vermicelli Galante)

Cooking time: 70 minutes

1½ pounds eye of round beef	½ cup white wine
½ cup flour	½ pound peeled tomatoes
4 tablespoons oil	(2 medium)
2 slices bacon	1 bouillon cube
1 large onion	1 pound vermicelli
2 whole cloves	1 cup grated Cheddar cheese
Salt and pepper to taste	

Roll the meat in flour until it is well covered and brown well on all sides in the oil. Add the thinly sliced bacon and onion, and sauté together with the meat. When all is well browned, add whatever flour remains, the whole cloves, and salt and pepper. Pour in the white wine and allow half of it to evaporate. Add the cut-up tomatoes and the bouillon cube dissolved in 1 cup of hot water. Stir a minute or so, then cover the saucepan and simmer over a moderate flame for 60 minutes. Be sure to stir from time to time and add a little water whenever necessary. When the sauce is almost done, cook the vermicelli in abundant boiling salted water for 10 minutes. In the meantime, remove the meat from the saucepan. Pass the sauce through the fine blade of a food mill or blend in a blender. Drain the cooked vermicelli and put in a serving bowl. Add three fourths of the sauce and half of the grated cheese. Mix well. Serve with the rest of the cheese sprinkled on top.

The meat may be served as a second course, thinly sliced with sauce spooned over each slice and accompanied by whatever vegetable you desire. Serves 4.

VERMICELLI SYRACUSE
(*Vermicelli alla Siracusana*)

Cooking time: 30 minutes

2 cloves garlic	25 pitted olives
4 tablespoons oil	1 tablespoon capers
1 pound peeled tomatoes (3 or 4 medium)	4 basil leaves (or ¼ teaspoon dried)
⅔ cup diced eggplant	2 tablespoons chopped anchovy fillets
Salt and pepper to taste	
¼ pound roasted peeled yellow peppers	1 pound vermicelli

Sauté the coarsely chopped garlic in the oil until golden, then remove garlic and add the cut-up tomatoes. Cook for 3 minutes. In the meantime dice the eggplant. Add together with salt and pepper to taste, and cook for 5 minutes. Cut the roasted peppers into strips and add together with the pitted olives, the capers, and the chopped basil. Stir. Simmer for 10 minutes. Finely chop the anchovies. Add to the sauce just 2 minutes before seasoning the vermicelli. After the vermicelli has been boiling for 10 minutes, drain and put in a serving bowl. Pour on all of the sauce and mix well. Serve with a dusting of freshly ground pepper. Serves 4.

VERMICELLI WITH CREAM
(*Vermicelli alla Panna*)

Cooking time: 20 minutes

1 pound vermicelli
½ cup grated Swiss cheese
½ cup grated Parmesan cheese
6 tablespoons butter

¾ cup heavy cream
Salt to taste
Pinch of cayenne

Put the vermicelli in abundant boiling salted water and boil for 10 minutes. While this is cooking, mix the two cheeses. As soon as the vermicelli is cooked, drain and add the butter in dabs. Mix well. Add the cream and half of the grated cheeses. Mix again. Add salt. Serve with the rest of the cheese and the cayenne sprinkled on top. Serves 4.

VERMICELLI DELICIOUS
(*Vermicelli Deliziosi*)

Cooking time: 60 minutes

¼ pound pork, slightly fatty
2 tablespoons oil
1 small onion
¼ pound turkey breast
1 carrot
1 stalk celery
2 tablespoons flour
Salt and pepper to taste

½ cup white wine
¼ pound ripe tomatoes (1 medium)
2 basil leaves (or ¼ teaspoon dried)
1 pound vermicelli
4 tablespoons butter
1 cup grated Parmesan cheese

Slice the meat *very* thinly and put in saucepan with the oil. Brown over high flame for 3 minutes. Add the sliced onion and continue to brown for 2 minutes. Slice the breast of turkey into very thin slices and add. When browned, add the sliced carrots and the celery. Now add the flour, salt, and pepper, and stir for 1 minute. Pour in the white wine, continuing to stir while it evaporates. Add the cut-up tomatoes and the basil leaves. Stir for a minute or so, then add 1½ cups hot water, cover the saucepan and simmer for 40 minutes. Cook the vermicelli in abundant boiling salted water for 10 minutes. In the meantime, put the entire contents of the saucepan (including meat) through the fine blade of a food mill or blend in a blender. If using a food mill, you must persist in passing the meat through. If you have difficulty, keep returning the liquid sauce to the mill to help pass the meat. The resulting sauce will be quite thick. Drain the cooked vermicelli and put in a serving bowl. Add the sauce, the dabs of butter, and half the grated cheese. Mix well and serve with the rest of the cheese sprinkled on top. Serves 4.

VERMICELLI WITH TURKEY RAGÙ
(*Vermicelli al Ragù di Tacchino*)

Cooking time: 60 minutes

4 slices lean bacon	2 basil leaves (or ¼ teaspoon
3 tablespoons oil	dried)
2 pounds turkey drumsticks	Salt and pepper to taste
2 tablespoons flour	1 chicken bouillon cube
1 medium onion	1 pound vermicelli
1 clove garlic	4 tablespoons butter
½ cup white wine	1 cup grated Parmesan cheese
¾ pound peeled tomatoes (3 medium)	

Slice the bacon and put it in a saucepan with the oil. Roll the drumsticks in flour and brown together with the bacon. Also add the coarsely chopped onion and the unpeeled clove of garlic. Sauté for 5 minutes, making sure to turn the drumsticks often in order to brown evenly. Pour in the white wine. When evaporated, add the cut-up tomatoes and the basil leaves. Add salt and pepper to taste. Dissolve the bouillon cube in 1 cup of hot water and add. Stir and allow to come to a boil, then lower flame and simmer for 50 minutes. Test the drumsticks for doneness with a fork from time to time. When the sauce has been cooking for almost 50 minutes, start cooking the vermicelli in abundant boiling salted water for 10 minutes. In the meantime, pass the sauce through a food mill or blend in a blender. Set aside the turkey drumsticks. Put the drained vermicelli in a serving dish. Add the butter in dabs, three fourths of the sauce (set aside the rest to spoon over the turkey), and half of the Parmesan. Mix well and serve with the rest of the cheese sprinkled on top. The drumsticks may be served as a second course. Serves 4.

VERMICELLI SICILIAN STYLE
(*Vermicelli alla Siciliana*)

Pedro, the owner of the restaurant Al Ficodindia in Palermo taught me how to cook this tasty dish invented by the fishermen of the island.

Cooking time: 50 minutes

1½ pounds fresh tuna	¾ pound peeled tomatoes (3
1 tablespoon flour	medium)
4 tablespoons olive oil	3 basil leaves (or ¼ teaspoon
1 medium onion	dried)
2 cloves garlic	2 fresh mint leaves
Salt and pepper to taste	1 pound vermicelli
1 cup white wine	

Choose a nice piece of tuna, preferably the tail section. Clean it, wash it, and dry it with a paper towel. Sprinkle with the flour, then brown it in the hot oil in a saucepan. Cut up the onion and the garlic in large pieces, arrange around the fish, and continue to sauté, making sure to turn the fish often to brown it evenly. Add salt and pepper. Add the white wine and continue to stir until half of it has evaporated. Add the coarsely chopped tomatoes, basil leaves, and the mint. Stir and cover. Simmer for 30 minutes over a low flame. (When the fish is cooked, remove it from the saucepan but continue to cook the sauce.) Pass the sauce through the fine blade of a food mill or blend in a blender. If the sauce seems to be too thick, add a little hot water. Cook the vermicelli in abundant boiling salted water for 10 minutes and drain. Add the sauce, setting aside a little to spoon over the tuna, which may be served as a second course. Serves 4.

VERMICELLI WITH SEAFOOD LASPEZZINA
(*Vermicelli ai Frutti di Mare alla Spezzina*)

Cooking time: 50 minutes

1 clove garlic	Salt and pepper to taste
4 tablespoons oil	¼ cup white wine
2 ounces squid	1 pound tomatoes, peeled (3 or
3 ounces shrimp	4 medium)
1 pound mussels (with shells)	1 pound vermicelli
(3 ounces without shells)	1 tablespoon chopped parsley

Crush the garlic and chop very finely. Sauté in the oil until almost golden. Add the squid, which you have already cut into strips, and the shrimp. Sauté for 1 minute, then add the mussels (in shell), taking care to set aside their liquid for later use. Add salt and pepper. Add the wine and the thinly sliced tomatoes. Cook for 35 minutes. In the meantime, you have put on the water to boil for the vermicelli. About 10 minutes before the sauce is ready, put the vermicelli in abundant boiling salted water and cook for 10 minutes. Stir the sauce often. While the vermicelli is cooking, add the mussel liquid and the parsley to the sauce. Drain the cooked vermicelli and put in a serving bowl. Add the sauce and mix well. Serve, making sure that each serving has its share of the seafood.

Variation: Cherrystone clams (or quahogs) may be substituted for the mussels.

Serves 4.

Preparation for mussels: Wash the mussels under running water and, if needed, clean with a brush; then place them in a saucepan over a low fire and cook for 5 minutes.

NOTE: There is no need to add any water to the saucepan for the mussels will cook in their own juice.

VERMICELLI WITH GARLIC AND OIL, NEAPOLITAN STYLE
(*Vermicelli Aglio e Olio alla Napolitana*)

Cooking time: 20 minutes

1 pound vermicelli	¼ hot red pepper
2 cloves garlic	2 tablespoons chopped parsley
5 tablespoons olive oil	Salt and pepper to taste

Start cooking the vermicelli in abundant boiling salted water. It should cook for approximately 10 minutes. In the meantime, sauté the sliced garlic in the oil in a small saucepan. When it is golden add the red pepper and the chopped parsley. When you add the parsley, have ready in your hand a small ladleful of the boiling water in which the vermicelli is cooking. This is because you must add the water to the saucepan almost immediately in order not to burn the parsley. Add a pinch of salt and pepper, and simmer slowly until the vermicelli is cooked. Drain the vermicelli and put in a serving bowl. Add the contents of the saucepan, mix well, and serve.

Variation: When sautéing the garlic in the oil, fry ½ cup of day-old bread cubes until golden. Remove and set aside to drain on a paper towel. After mixing the sauce with the vermicelli, sprinkle the croutons on top. Serves 4.

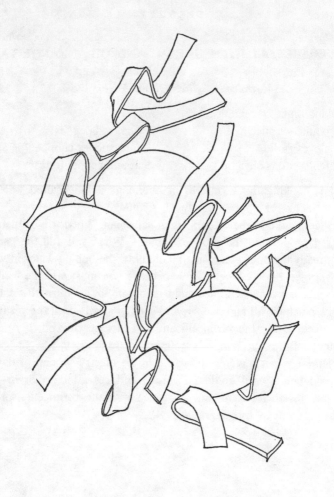

CHAPTER II

Noodles and Family

The Italians are great eaters of noodles, which they call *"fettuccine,"* which means, literally, "little ribbons." The most famous restaurant in Italy, specializing in the preparation of fettuccine, is situated in Rome at Piazzo Augusto. Alfredo all'Augusteo, even better known under the name Alfredo l'Originale, for the past half century has been host to thousands of persons each month, many of whom are internationally known personalities.

For example, in 1927 Mary Pickford and Douglas Fairbanks, Sr., presented Alfredo with a solid gold fork and spoon, on the handles of which was inscribed: "To Alfredo, the King of the Noodles," followed by the signatures of the two great silent film stars.

President Nixon lunched at Alfredo's with his wife and daughter Julie in 1963, when he was vice president. Elizabeth Taylor is a habitué of the place when she is in Italy, as is Thomas Pain, a NASA executive, whom Alfredo jokingly asked if he could be the first man to prepare noodles on the moon!

Fettuccine all'Alfredo, which are really very easy to prepare (see Index), have four secrets. The eggs used in the noodles come from Alfredo's own farm, as do the butter and the cheese. The fourth secret is the amount of time required to cook the fresh pasta.

For Alfredo, as for all Italian gourmets, the pasta for fettuccine, to be really delicious, must be homemade. That is why the recipes for preparing fettuccine (together with the appropriate sauces) are not found in this chapter but in that entitled "Homemade Pasta."

Naturally, since in America you can find very good egg noodles on the market if you don't want to—or don't have the time to— make your own noodles, in the same chapter I have shown how one can prepare and season commercially sold noodles.

In the pages that follow you will find out how to cook three types of pasta that make up the noodle family: lasagnette, which are simply noodles prepared without eggs and which may be sold simply as "noodles," linguine, and pappardelle. Linguine are thin noodles that are exactly like spaghetti except only one half its length; whereas pappardelle are very wide noodles resembling fettuccine but twice its thickness.

I also want to specify that the sauces I suggest in this chapter may be used for any type of noodle whatsoever: yellow or green, with or without eggs. All that one needs to change is the amount of time required for cooking the pasta—and this is usually indicated on the package of the pasta you have purchased. However, I do advise most strongly, if you want to succeed in making deliciously succulent noodles, to refer to the fettuccine recipes, which are the best to be found in Italy.

CURLY LASAGNETTE OUR STYLE
(*Lasagnette Ricci a Modo Nostro*)

Cooking time: 40 minutes

½ pound sausages
3 tablespoons oil
2 cloves garlic
¼ pound fresh mushrooms, sliced
¾ pound ripe tomatoes (2 or 3 medium)

Salt and pepper to taste
½ cup shelled green peas
1 pound curly lasagnette
½ cup heavy cream
1 cup grated Parmesan cheese

Slice the sausage and brown in a saucepan with the oil and whole cloves of garlic. Add the mushrooms, stir, and continue to cook. Add the unpeeled tomatoes, cut in pieces, salt and pepper. Bring to a boil, then lower the flame and simmer covered for 20 minutes. In the meantime, boil the peas (if fresh) and add. Cook for 10 minutes more. After adding peas, start cooking the curly lasagnette, which you have previously broken into pieces 3 inches long. Boil for 8 minutes in salted water. Drain and turn onto a large serving platter. Pour on the entire contents of the saucepan. Mix well. Add the heavy cream and half of the Parmesan. Mix again. Serve with the rest of the cheese sprinkled on top. Serves 4.

LASAGNETTE WITH CHICKEN SAUCE
(*Lasagnette al Sugo di Pollo*)

This very simple recipe is a classic Italian dish prepared with chicken, which is used by the Italians as frequently as hamburgers by the Americans.

Cooking time: 40 minutes

1 1½-pound spring chicken
1 tablespoon flour
4 tablespoons oil
1 medium onion, chopped
1 clove garlic, chopped
1 pinch marjoram (⅛ teaspoon)

1½ pounds ripe tomatoes (5 medium)
Salt and pepper to taste
1 pound lasagnette
1 cup grated Parmesan cheese

Cut the chicken into 12 pieces (dividing each fourth into 3 pieces). Coat with flour and brown in the hot oil in a large saucepan. When golden brown add the onion and the garlic and the marjoram. Peel and cut up the tomatoes, and add with salt and pepper. Stir well and allow to simmer for 30 minutes. In boiling water add the lasagnette a little at a time to prevent its sticking together. Stir often. Boil for 10 minutes. Drain and put into a serving bowl. Remove the pieces of chicken from the sauce. Pour the sauce over the cooked pasta. Toss together with half of the Parmesan. Serve with the rest of the Parmesan sprinkled on top. The chicken may, if desired, be served as a second course together with a vegetable such as peas or beans. Serves 4.

LASAGNETTE WITH PEAS AND MUSHROOMS
(*Lasagnette ai Piselli e Funghi*)

Cooking time: 40 minutes

3 slices lean bacon	2 basil leaves (or ⅛ teaspoon dried)
3 tablespoons olive oil	
1 medium onion, thinly sliced	Salt and pepper to taste
½ cup shelled peas	1 pound lasagnette
¼ pound fresh mushrooms	4 tablespoons butter
⅓ pound ripe tomatoes (1 medium)	1 cup grated Parmesan cheese

Cut the bacon into matchstick strips. Sauté in the oil in a saucepan until golden brown. Add the onion and continue to sauté until golden. Add 1½ cups of hot water and the peas. Cook for 15 minutes. In the meantime wash and slice the mushrooms and add to the peas together with the cut-up tomatoes. Bring to a boil and cook for 5 minutes more. Chop the basil and add. Add salt and pepper. Cook for 20 minutes over a low flame. When the sauce is almost done, cook the lasagnette in boiling water for 10 minutes. (Add it a little at a time to prevent its sticking together, and stir often.) Drain and put in a serving bowl, putting dabs of butter here and there on the pasta. Mix well. Pour on the sauce and half of the Parmesan and mix again. Serve with the rest of the cheese sprinkled on top.

Variation: Cooked ham and 1 more tablespoon of butter may be substituted for the bacon. Serves 4.

HOME-STYLE LASAGNETTE
(*Lasagnette Casarecce*)

Cooking time: 30 minutes

Generous ½ pound pork, fatty
1 large onion, finely chopped
3 tablespoons olive oil
1 stalk celery, finely chopped
Salt and pepper to taste
1 tablespoon flour
½ cup red wine
1 bouillon cube

½ cup plus 2 tablespoons
  tomato paste
1 teaspoon chopped basil (or ¼
  teaspoon dried)
1 pound lasagnette
1 cup grated Parmesan cheese
  (or pecorino cheese)

The meat should be very finely ground. Sauté it in a saucepan with the onion and the oil over a fairly high flame for 6 minutes. Add the celery, salt, and pepper. Stir. Add the flour and stir again. Pour in the red wine and allow half of it to evaporate. Dissolve the bouillon cube in 1½ cups hot water in which you have also diluted the tomato paste. Pour into the saucepan. Add finely chopped basil, stir, and cook covered over moderate flame for 25 minutes. When almost done, cook the lasagnette in boiling water for 10 minutes. (Add it a little at a time to prevent its sticking together, and stir often.) Drain and put in serving dish. Pour on all the sauce and half the cheese. Mix well. Serve with rest of cheese sprinkled on top. Serves 4.

LASAGNETTE POMPADOUR
(*Lasagnette Pompadour*)

The marquise of Pompadour (1721–64) especially loved this way to prepare pasta. Protectress of the arts and the letters, she desired to be sponsor of this recipe prepared by the chef of King Louis XV.

Cooking time: 30 minutes

1 medium onion, sliced
4 tablespoons olive oil
1 small piece dried red pepper
1 clove garlic, sliced
1 carrot, sliced
1 stalk celery, sliced
1 tablespoon flour

½ cup white wine
Salt and pepper to taste
1¼ pounds ripe tomatoes (4
  medium)
1 pound lasagnette
4 tablespoons butter
1 cup grated Parmesan cheese

Sauté the onion in a saucepan with the olive oil and the red pepper. When golden, add the garlic, the carrot, and the celery. Sauté for 2 minutes. Add the flour. Stir. Pour in the white wine. When half of the wine has evaporated, add salt and pepper and the peeled, cut-up tomatoes. Stir and cook for 25 minutes. In the meantime the water has been heating. When it has come to a boil and the sauce is almost done, cook the lasagnette for 10 minutes. (Add it a little at a time to prevent its sticking together, and stir often.) While the pasta is cooking, pass the sauce through the medium blade of a food mill. Turn the drained lasagnette onto a serving platter. Add the butter in dabs and toss well. Add the sauce and half of the Parmesan. Mix well and serve with the rest of the cheese sprinkled on top. Serves 4.

LASAGNETTE WITH BUTTER AND TOMATOES
(*Lasagnette al Burro e Pomodoro*)

Cooking time: 30 minutes

1 small onion, thinly sliced

2 tablespoons olive oil

1 pound ripe tomatoes (3 or 4 medium)

1 clove garlic

3 basil leaves (or ¼ teaspoon dried)

Salt and pepper to taste

1 pound lasagnette

6 tablespoons butter

1 cup grated Parmesan cheese

In a saucepan sauté the onion in the olive oil until golden. Peel the tomatoes, cut up, and add with their juice to the saucepan. Mash the garlic with a garlic press or with the flat blade of a knife. Chop together with the basil leaves and add to the sauce. Add salt and pepper. Simmer 20 minutes. While the sauce is cooking, put the water for cooking the pasta on to boil. When the sauce is almost done, cook the lasagnette in boiling water 10 minutes. (Add it a little at a time to prevent its sticking together, and stir often.) Drain and return to the pot in which it was cooked. Add the butter, cut in pieces, all the sauce, and half of the Parmesan. Toss well, making sure that the butter and the tomato sauce are well mixed. Serve with the rest of the cheese sprinkled on top. Serves 4.

LASAGNETTE WITH ANCHOVY BUTTER
(*Lasagnette al Burro d'Acciughe*)

Cooking time: 20 minutes

5 tablespoons butter	½ cup white wine
2 (2-ounce) cans anchovy fillets	Salt and pepper to taste
	2 tablespoons chopped parsley
2 tablespoons flour	1 pound lasagnette

Put the salted water for the lasagnette on to boil. In the meantime melt 2 tablespoons of the butter in a medium-size saucepan. Add the anchovies and sauté, mashing them continuously with a fork in order to reduce them to a creamy texture. Add the flour and stir. Add the white wine and, stirring rapidly, allow to boil for 3 minutes. You should have a rather thick, creamy mixture. Add a scant ½ cup of boiling water, salt and a generous amount of pepper. Stir. Add the parsley and allow to simmer slowly until the lasagnette are cooked. As soon as the water begins to boil, add the lasagnette a little at a time in order to prevent its sticking together. Be sure to stir often while it is cooking. Boil for 10 minutes. Drain and turn onto a serving platter. Add the remaining butter to the sauce. Remove from the fire and stir in order to melt the butter. Pour over the pasta, toss well, and serve. This pasta is also good served cold.
Serves 4.

LASAGNETTE PICCOLO MONDO
(*Lasagnette Piccolo Mondo*)

This recipe is a specialty of the famous restaurant Piccolo Mondo in Rome.

Cooking time: 20 minutes

3 slices lean bacon	¼ pound mushrooms
6 tablespoons butter	1 tablespoon lemon juice
½ cup shelled peas	1 pound lasagnette
Salt and pepper to taste	1 cup grated Parmesan cheese
1 clove garlic	

Cut the bacon into thin matchstick strips. Put into saucepan with 1 tablespoon of the butter and sauté. Do not allow to brown. If the peas are raw, add them together with 1 cup of hot water; if already cooked add only ¼ cup hot water. Salt and pepper to taste. Cook until the peas are tender. In another small saucepan sauté the whole clove of garlic in the rest of the butter until golden. Slice the mushrooms and add with the lemon juice, salt, and pepper. Cook covered over a moderate flame until most of the liquid has evaporated. Remove garlic. In the meantime put the water on to boil. Boil the lasagnette 10 minutes, adding it to the water a little at a time to prevent its sticking together. Stir often. Drain and turn onto a serving plate. Add the contents of both saucepans. Mix well together with half of the grated cheese. Serve with the rest of the cheese sprinkled on top.

Variation No. 1: ⅓ cup chopped ham may be substituted for the bacon.

Variation No. 2: ⅓ cup crumbled or sliced sausage meat may be substituted for the bacon.

Serves 4.

COMPANY LINGUINE
(Linguine alla Forestiera)

Cooking time: 40 minutes

¾ pound tomatoes, coarsely chopped (2 medium)	8 to 10 green olives, sliced
1 stalk celery, sliced	2 tablespoons flour
1 bouillon cube	2 basil leaves (or ⅛ teaspoon dried)
¾ cup thinly sliced mushrooms	Salt and pepper to taste
1 tablespoon lemon juice	1 pound linguine
1 clove garlic	1 cup grated Cheddar cheese
5 tablespoons olive oil	

Put the first 3 ingredients in a small saucepan with ½ cup water and allow to boil for 5 minutes. Put through the fine blade of a food mill or put in a blender. Mix the mushrooms together with the lemon juice. Sauté the garlic in the oil until almost golden. Add the mushrooms with the lemon juice and the olives and cook over a high flame until most of the liquid evaporates. Add the flour and stir. Add the tomato mixture, the coarsely chopped basil, and the salt and pepper. Simmer for 25 minutes over a low flame. When the sauce is almost

done, cook the linguine in abundant rapidly boiling salted water for
7 minutes. Drain. Add the sauce and half of the grated cheese. Mix
well. Serve with the rest of the cheese sprinkled on top.
Serves 4.

LINGUINE CONTINENTAL
(*Linguine alla Continentale*)

Cooking time: 40 minutes

2½ pounds dried mushrooms	2 tablespoons flour
Scant ½ pound beef	⅓ cup white wine
1 carrot	⅓ cup tomato paste
1 stalk of celery	1 bouillon cube
1 medium onion, finely chopped	1 pound linguine
4 tablespoons olive oil	4 tablespoons butter
Salt and pepper to taste	1 cup grated Parmesan cheese

Wash the dried mushrooms and put in 1 cup hot water to soak.
Grind the beef, carrot, and celery together in the meat grinder.
Sauté the onion in the oil until almost golden, then add the ground
meat mixture. Add salt and pepper. Stir. Cook over high flame to
brown, then add the flour. Stir again. Pour in the white wine and,
when half of it has evaporated, add the mushrooms, which you have
removed from the water, squeezed dry, and chopped (do not throw
the water away). Add the tomato paste and stir for 3 minutes over
a moderate flame. Dissolve the bouillon cube in the mushroom
water and add. Stir and cook for 25 minutes. If the sauce seems to be
too thick, add ½ cup of hot water. When the sauce is almost done,
cook the linguine in abundant rapidly boiling salted water for 7
minutes. Drain. Add the butter, cut in pieces, to the drained linguine,
mixing well. Pour on the sauce with half of the grated cheese. Mix.
Sprinkle the rest of the cheese on top. Serves 4.

HARVEY'S LINGUINE
(*Linguine di Harvey*)

This recipe I invented in Rome and taught it to my friend Joe Pasternak several years later in Hollywood. Joe, a very good cook himself and author of the cookbook *How to Cook with Love and Paprika* served this dish at his Bel Air house when entertaining Zsa Zsa Gabor and Gene Kelly.

Cooking time: 40 minutes

2½ pounds dried mushrooms	⅓ cup white wine
1 small onion, finely chopped	2 thin slices cooked ham
3 tablespoons olive oil	1 pound linguine
Scant ½ pound ground pork (with fat)	3 egg yolks
¼ pound sausage	¼ cup heavy cream
Salt and pepper to taste	4 tablespoons butter
	1 cup grated Cheddar cheese

Put the dried mushrooms to soak in ½ cup of hot water. Sauté the onion in a saucepan with the olive oil until almost golden. Add the pork, the peeled sausage, and salt and pepper, and brown well. Pour in the white wine and cook over a fairly high flame until half of it has evaporated. Squeeze the mushrooms dry and cut into strips. Add to the sauce together with ⅔ of the water in which they were soaking (or juice from can). Cook over a very slow fire for 25 minutes. Add the ham cut into julienne strips. Now start cooking the linguine in rapidly boiling salted water for 7 minutes. While it is cooking, beat the egg yolks, the cream, and a generous pinch of pepper together in a small bowl. Put the drained linguine in a preheated serving dish. Add the butter, cut in pieces, and the entire contents of the saucepan together with half of the grated cheese. Toss well. Put the remaining cheese in the bowl with the eggs and cream. Beat slightly. Pour over the pasta. Mix well and serve. Serves 4.

LINGUINE OCIE
(*Linguine alla Ocie*)

In December 1970, my mother-in-law Ocie visited us in Rome. Our friend Chef Ovidio prepared a celebration dinner for her and named this dish after our mother.

Cooking time: 40 minutes

1 pound ripe tomatoes, peeled (3 or 4 medium)	2 basil leaves (or ⅛ teaspoon dried)
1 medium onion, thinly sliced	4 tablespoons butter
1 chicken bouillon cube	2 tablespoons flour
4 slices lean bacon	Salt and pepper to taste
¼ pound chicken breast	¼ cup white wine
4 tablespoons olive oil	1 pound linguine
½ clove garlic, crushed	1 cup grated Cheddar cheese

Put the first 3 ingredients in a saucepan with ½ cup hot water, bring to a boil, and let cook for 8 minutes. In the meantime, cut the bacon and the chicken breast into very thin julienne strips—about the same size as the linguine. Sauté the bacon and chicken in another saucepan with the olive oil until browned. With a small spatula or with the blade of a knife make a paste out of the garlic, the finely chopped basil, and the butter. Add the flour to the browned meat. Add salt and pepper. Stir. Pour in the white wine and allow half of it to evaporate. In the meantime, put the tomato mixture through the fine blade of a food mill or blend in a blender. Pour the tomato sauce into the saucepan with the meat, bring to a boil, and then simmer slowly for 20 minutes. Add the paste you have prepared and simmer for 5 minutes more. Ten minutes before the sauce is done, cook the linguine in rapidly boiling salted water for 7 minutes. Drain. Put the pasta in a serving dish and pour on the sauce. Mix together with half of the cheese. Serve with the rest of the cheese sprinkled on top. Serves 4.

LINGUINE TRASTEVERE
(*Linguine di Trastevere*)

All of the *trattorias* in Trastevere, the oldest section of Rome, like to prepare pasta this way.

Cooking time: 40 minutes

¾ cup diced pork (slightly
  fatty)
4 tablespoons olive oil
1 medium onion, chopped
¼ pound fresh mushrooms,
  sliced
1 stalk celery, chopped
Salt and pepper to taste

2 tablespoons flour
⅓ cup red wine
⅓ cup tomato paste
1 bouillon cube
¼ cup shelled green peas
1 pound linguine
4 tablespoons butter
1 cup grated Parmesan cheese

Dice the meat and brown it in a saucepan with the oil and onion. Add the mushrooms, celery, salt, and pepper. Stir from time to time. When all is well browned, add the flour. Stir. Pour in the red wine. When it is half evaporated, add the tomato paste and stir for 1 minute. Dissolve the bouillon cube in 1½ cups of hot water and add. Bring to a boil over a high flame, then lower the flame and cook for 25 minutes. In the meantime boil the peas (if fresh). Cook the linguine in rapidly boiling salted water for 7 minutes. While it is cooking, add the peas to the sauce and continue to simmer. Add the butter and the sauce to the drained linguine. Toss with half of the Parmesan. Serve with the rest of the cheese sprinkled on top. Serves 4.

LINGUINE VENETIAN STYLE
(*Linguine alla Veneta*)

Cooking time: 30 minutes

1 large onion
4 tablespoons olive oil
½ pound sausages
½ cup white wine
1½ pounds ripe tomatoes,
  peeled (5 medium)

Salt and pepper to taste
1 pound linguine
1 cup grated Parmesan cheese

Slice the onion *very* thinly and sauté it in the hot olive oil until golden. Peel the sausages, crumble them up, and sauté them in the oil until well browned. Add the white wine. When half of it has evaporated, add the tomatoes, cut in pieces. Add salt and pepper. Simmer for 25 minutes over moderately low fire. Cook the linguine in rapidly boiling salted water for 7 minutes. Drain. Pour the sauce over the cooked drained linguine. Toss together with half of the grated Parmesan. Serve with the rest of the cheese sprinkled on top. Serves 4.

LINGUINE WITH PESTO
(*Linguine al Pesto*)

A Genoese specialty.

Cooking time: 10 minutes

1 large bunch basil leaves (or ½ teaspoon dried)	⅔ cup grated Parmesan cheese
2 cloves garlic	⅔ cup grated pecorino cheese (or any sharp cheese)
4 tablespoons first-quality olive oil	Salt and pepper to taste
	1 pound linguine

Pass the basil, the garlic, the olive oil, ⅓ cup Parmesan, ⅓ cup pecorino, salt, and pepper through the blender until a creamy paste results. Cook the linguine in rapidly boiling salted water for 7 minutes. Drain. Pour paste over very hot drained linguine. Toss well. Sprinkle remaining cheese on top. Serves 4.

LINGUINE WITH TURKEY
(*Linguine al Tacchino*)

In Italy—where turkey is very expensive, compared to the United States, and is eaten only at Christmas, and then not by the lower class—this recipe is considered very exceptional and very expensive. But it is greatly enjoyed at that time of the year.

Cooking time: 60 minutes

1½ pounds turkey drumsticks	1 chicken bouillon cube
Flour	1 pound ripe tomatoes (3 medium)
4 tablespoons olive oil	
1 medium onion, thinly sliced	1 pound linguine
1 carrot, thinly sliced	4 tablespoons butter
1 stalk celery, thinly sliced	2 basil leaves (or ⅛ teaspoon dried)
1 clove garlic, unpeeled	
1 bay leaf	1 cup grated Parmesan cheese
Salt and pepper to taste	

Have your butcher cut the drumsticks into ½-inch wheels, using an electric bone saw. Flour each wheel and brown on both sides in a saucepan with the hot olive oil. Add the onion and sauté for 3 minutes. Add the carrot, celery, garlic, bay leaf, and salt and pepper. Stir for 2 minutes. Add the bouillon cube dissolved in ⅔ cup hot water. Add the cut-up tomatoes, stir, and bring to a boil over a high flame. Cook covered for 40 minutes over a moderate flame. When the sauce is almost done, cook the linguine in rapidly boiling salted water for 7 minutes. While the linguine is cooking, make a paste of the butter, finely chopped basil, a pinch of pepper, and 1 tablespoon grated Parmesan. Remove the turkey wheels from the sauce and place on a platter. Put the remaining sauce through a food mill or blend in a blender. Add the paste you have made to the sauce. Set aside 5 tablespoons of the sauce to spoon over the turkey, and pour the rest over the drained linguine. Toss with half of the grated cheese. Serve with the rest of the cheese sprinkled on top. The turkey may be served as the second course if you wish. Serves 4.

LINGUINE WITH WALNUTS
(*Linguine alle Noci*)

Cooking time: 30 minutes

1 cup shelled walnuts	Salt and pepper to taste
1 small onion, chopped	1 pound linguine
4 tablespoons butter	2 egg yolks
1 pound ripe tomatoes (3 medium)	1 cup grated Swiss cheese

Soak the walnuts in hot water for ½ hour in order that the brown skin may be easily removed. Make a paste of the walnuts by putting them through the blender or by using a mortar and pestle. Set aside for use later. In a saucepan sauté the onion in 2 tablespoons of the butter until just hot, then add the cut-up tomatoes. Boil for 10 minutes, then put through the blender. Add salt and pepper. Heat the walnut paste in a double boiler with the remaining 2 tablespoons of butter, stirring until well blended. Keep *lukewarm*. Cook the linguine in rapidly boiling salted water for 7 minutes. Put the drained linguine in a serving dish, pour the tomato mixture over it, and toss. Add the egg yolks to the walnut mixture and beat. Pour over the linguine. Mix together with half of the grated cheese. Serve with the rest of the cheese sprinkled on top. Serves 4.

MAMMA CORSETTI'S PAPPARDELLE
(Pappardelle Mamma Corsetti)

This is the recipe of Elena Corsetti, proprietress of the Roman restaurant Il Galeone.

Cooking time: 25 minutes

¼ cup finely chopped ham	Salt and pepper to taste
2 tablespoons butter	1 pound pappardelle
¼ cup shelled green peas	1½ cups grated Parmesan
1 cup heavy cream	cheese

Sauté the finely chopped ham in the butter in a small saucepan. Allow to brown for 3 minutes. Add the peas and cook for 15 minutes. Pour in the cream, bring to a boil, and remove from the fire. Add salt and pepper. Cook the pappardelle in abundant boiling salted water for 8 minutes. Drain and turn onto a serving platter. Add half the sauce and half the grated cheese. Mix well. Pour on the rest of the sauce and sprinkle the rest of the Parmesan on top. Serves 4.

PAPPARDELLE WITH CHICKEN SAUCE
(Pappardelle con Sugo di Pollo)

Richard Burton is very fond of these pappardelle, which he eats at Gino's, one of the best restaurants in the ancient Trastevere area of Rome.

Cooking time: 40 minutes

1 pound pappardelle	1 stalk celery
1 3-pound chicken	6 rosemary needles (or ¼
3 slices fatty bacon	teaspoon dried)
1 medium onion	1 chicken liver (optional)
1 clove garlic	½ cup red wine
½ cup oil	⅓ cup tomato paste
2 tablespoons flour	1 chicken bouillon cube
Salt and pepper	1 whole clove
1 carrot	1 cup grated Parmesan cheese

Make noodle dough for pappardelle as directed in Chapter VII (see Index). Cut the dough into strips 1 inch wide and 8 inches long. Clean the chicken and cut it into fourths. Chop the bacon, the onion, and the garlic together so finely that they form a paste. Sauté in the oil in a fairly large saucepan until golden. Flour the chicken and brown (do *not* use more than 2 tablespoons of flour) on all sides. Add salt and pepper. While the chicken is browning, chop together very finely the carrot, the celery, and the rosemary, and, if you like, the chicken liver. Sauté over a low fire, taking care that the ingredients do not stick to the bottom of the pan. Add the red wine and allow half of it to evaporate. In the meantime, dilute the tomato paste in 1½ cups of hot water in which the bouillon cube has already been dissolved. Add to the saucepan and stir. Taste for salt. Add the whole clove. Cover the saucepan and simmer slowly for 30 minutes. Stir from time to time and test the chicken for doneness. A few minutes before the sauce is done, cook the pappardelle by adding a few at a time to boiling salted water. Boil for 8 minutes. Drain and turn onto a serving platter. Remove the whole clove from the sauce. Pour the sauce over the pasta, making sure to save some to spoon over the chicken later. Add the grated Parmesan and mix well. The chicken may be used as a second course if desired. Serves 4.

PAPPARDELLE WITH LAMB SAUCE
(*Pappardelle al Sugo di Agnello*)

Cooking time: 45 minutes

4 tablespoons oil	1 clove garlic
2 slices bacon, chopped	Generous ½ pound lamb
1 medium onion	½ cup red wine
1 stalk celery	Salt and pepper to taste
1 carrot	2 tablespoons butter
2 leaves fresh sage (or ¼ teaspoon dried)	1 tablespoon cognac
6 rosemary needles (or ¼ teaspoon dried)	1 pound pappardelle
	1 cup grated Parmesan cheese

Put into a saucepan the oil and the next 7 ingredients, all finely chopped, and the lamb, cut into bite-size pieces. Sauté until the meat is well browned. Add the red wine, salt, and pepper, and simmer for 40 minutes. When the meat is tender, remove it from the saucepan. Remove whatever bones there may be and chop the meat *very* finely. Return to the saucepan and allow to come to a boil again. Simmer for a few minutes. A thick sauce will result. Add the butter and the cognac. Simmer for a few minutes more. Cook the pappardelle in abundant boiling salted water for 8 minutes. Drain, and turn onto a serving platter. Add half of the sauce. Mix well. Add the rest of the sauce and the Parmesan, mix well, and serve. Serves 4.

PAPPARDELLE WITH MEAT BALLS
(*Pappardelle alle Polpettine di Carne*)

Cooking time: 65 minutes

3 slices day-old bread	5 tablespoons oil
⅔ cup milk	1 pound ripe tomatoes, peeled
1 pound ground beef	(3 medium)
2 eggs	2 basil leaves (or ⅛ teaspoon
2 tablespoons chopped parsley	dried)
Salt and pepper to taste	Salt and pepper to taste
1½ cups grated Parmesan cheese	1 bouillon cube
	2 tablespoons flour
1 medium onion	1 pound pappardelle
1 stalk celery	4 tablespoons butter

Put the bread in the cold milk to soak. Squeeze as much milk as possible from the bread and add bread to meat, together with the eggs, the parsley, salt and pepper, and ⅔ cup of grated Parmesan. Mix. Put the whole mixture through the fine blade of a meat chopper. In a saucepan, sauté the cut-up onion and celery in 2 tablespoons of the oil. When golden, add the cut-up tomatoes, the basil leaves, and salt and pepper. Dissolve the bouillon cube in 1 cup of hot water and pour into the saucepan. Cook over a moderate flame for 45 minutes. Make meat balls with the meat mixture the size of half a walnut. Roll in flour and sauté in a skillet with 3 tablespoons hot oil over moderate heat. When they begin to brown, remove from the skillet, put on a plate, and set aside for use later. Put the sauce through the fine blade of a food mill or blend in a blender. Return to the saucepan, add the meat balls, and continue to cook for 5 minutes more. Before the sauce is ready, cook the pappardelle in rapidly boiling salted water for 8 minutes. Drain and put in a serving bowl. Add the butter in dabs, the sauce with the meat balls, and half of the remaining cheese. Mix well and serve with the rest of the cheese sprinkled on top. Make sure the meat balls are equally divided and arranged nicely on each serving. Serves 4.

PAPPARDELLE WITH DUCK
(*Pappardelle all'Anitra*)

Cooking time: 70 minutes

1 2½-pound duck	4 tablespoons oil
3 thin slices cooked ham	1 medium onion
2½ cloves garlic	1 cup red wine
15 rosemary needles (or ½ teaspoon dried)	2 tablespoons tomato paste
Salt and pepper	2 chicken bouillon cubes
5 slices bacon	1 pound pappardelle
4 tablespoons flour	6 tablespoons butter
	1 cup grated Cheddar cheese

Clean the duck and set aside the cleaned liver, heart, and gizzard. Finely chop the ham, ½ clove of garlic, and 4 needles of rosemary. Add salt and pepper to the mixture and put into the interior of the duck. The bacon should be sliced in long, wide, very thin slices. Rub salt and pepper over the entire surface of the duck. Cover it as much as possible with the bacon slices—particularly the breast and the drumsticks, and truss the duck with kitchen twine in order to keep the bacon in place. Flour it and put it in a large saucepan with the oil, which has been preheated. Brown well on all sides over a moderate flame. Add the sliced onion, the 2 unpeeled cloves of garlic, and the rest of the rosemary. Cut the liver, heart, and gizzard into strips and add. When well browned add flour if there is any left and pour in the red wine, stirring and turning the duck very carefully. When half of the wine has evaporated, add the tomato paste and stir for 1 minute until blended in the sauce. Dissolve the 2 bouillon cubes in 2 cups of hot water and add. Cook for 55 minutes over a moderate flame, being very careful to stir from time to time and turn the duck often, making sure that nothing sticks to the bottom of the pan. If the duck is young, it may cook sooner, so be sure to check from time to time. Cook the pappardelle in boiling salted water for 8 minutes. While it is cooking, remove the twine from the duck and also remove the filling. Pass the sauce and the filling through the fine blade of a food mill or blend in a blender. The sauce will be fairly thick. Save one third of the sauce to spoon over the duck. Put dabs of butter over the cooked drained pappardelle and mix well. Add the sauce and half of the grated cheese and mix well. Serve with the rest of the cheese sprinkled on top. Cut the duck into fourths and serve as a second course accompanied by whatever vegetable you desire. Serves 4.

AUTHOR'S GREEN PAPPARDELLE
(*Pappardelle Verdi dell'Amatore*)

My friends, knowing that I love to cook, often request that I prepare dinner for them at my home. This recipe was prepared by me especially for Esther Williams and Fernando Lamas.

Cooking time: 40 minutes

3 slices bacon	½ cup white wine
4 tablespoons oil	1 pound ripe tomatoes, peeled
½ pound chicken thighs	(3 medium)
2 tablespoons flour	1 chicken bouillon cube
1 medium onion	1 pound pappardelle
1 stalk celery	1 cup grated Parmesan cheese
Salt and pepper to taste	

Slice the bacon into wide, very thin slices and brown in a saucepan with the oil. Roll the chicken thighs in flour and brown. Add the coarsely chopped onion and celery, salt and pepper, and sauté until golden. If any flour is left over, add it and stir. Pour in white wine and allow half of it to evaporate. Add the cut-up tomatoes and the bouillon cube dissolved in ¾ cup hot water. Stir and bring to a boil, then lower the flame and simmer for 30 minutes. If you plan to make your own green pappardelle, prepare them as directed in Chapter VII (see Index). Cut the rolled-out pasta dough into strips 8 inches by 1 inch. Just before the sauce is done, cook the pappardelle in abundant boiling salted water for 8 minutes. While this is cooking, remove the chicken and bacon from the saucepan and put the sauce through a food mill or blend in a blender. Return sauce to the saucepan. Cut the bacon into small pieces. Debone the thighs and cut the meat into bite-size pieces. Return to the saucepan together with the bacon. Simmer sauce while you drain the pasta and put it in a serving bowl. Add the sauce and half the grated cheese. Mix well and serve with the rest of the cheese sprinkled on top. Serves 4.

BRAISED BREAST OF VEAL WITH BUCATINI
(*Petto di Vitello Stufato con Bucatini*)

Cooking time: 50 minutes

2 large onions	1 tablespoon flour
¾ cup butter	2 cups broth
Generous ½ pound breast of veal	1 pound bucatini
	1 cup grated Parmesan cheese
Salt and pepper to taste	

Put the *very* finely chopped onion in a saucepan with 3 table-spoons butter and sauté until almost golden. Cut the breast of veal into walnut-size pieces and add to the saucepan. Brown well. Add salt and pepper. Add flour and stir continuously for a few minutes. Add the broth and stir. Bring to a boil, then lower the flame and simmer for 50 minutes. Cook the bucatini in abundant boiling salted water for 10 minutes. Drain. Add the rest of the butter and the sauce. Mix well together with the grated Parmesan. The pieces of meat may be served with the bucatini if desired. Serves 4.

TOMATOES STUFFED WITH BUCATINI
(*Pomodori Ripieni con Bucatini*)

Cooking time: 50 minutes

8 large tomatoes	1 pound bucatini
½ pound mushrooms	4 tablespoons butter
1 tablespoon lemon juice	6 tablespoons grated Parmesan
6 tablespoons oil	cheese
3 thin slices cooked ham	1 bouillon cube
Salt and pepper to taste	

Preheat oven to 400° F.

Remove the top part of each tomato and remove the pulp with a spoon, being very careful not to break the skins. Turn the tomatoes upside down on a rack in order that excess liquid may be drained off. Wash and thinly slice the mushrooms. Put into a skillet with a tablespoon of lemon juice and 2 tablespoons of oil, and cook until most of the liquid has evaporated. Dice the ham and add to the mushrooms. Remove from the fire. Add salt and pepper. Break the bucatini into 3-inch lengths. Cook in rapidly boiling salted water for 10 minutes. Drain. Season with the mushroom mixture, half of the butter, and a little Parmesan. Mix well and stuff into each tomato. Arrange the tomatoes in a baking dish. Dissolve the bouillon cube in a cup of hot water. Add the remaining 4 tablespoons of oil. Pour into the baking dish containing the stuffed tomatoes. Sprinkle each tomato with Parmesan and put a generous dab of butter on each tomato. Put in a 400° oven and bake for about 15 minutes.

Variation: Add ⅓ cup Béchamel Sauce (see Index) flavored with freshly grated nutmeg to the bucatini before filling the tomatoes.

Serves 4.

BUCATINI WITH HOT SAUCE
(*Bucatini all'Arrabbiata*)

Cooking time: 20 minutes

¼ pound fresh mushrooms	⅓ cup white wine
1 tablespoon lemon juice	Salt and pepper to taste
2 cloves garlic	1 pound tomatoes, peeled
3 tablespoons oil	(3 medium)
1 small dried red pepper	1 pound bucatini
2 tablespoons flour	2 tablespoons chopped parsley

Wash the mushrooms and slice very thinly. Put in a dish with the lemon juice and mix. This prevents them from turning dark. Crush the garlic and chop finely. Sauté in the oil in a saucepan but do not allow to color. Add the red pepper, cut in slices, the flour, and the mushrooms. Mix well over a high flame. Add white wine, salt, and pepper. Cut up the tomatoes and add. Cook over a moderate flame for 15 minutes, stirring from time to time. Cook the bucatini in abundant boiling salted water for 10 minutes. While it is cooking, add the parsley to the sauce and continue to simmer. The sauce should be fairly thick. Drain the bucatini and put in a serving bowl. Pour on the sauce and mix well. This dish may also be served cold. Serves 4.

BUCATINI WITH CHICKEN
(*Bucatini al Pollo*)

Cooking time: 25 minutes

1 2-pound spring chicken	2 medium-size ripe tomatoes,
2 tablespoons oil	peeled
1 tablespoon flour	1 pound bucatini
Salt and pepper to taste	4 tablespoons butter
2 cups chicken broth	⅔ cup grated Parmesan cheese

Cut up the chicken into small pieces (remove the small bones). Put in a saucepan with the oil, and brown. When well browned add the flour, salt, and pepper. Stir. Add the broth and the cut-up tomatoes. Cook for 25 minutes over a moderately low flame, taking care to stir often, as the chicken tends to stick to the bottom of the pan. When it is almost done, cook the bucatini in abundant boiling salted water for 10 minutes. Drain and turn onto a serving platter. Season with the entire contents of the saucepan, the butter, and the grated cheese. Serves 4.

HOST'S BUCATINI
(*Bucatini all'Uso dell'Oste*)

Easy and inexpensive to prepare, this dish is a delight for those evenings when you are pressed for time and watching the budget; it is a very pleasant dish and liked by all.

Cooking time: 40 minutes

3 slices bacon	2 tablespoons flour
4 tablespoons oil	1 bay leaf
Generous ¼ pound sausage	⅓ cup white wine
1 medium onion	1 pound ripe tomatoes (3
1 stalk celery	medium)
1 clove garlic	1 pound bucatini
Salt and pepper to taste	1 cup grated Parmesan cheese

Cut the bacon into julienne strips and brown slightly in the oil. Peel the sausage and add. While browning keep crushing it with a spatula or wooden spoon in order to crumble it and allow it to brown nicely. In the meantime, slice the onion and the celery very thinly and add. Crush and finely chop the garlic, and add together with the salt and pepper. Now add the flour and the bay leaf. Stir for a minute or so. Pour in the white wine and allow to evaporate a little, then add the tomatoes, peeled and cut in pieces. Stir and cook over a moderate fire for 30 minutes more. If the sauce tends to become too thick, add ½ cup hot water. Stir from time to time. When the sauce is almost done, cook the bucatini in abundant boiling salted water for 10 minutes. Drain and turn onto a serving dish. Pour the sauce over all. Mix together with half of the Parmesan. Serve with the rest of the Parmesan sprinkled on top.
Serves 4.

BUCATINI WITH SAUSAGE
(*Bucatini con Salsiccia*)

Cooking time: 40 minutes

1 small onion, chopped	1½ pounds fresh tomatoes
4 tablespoons oil	(5 medium)
½ pound sausage	1 tablespoon tomato paste
¼ pound chicken giblets (liver, heart, gizzard)	1 pound bucatini
	1 cup grated Parmesan cheese
Salt and pepper to taste	

Sauté the onion in the oil. Add the peeled chopped sausage and the chicken giblets, cut in pieces. Sauté for 5 minutes. Add salt and pepper. Peel the tomatoes and chop coarsely. Add tomato paste and cook for 35 minutes. Cook the bucatini in abundant boiling salted water for 10 minutes, and drain. Add the sauce and half of the grated Parmesan. Mix well. Serve with the rest of the cheese sprinkled on top. Serves 4.

BUCATINI WITH VEAL
(*Bucatini alla Noce di Vitello*)

Cooking time: 1 hour and 35 minutes

1 ounce dried mushrooms (or ¼ pound fresh)	1 carrot
	Salt and pepper to taste
2 slices bacon	2 basil leaves (or ⅛ teaspoon
2 pounds veal roast	dried)
4 tablespoons oil	1 pound bucatini
1 large onion	4 tablespoons butter
1 stalk celery	1 cup grated Parmesan cheese

Put the mushrooms in 1 cup of hot water to soak. Dice the bacon. With the sharp point of a knife make holes in the veal and force a piece of bacon into each hole. Brown the meat in the oil in a fairly large saucepan, turning it continuously to brown it evenly. Chop the onion very finely. Add to the saucepan and sauté until softened. Add the finely chopped celery and carrot. Squeeze the mushrooms dry and chop coarsely. (Thinly slice fresh.) Add, together with salt and pepper and basil. Pour in enough lukewarm water to half cover the meat. Cook for 80 minutes. When the sauce is almost ready, cook the bucatini in boiling salted water for 10 minutes. Drain. Add the butter and ⅔ of the sauce produced by the meat. Mix well together with half of the Parmesan. Serve with the rest of the cheese sprinkled on top. Slice the meat and spoon some sauce over each slice. Serve as a second course with a green vegetable. Serves 4.

BUCATINI GRATIN
(*Bucatini Gratinati*)

Cooking time: 20 minutes

½ cup butter	1 pound bucatini
½ cup flour	Salt and white pepper to taste
4 cups milk	1 cup grated Parmesan cheese
¼ teaspoon nutmeg	

Preheat oven to 375° F.

Make a Béchamel Sauce (see Index) with 6 tablespoons of the butter, flour, and the milk. Add the nutmeg. Break the bucatini into

small pieces. Cook in abundant boiling salted water for 10 minutes.
Drain. Add salt and white pepper and the ¾ cup grated Parmesan to
the Béchamel Sauce. Grease a baking dish with the rest of the butter.
Mix the pasta and the Béchamel Sauce and put in the baking dish.
Level off nicely. Top with a few dabs of butter and a sprinkling of
cheese. Bake in a 375° oven until golden on top. Allow to rest a few
minutes before serving.

Variation: For a more "company dish" add 4 slices of crisp bacon,
crumbled, and ½ cup thinly sliced mushrooms that have been
sautéed in butter. Serves 4.

BUCATINI ALL'AMATRICIANA
(*Bucatini all'Amatriciana*)

The management of the Hotel Restaurant Shangri-La Corsetti,
located on the outskirts of Rome on the way to the sea, kindly gave
us this delicious recipe, which was a favorite of former King Farouk
of Egypt.

Cooking time: 30 minutes

3 slices bacon	Salt and pepper to taste
1 tablespoon oil	1 pound bucatini
½ cup white wine	1 cup grated Parmesan cheese
½ pound tomatoes, peeled (2 medium)	⅔ cup grated pecorino cheese (or any sharp cheese)

Cut the bacon into strips. Brown in the oil. Add the wine. Cook
for a few minutes, then add the tomatoes, cut in pieces. Add salt
and pepper. Cook for about 30 minutes. Cook the bucatini in abundant boiling salted water for about 10 minutes. Drain. Add the sauce
with half the grated cheeses. Mix well. Sprinkle the rest of the cheese
on top.

Variation: If you like a more piquant sauce, sauté 1 small dried red
pepper with the bacon. Remove the pepper. Serves 4.

BUCATINI WITH TUNA
(*Bucatini al Tonno*)

Cooking time: 25 minutes

2 cloves garlic

5 tablespoons oil

¼ dried red pepper, chopped
(or ½ teaspoon paprika)

1 (7-ounce) can tuna, coarsely chopped

½ cup tomato paste

2 tablespoons chopped parsley

1 pound bucatini

Crush and finely chop the garlic. Sauté in the oil in a saucepan, but do not allow it to color. Add the red pepper (or paprika). Add the tuna and sauté for 2 minutes more. Dilute the tomato paste in 2 cups of hot water and add to the saucepan together with 1 tablespoon of parsley. Cook over a slow flame for 20 minutes. Drain the bucatini after having cooked it in abundant boiling salted water for 10 minutes. Mix with the sauce and the rest of the parsley. Serves 4.

BUCATINI ALLA GRIMALDI
(*Bucatini alla Grimaldi*)

A favorite of the Prince of Monaco.

Cooking time: 50 minutes

Scant ½ pound lobster meat
(tail)

½ cup plus 2 tablespoons butter

Salt to taste

1 pound bucatini

Cayenne pepper to taste

Prepare the lobster as directed in Lobster all'Americana (see Index). Slice into medallions and sauté in 2 tablespoons of the butter. Add salt. Cook the bucatini in abundant boiling salted water for 10 minutes. Drain and turn onto a fairly large serving platter. Add the remaining butter in dabs and toss well. Arrange the lobster medallions on top. Pour the lobster sauce over all and dust with the cayenne pepper. Serves 4.

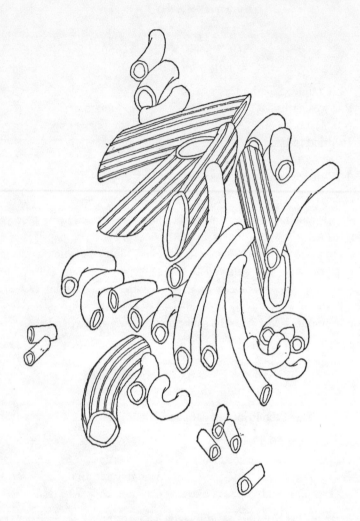

CHAPTER III

Macaroni and Family

Among the Italian people, macaroni and spaghetti are the pastas most commonly served at home, while the contrary is true in restaurants, for the very reason that they are eaten too often at home.

In Europe, macaroni represents the typical Italian national dish, a reason for which Italians (especially in France) are colloquially referred to as "macaroni's," which, of course, is neither very elegant nor very courteous! Why is this type of pasta considered rather commonplace in our times? Probably because of its shape, which is less slender than that of spaghetti or less artistic than that of fusilli, for example.

What is certain, however, is that up until the beginning of this century macaroni was considered a dish fit for kings. In England it is well known that Queen Elizabeth likes macaroni very much, particularly when it is baked au gratin.

The great Italian composer Rossini, with typically Latin exaggeration, used to say that it is easier to compose a successful opera than to prepare a good plate of macaroni! He loved macaroni so that he invented a sauce (the recipe for which he kept secret) that he injected into the cooked macaroni with a hypodermic needle!

Alexandra Feodorovna, wife of Czar Nicholas II, sent one of her chefs to Naples to learn how to prepare macaroni. As a result, this chef invented "Queen's Macaroni" for her.

Pauline Bonaparte, sister of Napoleon, ate macaroni several times a week, as did Margaret of Valois, better known as Queen Margot, to mention only a few.

I must also mention the fact that it was Ferdinand II (King of Sicily) who commissioned a certain Mr. Spadaccini to invent a fork with which macaroni could be eaten by the members of his court, where, as in all of Italy before 1516, macaroni was eaten with one's hands.

Before you turn the page, I would like to mention that I have included six recipes for lasagne in this chapter whereas you will find all other lasagne recipes listed in Chapter VII: HOMEMADE PASTA. The reason for this is that lasagne made from a batter without eggs is associated with the macaroni family and is prepared in a similar fashion, and lasagne made from an egg batter is considered an oven-pasta and *should only* be cooked in the oven.

ELBOWS WITH CREAM
(*Elbow alla Crema*)

This recipe comes from Florence, and was given to me by the owner of the restaurant Giannino in San Lorenzo: a typical Tuscan restaurant where a delicious pizza is also served.

Cooking time: 20 minutes

1 pound elbow macaroni	Salt and pepper to taste
2 egg yolks	4 tablespoons butter
1 cup heavy cream	1⅓ cups grated Gruyère cheese

While the macaroni is cooking in abundant boiling salted water (12 minutes), beat the egg yolks with the cream, salt, and pepper. Drain the cooked macaroni and put in a preheated serving bowl. Add the butter in dabs and mix well. Add the egg-cream mixture and the grated Gruyère. Toss until well mixed and serve.
Variation: Substitute ½ cup grated mozzarella for the Gruyère.
Serves 4.

ELBOWS WITH HONEY
(*Elbow al Miele*)

Simple and inexpensive to prepare, this dish is a delight for those evenings when you are pressed for time and watching the budget yet want to serve something different and delicious.

Cooking time: 12 minutes

1 pound elbow macaroni	¼ pound butter
⅔ cup sugar	⅓ cup cream
⅔ cup honey	

While the macaroni is cooking in abundant boiling salted water (12 minutes), put the sugar in a small saucepan with 1 tablespoon of water and caramelize until golden brown. Add 2 tablespoons of water and stir. Remove from fire and add the honey and the butter. As soon as the macaroni is cooked, drain and put in a serving bowl. Add the contents of the saucepan and the cream. Mix and serve.
Serves 4.

ELBOWS WITH SALMON
(*Elbow al Salmone*)

Cooking time: 20 minutes

1 small onion	Salt and pepper to taste
3 tablespoons oil	4 tablespoons butter
2 tablespoons flour	2 tablespoons chopped parsley
1 pound canned salmon	1 pound elbow macaroni

While you are waiting for the water for cooking the macaroni to come to a boil, finely chop the onion and put in a saucepan with the oil. Sauté until golden. Add the flour and stir for one minute. Add the salmon, setting aside the juices. Stir one minute more. Salt and pepper to taste. Add the salmon juices, stirring continuously. Add the butter and the parsley. Stir and simmer slowly until the macaroni has cooked in rapidly boiling salted water for 12 minutes. Drain. Add the sauce, including the salmon which will have disintegrated in the cooking. Toss until well mixed and serve. Serves 4.

ELBOWS IN HOT SAUCE
(*Elbow in Salsa Forte*)

An excellent dish for a country weekend.

Cooking time: 40 minutes

1 medium onion	3 basil leaves (or ¼ teaspoon
2 cloves garlic	dried)
5 tablespoons oil	Salt and pepper to taste
½ dried red pepper	1 pound elbow macaroni
2 tablespoons flour	3 tablespoons chopped parsley
⅓ cup white wine	Pinch of cayenne pepper
1½ pounds tomatoes, peeled	
(5 medium)	

Thinly slice the onion and the garlic, and sauté in the oil with the red pepper. When barely golden, add the flour and stir. Add the white wine and allow half to evaporate. Add the cut-up tomatoes, the basil leaves, and salt and pepper. Stir and cook for 30 minutes over a moderate flame. Cook the macaroni in abundant boiling

salted water for 12 minutes. In the meantime, put the sauce through the fine blade of a food mill or blend in a blender. Drain the cooked elbows and put in a serving bowl. Add the sauce, the parsley, and a generous pinch of cayenne. Toss until well mixed and serve.
Serves 4.

ELBOWS GARDENER STYLE
(*Elbow alla Giardiniera*)

Of course this recipe can be prepared with canned or frozen vegetables but if you have the time to prepare it with fresh vegetables, the praise from your family or friends will be worth it.

Cooking time: 30 minutes

3 slices bacon	1 bouillon cube
3 tablespoons oil	Salt and pepper to taste
1 medium onion	½ cup shelled green peas
1 clove garlic	Scant ½ cup asparagus tips
3 basil leaves (or ¼ teaspoon dried)	1 pound elbow macaroni
	4 tablespoons butter
2 tablespoons flour	1 cup grated Parmesan cheese

Cut the bacon into spaghetti-like strips and brown in the oil with the finely chopped onion. Finely chop the crushed clove of garlic with the basil leaves, and add. Sauté for 1 minute more. Add the flour and stir. Dissolve the bouillon cube in 1½ cups of hot water and pour into the saucepan. Add salt and pepper. When the sauce comes to a boil, add the peas and cook over a moderately high flame. Cut the asparagus tips in 1-inch lengths and add. Cook for 15 minutes more. In the meantime, cook the macaroni in abundant boiling salted water for 12 minutes. Drain and put in a serving bowl. Add the contents of the saucepan, the butter in dabs, and half the grated cheese. Mix well and carefully in order not to break the asparagus. Serve with the rest of the cheese sprinkled on top. Serves 4.

ELBOWS VENETIAN STYLE
(*Elbow alla Veneta*)

Cooking time: 30 minutes

3 ounces dried mushrooms (or ¾ pound fresh)
6 slices lean bacon
3 tablespoons oil
1 large onion
½ cup red wine

1 bouillon cube
½ cup tomato paste
Salt and pepper to taste
Pinch of orégano
1 pound elbow macaroni
1 cup grated Parmesan cheese

Put the dried mushrooms in 1 cup of hot water to soak. Cut the bacon into julienne strips, put in a saucepan with the oil, and brown. Cut the onion into julienne strips and sauté until golden. Add the red wine and allow to evaporate over a fairly high flame. Remove the mushrooms from the water and slice thinly. Add. Dilute the bouillon cube and the tomato paste in the mushroom water and add (¾ cup hot water if fresh mushrooms are used). Add salt and pepper. Stir. Add orégano. Simmer for 20 minutes. When the sauce is almost done, cook the macaroni in abundant boiling salted water for 12 minutes. Drain and put in a serving bowl. Add the sauce and half the grated Parmesan. Toss until well mixed. Serve with the rest of the cheese sprinkled on top. Serves 4.

CITIZEN'S ELBOWS
(*Elbow alla Cittadina*)

Cooking time: 30 minutes

½ pound spinach (or 10-ounce package frozen, chopped)
1¼ pounds tomatoes (4 medium)
1 medium onion
4 tablespoons oil
Salt and pepper to taste

2 basil leaves (or ⅛ teaspoon dried)
6 tablespoons butter
6 eggs
⅔ cup grated Gruyère cheese
⅓ cup grated Parmesan cheese
1 pound elbow macaroni

Wash the spinach well and cook in very little water until tender. Peel the tomatoes. Finely chop the onion, put in a saucepan with 2 tablespoons of the oil, and sauté until golden. Add the cut-up tomatoes, salt and pepper, chopped basil leaves and butter, and cook for 25 minutes. In the meantime, break the eggs into a bowl together with salt, 1 tablespoon of the mixed grated cheeses and the spinach, which has been squeezed as dry as possible and finely chopped. Beat until well mixed. Divide this mixture into 3 parts and also divide the remaining 2 tablespoons of oil into 3 parts. Make 3 small omelets in a skillet with the oil. Put the omelets on a bread board and cut into half-inch squares. Add these little squares to the sauce about 5 minutes before you are to use it. When the sauce is almost done, cook the macaroni in abundant boiling salted water for 12 minutes. Drain well and put in a serving bowl with all the sauce and half the remaining grated cheeses. Mix well and serve with the rest of the cheese sprinkled on top. Serves 4.

PRINCE'S ELBOWS
(Elbow del Principe)

Cooking time: 40 minutes

3 slices bacon

3 tablespoons oil

¼ pound chicken breast

¼ pound fresh mushrooms

2 tablespoons flour

Salt and pepper to taste

¼ cup tomato paste

1 chicken bouillon cube

1 pound elbow macaroni

1 cup grated Parmesan cheese

½ cup heavy cream

Cut the bacon into spaghetti-like strips and sauté in the oil in a saucepan. Cut the chicken breast in the same manner and sauté. Do the same with the mushrooms. Stir. Add the flour, salt, and pepper. Dilute the tomato paste and the bouillon cube in 1½ cups of hot water and pour into the saucepan. Stir and cover. Simmer over a moderate fire for 25 minutes. When the sauce is almost done, cook the macaroni in abundant boiling salted water for 12 minutes. Drain well and put in serving bowl together with all the sauce and half the grated cheese. Toss until well mixed. Add the cream and mix again. Serve with the rest of the cheese sprinkled on top. Serves 4.

ELBOWS WITH FRESH MUSHROOMS
(*Elbow con Funghi Freschi*)

Cooking time: 20 minutes

½ pound mushrooms	2 tablespoons flour
1 tablespoon lemon juice	1 chicken bouillon cube
2 cloves garlic	3 tablespoons chopped parsley
5 tablespoons oil	1 pound elbow macaroni
Salt and pepper to taste	1 cup grated Parmesan cheese

Wash and slice the mushrooms. Put in a bowl with the lemon juice and mix. Finely chop the garlic and sauté in the oil in a saucepan. When barely golden, add the mushrooms with the lemon juice, salt and pepper. Cook for 10 minutes. When most of the liquid has evaporated, add the flour and stir. Dissolve the bouillon cube in ½ cup hot water and pour into the saucepan. Add the parsley, stir, and allow to simmer over a low flame. At this point the water for the macaroni should be boiling. Cook the elbows in abundant boiling salted water for 12 minutes. Drain and put in a serving bowl. Add the sauce (which has been simmering while the macaroni has been cooking) and half the grated cheese. Mix well. Serve with the rest of the cheese sprinkled on top. Serves 4.

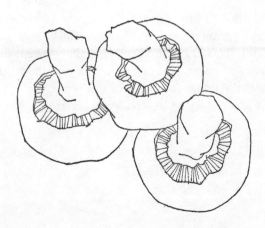

LASAGNE, HUNTER STYLE
(*Lasagne alla Cacciatore*)

One of my best friends is Tonino, owner of the famous *trattoria* Tonino's, which is situated in a seventeenth-century cave in Sacrafano, a small village 14 miles from Rome. On January 6, 1971, my wife and I had our wedding luncheon in this earthy atmosphere, and we and our guests enjoyed this lasagne dish invented especially for us by Tonino.

Cooking time: 50 minutes

1¾ pounds ripe tomatoes (5 or 6 medium)	Pepper
	½ cup Marsala wine
¼ cup oil	1 pound lasagne
3 tablespoons butter	¾ cup grated Parmesan cheese
1 small onion	1 tablespoon chopped basil
2 cloves garlic	(or 1 teaspoon dried)
3 slices bacon	1 tablespoon chopped parsley
1 2½-pound chicken	

First peel the tomatoes, remove the seeds, and cut them up. Then put into a saucepan the oil, butter, chopped onion, and the whole cloves of garlic. Sauté over a very low heat for 3 minutes or until the onion is softened but not colored. Add the bacon, cut in julienne strips, the cut-up chicken, and the pepper. Brown over high heat until bacon is a lovely golden color. Lower the heat and cook for 20 minutes. Remove the garlic and add the wine. Allow it to evaporate for 3 minutes, then add the tomatoes. Cover the saucepan and cook for 20 minutes, stirring from time to time. Add a little hot water if necessary. Cook the lasagne in abundant boiling salted water for 8 minutes. Drain and put in a serving dish. Mix with the sauce and the grated Parmesan. Arrange the pieces of chicken on top. Sprinkle the chopped basil and parsley on top and serve. Serves 4.

LASAGNE WITH ANCHOVY SAUCE
(*Lasagne alla Salsa di Acciughe*)

For those who love anchovies here is another dish made with those little fish, which are a delicacy especially for the people from the southern part of Italy.

Cooking time: 20 minutes

1 (2-ounce) can anchovy fillets	1 pound lasagne
4 tablespoons oil	1 tablespoon chopped parsley
Pepper	

Sauté the anchovies in a small saucepan with the oil, crushing them continuously with a fork until they become completely disintegrated. Add 2 tablespoons of water and a generous pinch of pepper. Cook over very low heat for 12 minutes. Salt probably will not be needed since the anchovies are salty, but taste the sauce and add salt if necessary. Cook the lasagne in abundant boiling salted water for 8 minutes. Drain and put in serving bowl. Add the anchovy sauce and the chopped parsley. Toss until well mixed and serve while hot. Serves 4.

LASAGNE WITH FRESH TOMATO
(*Lasagne al Pomodoro Fresco*)

Cooking time: 30 minutes

1½ pounds ripe tomatoes (5 medium)	Salt and pepper to taste
1 small onion	1 pound lasagne
2 leaves sage (or ¼ teaspoon dried)	¼ pound butter
	1 cup grated Parmesan cheese

Wash the tomatoes, halve them, and put in a saucepan with the onion, cut in fourths, the sage, salt, and pepper. Boil for 25 minutes. Cook the lasagne in abundant boiling salted water for 8 minutes. In the meantime, put the tomato mixture through the fine blade of a food mill. Add the butter (do not return to the fire) and stir. Drain the cooked lasagne and mix with the tomato sauce and the grated Parmesan. Serve hot. Serves 4.

LASAGNE WITH ASPARAGUS
(Lasagne agli Asparagi)

Cooking time: 40 minutes

1 pound asparagus
1 medium onion
2 tablespoons oil
6 tablespoons butter
4 tablespoons flour
1 chicken bouillon cube

1 cup milk
Salt and white pepper to taste
1 pound lasagne
1 cup grated Parmesan cheese
¼ cup heavy cream

Cook the asparagus in boiling water for 10 minutes. Cut the onion into very thin julienne strips and sauté in a saucepan with the oil until golden. Add the butter and the flour. Stir until blended. Dilute the bouillon cube in ½ cup hot water and add. Stir. Add the milk, which you have previously brought to a boil, salt, and white pepper. Bring to a boil and add the asparagus, cut into 1-inch pieces. Simmer for 30 minutes over low heat, stirring often. When this sauce is almost ready, cook the lasagne in abundant boiling salted water for 8 minutes, being very careful to put them in the water a little at a time so that they do not stick together. Drain and put in a large serving bowl with all the sauce and half the grated Parmesan. Mix well. Add the cream and mix again. Dust with the rest of the grated cheese and serve. Serves 4.

LASAGNE WITH LEG OF MUTTON SAUCE
(Lasagne alla Salsa di Montone Arrosto)

Cooking time: for the mutton—2 hours
          for the lasagne—10 minutes

½ pound leg of mutton
Salt and pepper
3 tablespoons oil
4 tablespoons butter
2 cloves garlic, unpeeled
1 sprig rosemary (or ¼ teaspoon dried)

½ cup white wine
1 pound lasagne
1 anchovy fillet
1 cup grated Parmesan cheese

Rub the meat with salt and pepper and brown in a saucepan with the oil and butter. When nicely browned, add the unpeeled cloves of garlic and the sprig of rosemary. Sauté for 1 minute, then add the wine and enough water to half cover the meat. Cover the saucepan and cook over a very slow fire until cooked. Turn the meat from time to time and add more water if needed. When the meat is cooked, put the sauce through a sieve. Cook the lasagne in abundant boiling salted water for 8 minutes. In the meantime, set aside half of the sauce to use with the meat later. Mash the anchovy with a fork and add to the remaining sauce, allowing it to simmer until the anchovy has disintegrated. Drain the cooked lasagne and put in a serving bowl together with the sauce and half the grated cheese. Mix well. Serve with the rest of the cheese sprinkled on top. Serves 4.

LASAGNE, HOME STYLE
(*Lasagne all'Uso di Casa*)

Cooking time: 40 minutes

Scant ½ pound ground pork (slightly fatty)	½ cup tomato paste
	Salt and pepper to taste
4 tablespoons oil	1 bouillon cube
1 clove garlic	½ cup shelled green peas
2 basil leaves (or ⅛ teaspoon dried)	1 pound lasagne
	1⅓ cups grated Parmesan
2 tablespoons flour	cheese

Brown the finely ground pork in a saucepan with the oil. In the meantime, chop together very finely the crushed clove of garlic and the basil and add to the saucepan while the meat is browning. Cook for 2 minutes, add the flour and stir until well blended. Add the tomato paste, salt, and pepper, and stir. Dissolve the bouillon cube in 1½ cups hot water and add. Cook over moderate heat for 30 minutes, stirring from time to time. When the sauce is almost done, add the cooked green peas. Cook the lasagne in abundant boiling salted water for 8 minutes, being careful to add the pasta to the water a little at a time in order to prevent it from sticking together. Stir it often while it is cooking. Drain the cooked pasta and put in a serving bowl together with all the sauce and half the grated Parmesan. Toss until well mixed. Serve with the rest of the cheese sprinkled on top. Serves 4.

MEAT RAGÙ, WHITE
(*Ragù di Carne, Bianca*)

Cooking time: 70 minutes

1 medium onion   Salt and pepper to taste
3 slices bacon   1 bay leaf
2 tablespoons oil   1 teaspoon flour
1 carrot   1 cup white wine
1 stalk celery
Generous ¼ pound ground beef
  (not prime quality)

Finely chop the onion and the bacon, and sauté in a saucepan
with the oil. When golden in color add the finely chopped carrot
and celery. Sauté for 2 minutes. Add the ground meat, salt, pepper,
and the bay leaf, and brown for 10 minutes, stirring often. Add
the flour and stir for 1 minute, until well blended. Pour in the white
wine and allow half of it to evaporate, then add 2 cups of boiling
water. Cook over low heat for 60 minutes. Serves 4.

RAGÙ, PIEDMONT STYLE
(*Ragù alla Piemontese*)

This recipe was given to me by the chef of the restaurant Gatto
Néro in Torino.

Cooking time: 90 minutes

3 slices bacon   1 stalk celery
2 tablespoons oil   Salt and pepper to taste
Scant ½ pound beef (not prime   1 cup white wine
  quality)   2 medium-size ripe tomatoes
1 medium onion   2 basil leaves (or ⅛ teaspoon
2 carrots   dried)

Sauté the bacon, cut in julienne strips, in oil in a saucepan. Add
the meat, also cut in julienne strips, and brown, together with the
coarsely chopped onion, carrots, celery, salt, and pepper. When well
browned, add the wine and allow half of it to evaporate. Add the
peeled cut-up tomatoes and the basil and cook over moderate heat
for 90 minutes, stirring from time to time. If necessary add a little
water. When the ragù is ready, put it through the medium blade of

a food mill or blend in a blender. The ragù should be fairly thick in texture. Serves 4.

WHITE RAGÙ, PIEDMONT STYLE
(*Ragù alla Piemontese in Bianco*)

Cooking time: 90 minutes

3 slices bacon	1 stalk celery
3 tablespoons oil	1 bay leaf
1 large onion	Salt and white pepper to taste
Generous ¼ pound beef (not	1½ tablespoons flour
prime quality)	1 cup white wine
1 carrot	1 bouillon cube

Sauté the sliced bacon in the oil in a saucepan. Add the thinly sliced onion and continue to sauté, stirring often. Add the sliced meat, and brown, together with the sliced carrot, celery, bay leaf, salt, and white pepper. When well browned, add the flour and stir until well blended. Add the white wine and stir continuously for 2 minutes. Dissolve the bouillon cube in 2 cups of hot water and add. Stir until the mixture comes to a boil, then cover and cook slowly for about 80 minutes. Check from time to time and add water if needed. Put the ragù through the medium blade of a food mill or blend in a blender. It should be fairly thick. It is excellent on several varieties of pasta and for other uses. Serves 4.

ZITE WITH LEG OF MUTTON SAUCE
(*Zite col Sugo di Montone*)

Cooking time: 70 minutes

3 slices bacon	1 medium onion
1 clove garlic	1 cup tomato paste
10 rosemary needles (or ½	Salt and pepper to taste
teaspoon dried)	1 bay leaf
1 tablespoon chopped parsley	1 pound zite
½ pound leg of mutton	⅔ cup grated pecorino cheese
1 tablespoon flour	(or any sharp cheese)
4 tablespoons oil	⅔ cup grated Parmesan cheese

Take the thinly sliced bacon, crushed garlic, rosemary, and parsley, and chop *very* finely, pressing down from time to time with the flat side of the knife in order to form a homogeneous paste. With a sharp-pointed knife make several deep holes in the meat (holes wide enough for a finger to fit into easily) and fill each hole with this mixture. Tie the meat if necessary. Rub with flour and brown in a saucepan in which the oil is already hot. Brown nicely on all sides. Add the thinly sliced onion and sauté together with the meat. Dilute the tomato paste in 2 cups of hot water and pour into the saucepan. Stir and add salt and pepper. Add the bay leaf. The liquid should cover about half the surface of the meat. Simmer slowly for 60 minutes. When almost ready, cook the zite in abundant boiling salted water for 10 minutes. In the meantime, mix the cheeses together with a generous pinch of pepper. Drain the cooked zite and put in a serving bowl. Set aside a little sauce for the meat and put the rest on the pasta. Add cheese and mix well. Serve immediately. Slice the meat and spoon some sauce over each slice. Serve as a second course. Serves 4.

BAKED ZITE
(*Zite Pasticciate*)

Cooking time: 30 minutes

3 slices bacon	Salt and pepper to taste
2 tablespoons oil	4 tablespoons butter
2 tablespoons finely chopped onion	1 tablespoon flour
	1 cup milk
⅛ pound mortadella (sausage)	1 pound zite
¼ cup shelled green peas	1⅓ cups grated Parmesan
¼ cup tomato paste	cheese
1 chicken bouillon cube	

Preheat oven to 400° F.

Cut the bacon into spaghetti-like strips. Put in saucepan with the oil and brown. Sauté the finely chopped onion in the oil and when golden add the mortadella (cut like the bacon) and the peas. Stir for a minute or so over a moderate flame. Dilute the tomato paste and the bouillon cube in ½ cup of hot water and pour into the saucepan. Add salt and pepper. Stir. Simmer over moderate flame for 10 minutes. In a small saucepan melt the butter, then add the flour. Stir. Add the milk gradually, stirring constantly. A delicate béchamel sauce will result. When the béchamel begins to boil, add salt to taste and pour into the other saucepan. Stir well. Cook for 10 minutes over a very low flame. Cook the zite (broken in 3-inch lengths) in abundant boiling salted water for 10 minutes. Drain and put in a serving bowl with all the sauce and half the cheese. Mix very well as the ingredients must be well blended. Put in an ovenproof serving dish. Sprinkle the rest of the cheese on top and put in a hot oven for 5 minutes. Serves 4.

MEZZE ZITE WITH CHICKEN CASSEROLE
(*Mezze Zite Sformate al Pollo*)

Cooking time: 40 minutes

1 2-pound chicken	4 tablespoons butter
4 tablespoons oil	6 tablespoons flour
1 medium onion	2 cups milk
Salt and pepper to taste	1 pound mezze zite
1 chicken bouillon cube	1⅓ cups grated Parmesan
1 tablespoon tomato paste	cheese
2 basil leaves (or ⅛ teaspoon dried)	

Preheat oven to 400° F.

After cleaning and singeing the chicken, cut it into 8 pieces. Put in a saucepan with the oil and brown. Add the finely chopped onion, salt, and pepper, and sauté along with the chicken. Dilute the bouillon cube and the tomato paste in 1 cup hot water. Pour into the saucepan with the coarsely chopped basil leaves. Stir and cook covered for 25 minutes. In meantime, in a small saucepan, prepare a Béchamel Sauce (see Index) with the butter, the flour, and the milk. Add salt and pepper and stir continuously for 5 minutes. Check the chicken for doneness. If cooked, remove the pieces from the sauce and debone them. Chop the meat and return to the sauce in the saucepan. Continue to simmer. Be very careful to remove *all* bones. Cook the mezze zite in abundant boiling salted water for 10 minutes without breaking them. Drain and return to the pot in which they were cooked. Pour in all the sauce with the chicken, the béchamel, and half the cheese. Mix all well. Put in an ovenproof baking dish. Level off and sprinkle with the rest of the grated cheese. Put in a hot oven for 15 minutes. Allow to rest for 5 minutes after

removing from the oven. Cut into squares and serve with a pancake turner or a cake server. Serves 4.

ZITE ABRUZZI STYLE
(*Zite alla Abruzzese*)

Aunt Marie, an old lady from the little town of Opi, between
Naples and Rome, gave me this recipe which has been in her family
for over 4 generations.

Cooking time: 20 minutes

4 slices bacon	1 pound tomatoes, peeled
2 tablespoons oil	(3 medium)
1 small onion (or leek)	Salt and pepper to taste
½ dried red pepper	1 pound zite
½ cup white wine	1 cup grated Parmesan cheese

Put a large pot of salted water on the fire for cooking the zite. Cut
the bacon into thin strips and put in a saucepan with the oil. Brown
well, together with the coarsely cut up onion (or leek). When golden
add the red pepper and the wine. Allow the wine to evaporate. Add
the cut-up tomatoes. Salt to taste, stir, and cook 10 minutes. In the
meantime, the water should be boiling. Cook the zite for 10 minutes,
drain, and put in a serving bowl. Add the sauce and the cheese
mixed with a generous pinch of pepper. Mix well and serve immediately. Serves 4.

ZITE AGRIGENTO STYLE
(*Zite alla Maniera di Agrigento*)

This recipe is typically Sicilian. It was given to me by the restaurant La Caprice in Agrigento.

Cooking time: 50 minutes

½ pound ground pork	1 clove garlic
1 medium onion	4 tablespoons flour
1 carrot	1 cup tomato paste
1 stalk celery	1 chicken bouillon cube
Salt and pepper to taste	1 pound zite
3 tablespoons oil	4 tablespoons butter
2 basil leaves (or ⅛ teaspoon dried)	1 cup grated Parmesan cheese

Grind together the pork, the onion, the carrot, and the celery. Add salt and pepper to taste, and sauté in the oil in a saucepan for 5 minutes over a high flame. Finely chop the basil leaves together with the crushed clove of garlic and add. Stir for a few minutes. Add the flour and stir again. Dilute the tomato paste and the bouillon cube in 1½ cups boiling water and pour into saucepan. Stir and allow to simmer 45 minutes over moderately low flame. In the meantime, break the zite into 3-inch lengths. When the sauce is almost ready, cook the zite in abundant boiling salted water for 10 minutes. Drain well and put in a serving bowl with dabs of butter, all the sauce and half the grated cheese. Toss until well mixed. Serve with the rest of the cheese sprinkled on top. Serves 4.

EMPEROR'S ZITE
(Zite all'Imperatore)

Cooking time: 30 minutes

3 slices bacon	2 bay leaves
1 medium onion	Salt and white pepper to taste
2 tablespoons oil	2 cups milk
6 tablespoons flour	1 pound zite
4 tablespoons butter	1⅓ cups grated Gruyère cheese
1 chicken bouillon cube	

Sauté the thinly sliced bacon and onion in the oil in a saucepan. When almost golden, add the flour and the butter. Stir for 1 minute, then gradually pour in the bouillon cube dissolved in 1 cup of hot water. Stir well. Add the bay leaves, salt, and white pepper. Simmer slowly for 20 minutes, stirring from time to time. In the meantime, bring the milk to a boil. When the 20 minutes are up, pour the milk into the saucepan, stir, and simmer for 10 minutes more. Do not cover the saucepan. Cook the zite in abundant boiling salted water for 10 minutes. While this is cooking, put the sauce through the fine blade of a food mill or blend in a blender. Drain the zite and put in a serving bowl with all of the sauce and half the grated cheese. Mix well and serve with the rest of the cheese sprinkled on top. Serves 4.

ZITE WITH VEAL CHOPS, NEAPOLITAN STYLE
(*Lombate di Vitello con Zite alla Napolitana*)

Cooking time: 40 minutes

2 tablespoons oil	Nutmeg
½ tablespoon flour	1 pound zite
4 veal chops (1 pound)	4 tablespoons butter
Salt and pepper to taste	⅔ cup grated pecorino cheese
⅓ cup tomato paste	(or any sharp cheese)

Put the oil in a saucepan and heat it. Flour the veal chops and brown on both sides in the hot oil. Add salt and pepper. Dilute the tomato paste in a cup of hot water and pour over the veal chops. Add a generous pinch of nutmeg and stir. While the chops are cooking over a low flame, start cooking the zite, broken into 3-inch lengths, in abundant boiling salted water. Cook for 10 minutes. Drain and put in a serving plate with the butter. Add the sauce and the grated pecorino. Mix well and serve with the veal chops. Serves 4.

ZITE À LA MODE
(*Zite alla Moda*)

Cooking time: 80 minutes

4 tablespoons flour	2 bouillon cubes
1 2-pound piece veal	1 bay leaf
(preferably eye of the round)	4 cups milk
3 tablespoons oil	1 pound zite
3 whole cloves	6 tablespoons butter
3 medium onions	1¼ cups grated Parmesan
Salt and pepper to taste	cheese

Flour the meat and brown in a saucepan where the oil is already hot. Brown evenly on all sides. Stick a clove in each of the onions and brown along with the meat. Add salt and pepper to taste. Dissolve the bouillon cubes in 1½ cups of hot water and pour into the saucepan. Add the bay leaf, cover the saucepan, and simmer over a low flame for 40 minutes. Boil the milk separately and add when the liquid in the saucepan has evaporated. Simmer for 25 minutes more.

Test the meat for doneness from time to time. When the meat is cooked remove from saucepan and put the sauce through the fine blade of a food mill or blend in a blender. In the meantime, cook the zite (broken into 3-inch lengths) in abundant boiling salted water for 10 minutes. Drain and put in a serving bowl. Add the butter in dabs, the sauce (setting aside a little to use on the meat), and half the Parmesan. Mix well and serve with the rest of the cheese sprinkled on top. Slice the meat and serve as a second course with a little sauce spooned over each slice. Serves 4.

MARSHAL'S ZITE
(*Zite alla Maresciallo*)

Cooking time: 80 minutes

2 slices bacon	Salt and pepper to taste
1 medium onion	2 tablespoons flour
4 tablespoons oil	½ cup white wine
Generous ½ pound mutton (not the leg)	½ pound tomatoes, peeled (2 medium)
1 stalk celery	1 pound zite
1 carrot	1 cup grated Parmesan cheese
1 bay leaf	

Thinly slice the bacon and the onion, and sauté together in the oil in a saucepan. Add the thinly sliced mutton, celery, and carrot, the bay leaf, salt, and pepper. Stir over a high flame for 3 minutes. Add the flour and stir. Pour in the white wine and while it is evaporating cut up the tomatoes and add. Stir. Cover the saucepan and cook for 80 minutes over a moderate flame, adding a little water whenever necessary. About 10 minutes before the sauce is ready, cook the zite (broken into 3-inch lengths) in abundant boiling salted water for 10 minutes. Drain and put in a serving bowl. Add the sauce and half the grated cheese. Toss until well mixed and serve with the rest of the cheese sprinkled on top. Serves 4.

ZITE WITH MEATLESS SAUCE
(*Zite alla Salsa di Macro*)

Cooking time: 55 minutes

2 slices bacon	3 tablespoons oil
1 clove garlic	1 stalk celery
5 rosemary needles (or ¼ teaspoon dried)	1 medium onion
	Salt and pepper to taste
3 basil leaves (or ¼ teaspoon dried)	1 bouillon cube
	¾ cup tomato paste
Pepper	1 pound zite
1 2-pound leg of lamb	1 cup grated Parmesan cheese

Chop the bacon, garlic, rosemary, and basil together so finely they form a paste. Mix with a generous pinch of pepper. With a sharp-pointed knife make several deep holes in the meat and insert a little of this paste in each hole. Put the meat in a saucepan and brown in the oil over a high flame, turning often in order to brown evenly. Finely chop the celery and the onion, and sauté together with the meat. Add salt and pepper to taste. Dilute the bouillon cube and the tomato paste in 1½ cups of hot water, pour into saucepan, and simmer over moderate flame for 45 minutes. Stir from time to time. Toward the end of the 45 minutes test the meat for doneness. Cook the zite (in 3-inch lengths) in abundant boiling salted water for 10 minutes. Drain and put in a serving bowl. Set aside a little sauce for the meat and pour the rest over the zite together with half the grated cheese. Mix well and serve with rest of cheese sprinkled on top. Slice the meat and spoon some sauce over each slice. Serve as a very tasty second course. Serves 6.

SWEET MACARONI
(*Macaroni Dolci*)

Cold or warm this is a delicious dish.

Cooking time: 10 minutes

1 pound macaroni	½ teaspoon cinnamon
½ pound ricotta cheese	2 tablespoons butter
1 tablespoon sugar	

Break the macaroni into thirds. Cook in abundant boiling salted water for 10 minutes. In the meantime, put into a serving bowl the ricotta, the sugar, the cinnamon, and the butter. Add 2 tablespoons of the boiling water in which the macaroni is cooking and mix all very well. Drain the macaroni, mix with the ricotta mixture, and serve. Serves 4.

MACARONI LIGURIAN STYLE
(*Maccheroni alla Ligure*)

All the Italian chefs say that, when possible, you should use freshly grated Parmesan because it makes all dishes taste better.

Cooking time: 25 minutes

2 potatoes
¾ cup thin green beans
2 carrots
½ cup shelled peas
1 pound macaroni
4 marjoram leaves (or ¼ teaspoon dried)

4 tablespoons olive oil
Salt and pepper to taste
3 tablespoons grated Parmesan cheese

Peel and dice the potatoes. Clean the green beans and break them in half. Clean the carrots and slice into wheels. Cook all the vegetables, including the peas, in boiling salted water for 15 minutes. Add the macaroni and the marjoram and boil for 10 minutes more. Drain. Put on a serving plate. Add the olive oil, salt and pepper to taste, and mix. Sprinkle with the grated cheese and serve. Serves 4.

MACARONI WITH ANCHOVIES
(*Maccheroni con Acciughe*)

Cooking time: 12 minutes

1 pound macaroni
1 (2-ounce) can anchovy fillets
3 egg yolks
½ pound mozzarella cheese, diced

2 tablespoons butter
Salt and pepper to taste

Cook the macaroni in boiling salted water for 10 minutes. While it is cooking, remove 2 cups of the boiling water in which it is cooking and set aside. In a small saucepan put the anchovies, which you have crushed with a fork and reduced to a creamy paste. Add the egg yolks, the diced mozzarella, the butter, and the 2 cups of boiling water. Mix well and cook over a very low flame for 10 minutes. Salt and pepper to taste. When the macaroni is cooked, drain well and add the boiling sauce. Mix well and return to fire for a minute or two. Serve immediately. Serves 4.

FOUR CHEESES MACARONI
(*Maccheroni ai Quattro Formaggi*)

This is a great Italian recipe and is served in many restaurants throughout Italy. It was given to me by the chef of Da Gino, a *trattoria* in Trastevere, the oldest section of Rome.

Cooking time: 20 minutes

½ pound mozzarella cheese	1 cup grated Parmesan cheese
¼ pound Dutch cheese (or	¼ pound butter
Cheddar cheese)	1 pound macaroni
¼ pound Gruyère cheese	Salt and white pepper to taste

Dice half of the mozzarella, the Dutch cheese, and the Gruyère. The other half should be grated and mixed together with the grated Parmesan. Melt the butter in 2 tablespoons of boiling water and keep hot in the top of a double boiler. Cook the macaroni in abundant boiling salted water for 10 minutes, drain, and put in a preheated serving plate. Add the diced cheeses, half of the grated cheeses and half of the melted butter. Salt and pepper to taste. Mix quickly while the pasta is hot. Sprinkle the rest of the grated cheeses on top and dribble the rest of the butter over all. Serve immediately in order that the cheese is not completely melted before it arrives on the table. Serves 4.

PUREST MACARONI
(*Maccheroni Purissimi*)

Cooking time: 20 minutes

¼ pound breast of capon	Salt and pepper to taste
¾ cup butter	1 pound macaroni
½ cup tomato paste	1 cup grated Parmesan cheese

Grind the breast of capon. Sauté in 2 tablespoons of the butter. Do not allow to brown. Sieve the tomato paste, add the salt and pepper, and add to the capon. Cook for 20 minutes. Cook the macaroni in abundant boiling salted water for 10 minutes, and drain. Put in a serving bowl with the rest of the butter. Add the tomato sauce and half of the grated cheese. Mix well and serve with the rest of the cheese sprinkled on top. Serves 4.

MACARONI WITH VARIOUS CHEESES
(*Maccheroni ai Formaggi Vari*)

Cooking time: 25 minutes

3 slices lean bacon	½ cup cottage cheese
2 tablespoons oil	½ cup diced Edam cheese
2 tablespoons flour	½ cup diced Swiss cheese
1 bouillon cube	2 egg yolks
Salt and white pepper to taste	4 tablespoons cream cheese
1 pound macaroni	⅔ cup grated Parmesan cheese

While you are waiting for the salted water for the pasta to come to a boil, cut the bacon into very fine spaghetti-like strips. Put in a medium-size saucepan with the oil, and brown. Add the flour, and stir. Dissolve the bouillon cube in ¾ cup hot water and add gradually, stirring continuously over a low flame. Add salt and white pepper to taste. Cook over a very low flame for 10 minutes. By this time the water has come to a boil. Cook the macaroni for 10 minutes. While it is cooking, finely dice the cottage, Edam, and Swiss cheeses. Remove the sauce from the fire and add the diced cheeses and stir. Beat the egg yolks in a small bowl together with the cream cheese and a pinch of white pepper. Drain the cooked macaroni. Add all the sauce and mix well. Add the egg mixture and toss until well mixed. Serve with the grated Parmesan sprinkled on top.

Variation 1: Ricotta may be substituted for the cottage cheese.

Variation 2: Add 1 cup of Béchamel Sauce (see Index) and 2 cups of plain tomato sauce to the above recipe and bake in a 375° oven for 25 minutes.

Serves 4.

MACARONI WITH EGGS
(*Maccheroni con le Uova*)

Cooking time: 15 minutes
   1 pound macaroni   White pepper
   10 tablespoons butter   4 eggs
   1½ cups grated Parmesan Salt to taste
     cheese

Cook the macaroni in abundant boiling salted water for 10 minutes, and drain. Put on a preheated platter with ⅔ of the butter and half of the cheese mixed with a generous pinch of white pepper. Fry the eggs in melted butter over a low flame. Salt slightly. When done, carefully arrange on the macaroni. Sprinkle with the rest of the cheese and serve immediately. Serves 4.

BAKER'S MACARONI
(*Maccheroni alla Fornaia*)

Cooking time: 15 minutes
   ¼ pound butter   1½ cups grated Gruyère cheese
   Salt   White pepper
   1 pound macaroni   1 cup heavy cream
   1½ cups grated Parmesan
     cheese

Add 1 tablespoon of the butter and 3 tablespoons of salt to 1 gallon of water in a large pot. When the water comes to a boil, add 1 pound of macaroni. When it comes to a boil again, cover and lower the flame. Simmer until the macaroni is tender, about 10 minutes. Drain and put on a serving platter. Add the grated cheeses, the remaining butter, and a generous pinch of white pepper. Mix well. Add the heavy cream, mix again, and serve. Serves 4.

MACARONI GRIMALDI
(*Maccheroni alla Grimaldi*)

Cooking time: 25 minutes

1 to 2 pounds lobster	1⅓ cups grated Parmesan
¾ cup butter	cheese
½ pound mushrooms, sliced	¼ teaspoon cayenne pepper
¼ cup sliced truffles	Salt and pepper to taste
1 pound macaroni	

Prepare the lobster as described in the recipe Lobster Sauce, American Style (see Index). Sauté in 4 tablespoons of the butter. Add the sliced mushrooms and very thinly sliced truffles previously sautéed in additional butter, and cover with the sauce in the above-mentioned recipe. Cook the macaroni in abundant boiling salted water for 10 minutes and drain. Put on a serving platter and mix with the remaining butter and the grated Parmesan (to which the cayenne pepper has been added). Arrange the lobster medallions attractively on top. Spoon the sauce over all and serve immediately. Serves 4.

LOBSTER SAUCE, AMERICAN STYLE
(*Aragosta, all'Americana*)

This sauce is really simple to prepare. It was given to me by Angelo Costa, chef of Pope John XXIII.

Cooking time: 30 minutes

1 2-pound lobster	Salt to taste
1 cup vinegar	4 tablespoons flour
⅔ cup butter	1 cup brandy
1 cup white wine	½ cup heavy cream
¼ cup tomato paste	1 teaspoon cayenne pepper

Immerse the lobster in a large pot of boiling water to which the vinegar has been added. Boil for 5 minutes, remove from the water, dry, and remove meat from the shell and save the shells for later use. Remove the meat in the tail section all in one piece and set aside. Discard the intestines. With a large chopping knife chop up the shell and the claws. Put in a saucepan with 4 tablespoons of butter and stir until the butter is absorbed. Add the white wine and allow to boil for 2 minutes, then add the tomato paste and 2 cups of water. Add salt and cover. Boil for 10 minutes. Stir from time to time, pressing down on the shells in order to release the juices. Remove from the fire and pass liquid through a very fine sieve. Squeeze the shells very well in order to remove as much juice as possible. In another saucepan put the rest of the butter with the flour and blend. Add the brandy gradually, stirring continuously. When well incorporated, add the liquid from the shells gradually. Allow to simmer and stir until a thin cream results. Remove from the fire and allow to cool for 2 minutes. Add the cream and the cayenne. Mix well with a wooden spoon. Cut the lobster tail into medallions and arrange in a skillet. Cover with part of the sauce and allow to heat over hot water, or continue to heat over a very low flame. Many delicious dishes may be prepared using this tasty sauce as a base. Serves 4.

MACARONI NEAPOLITAN STYLE
(*Maccheroni alla Napolitana*)

Cooking time: 40 minutes

¾ pound fresh mushrooms (or 7 tablespoons dried)
1 pound ripe tomatoes (3 or 4 medium)
1 medium onion
1 clove garlic
6 tablespoons oil
½ dried red pepper (whole)
Scant ½ pound ground beef
Salt and pepper to taste
2 basil leaves (or ⅛ teaspoon dried)
1 pound macaroni
1 cup grated Parmesan cheese

Put the dried mushrooms in warm water to soak. Cut up the tomatoes and boil for 5 minutes. Finely chop the onion and the garlic, and sauté in a saucepan in the oil and the red pepper. When barely colored, add the meat, salt, and pepper, and brown for 5 minutes. Add the chopped dried mushrooms, basil, and part of the water in which mushrooms have been soaking. Pass the tomatoes through the fine blade of a food mill, or blend in a blender and add. Simmer for 35 minutes until the sauce is fairly thick. Cook the macaroni in abundant boiling salted water for 10 minutes (do not overcook). Drain. Add the sauce and grated cheese. Toss until well mixed and serve immediately. Serves 4.

GUITAR MACARONI
(*Maccheroni alla Chitarra*)

Cooking time: 45 minutes

½ cup chopped ham fat
3 tablespoons oil
1 large onion
1 stalk celery
1 carrot
1 clove garlic
Generous ¼ pound ground pork

Salt and pepper to taste
1 tablespoon sugar (optional)
½ cup red wine
1¼ cups tomato paste
1 pound guitar macaroni
1 cup grated pecorino cheese
(or any sharp cheese)

Sauté the chopped ham fat in the oil in a saucepan. Add the finely chopped onion. When softened add the finely chopped celery, carrot, and garlic. Sauté for a few minutes more. Add the ground meat, salt, and pepper, and, if desired, the sugar. Brown the meat for 5 minutes. Pour in the red wine and allow to evaporate. Dilute the tomato paste in 2 cups of warm water and add to the saucepan. Simmer for 30 minutes. When the sauce is almost done, cook the macaroni in rapidly boiling salted water for 10 minutes. Drain well and put in a serving bowl. Mix with sauce and half of the grated cheese. Sprinkle the rest of the cheese on top and serve immediately. Serves 4.

MACARONI GALLANT
(*Maccheroni Galante*)

Cooking time: 40 minutes

3 slices bacon
6 tablespoons butter
⅓ pound turkey breast
2 cloves garlic
½ pound fresh mushrooms (or 5 tablespoons dried)
Salt and pepper to taste

1 pound canned tomatoes
3 basil leaves (or ¼ teaspoon dried)
1 pound macaroni
⅔ cup grated Gruyère cheese
⅓ cup grated Parmesan cheese

Dice the bacon, put in a saucepan with the butter, and sauté until barely golden. Add the diced turkey breast, and brown. Add the very finely chopped garlic. Coarsely chop the mushrooms (if dried, they should have been soaking in a cup of warm water) and add. Add salt and pepper. Pass the tomatoes through the fine blade of a food mill or blend in a blender. Add to the saucepan together with the chopped basil leaves. Simmer over a low flame for 40 minutes. Cook the macaroni in abundant boiling salted water for 10 minutes, and drain well. Mix together with the sauce and the grated cheeses and serve at once. Serves 4.

MACARONI WITH BEEF
(*Maccheroni con Umido*)

Cooking time: 1 hour and 45 minutes

¼ cup chopped salt pork	½ cup plus 2 tablespoons
1 stalk celery	concentrated tomato paste
1 large onion	1 tablespoon sugar (optional)
4 tablespoons oil	1 whole clove (optional)
Salt and pepper to taste	1 pound macaroni
1 pound beef (all in 1 piece)	1 cup grated Parmesan cheese

Finely chop the salt pork, the celery, and the onion, and sauté in a saucepan in the oil and salt and pepper until golden. Add the meat and brown evenly on all sides. Add the tomato paste and enough water to cover half the surface of the meat. Cook for 1½ hours over a very slow fire. If desired, add 1 tablespoon of sugar and a whole clove (which should be removed before adding the sauce to the pasta). Boil the macaroni in abundant boiling salted water for 10 minutes. Drain well. Put in a serving dish together with the sauce (remember to set aside a little to use on the meat) and half of the grated cheese. Mix well. Sprinkle the rest of the cheese over the pasta and serve. Slice the meat and serve as a second course with sauce spooned over it. Serves 4.

MACARONI WITH RICH SAUCE
(*Maccheroni al Sugo Ricco*)

Cooking time: 40 minutes

¼ pound chicken breast	1 tablespoon flour
¼ pound veal	1 bouillon cube
¼ pound pork	1 cup tomato paste
2 slices bacon	¼ cup chopped mortadella
6 tablespoons butter	sausage
1 small onion	3 eggs, hard-boiled
1 stalk celery	1 pound macaroni
Salt and pepper to taste	1 cup grated Parmesan cheese

Dice the chicken breast and grind the veal and pork together. Dice the bacon and sauté it in a saucepan in the butter until golden. Add the finely chopped onion, and sauté until transparent. Add the cut-up celery, the chicken, the ground meat, and salt and pepper. Brown for 10 minutes. Add the flour and stir. Dissolve the bouillon cube and the tomato paste in 2 cups of hot water and pour into the saucepan. Stir and simmer for 30 minutes. Add the coarsely chopped mortadella and the coarsely chopped egg yolks. Cook the macaroni in abundant boiling salted water for 10 minutes. Drain well. Add the sauce (which should be fairly thick) and half the cheese. Toss until well mixed. Serve with the rest of the cheese sprinkled on top.

Variation: By using large-size macaroni (such as rigatoni) and adding 3 cups of Béchamel (see Index), one can make a delicious timbale. Bake in a 375° oven for 20 minutes. Serves 4.

MACARONI WITH ASPARAGUS TIPS
(*Maccheroni con le Punte di Asparagi*)

Cooking time: 30 minutes

2 cups asparagus tips	1 pound macaroni
1 clove garlic	3 egg yolks
2 tablespoons oil	6 tablespoons butter
1 bouillon cube	1⅓ cups grated Gruyère cheese
Salt and white pepper to taste	1 tablespoon chopped parsley

Choose slender asparagus tips and cut in 1-inch lengths. Sauté the finely chopped garlic in the oil in a saucepan. When it is almost golden in color, add ¾ cup of hot water in which the bouillon cube has been dissolved. Add a little salt and a generous pinch of white pepper. Bring to a boil and add the asparagus. Cook over a moderate flame for 15 minutes. Cook the macaroni in abundant boiling salted water for 10 minutes. Beat the egg yolks in a small bowl. Drain the cooked macaroni and put in a serving bowl. Add the butter in dabs and mix. Add the sauce with the asparagus, half the grated cheese and mix again. Add the egg yolks and toss carefully in order not to break the asparagus. Serve with the rest of the cheese sprinkled on top along with the chopped parsley. Serves 4.

MACARONI WITH GREEN SAUCE
(*Maccheroni in Salsa Verde*)

Cooking time: 30 minutes

½ pound cooked spinach	1 cup grated Parmesan cheese
1 chicken bouillon cube	White pepper
1 pound macaroni	½ cup heavy cream
¼ pound butter	

Pass the cooked spinach through the fine blade of a food mill or blend in a blender. Put in a bowl together with the bouillon cube dissolved in 3 tablespoons of hot water. Cook the macaroni in abundant boiling salted water for 10 minutes. Drain well and put in a preheated serving bowl. Add the butter in dabs and mix. Add the spinach and mix. Add half of the grated cheese (mixed with a generous pinch of white pepper) and the cream. Toss until well mixed and serve with the rest of the grated cheese sprinkled on top. Serves 4.

MACARONI WITH SWEET CREAM
(*Maccheroni alla Panna Dolce*)

Cooking time: 20 minutes

⅓ cup sugar	1 cup heavy cream
1 pound macaroni	¼ teaspoon cinnamon
4 tablespoons butter	Salt to taste (optional)

While you are waiting for the water for cooking the macaroni to boil, put the sugar and 3 tablespoons of water in a small saucepan and heat over a moderate flame until caramelized, but just barely (a dark beige color). Add 4 more tablespoons of water and stir until the caramelized sugar is well diluted. Remove from the fire. As soon as the water for the macaroni comes to a boil, cook the macaroni for 10 minutes. Drain and put in a serving bowl. Add the butter in dabs and the caramelized sugar. Mix well. Add the cream and the cinnamon and toss until well mixed. Add salt if desired.
Serves 4.

QUEEN'S MACARONI
(*Maccheroni della Regina*)

This recipe is the prepared recipe of Queen Marie Josie, exiled from Italy; who now lives in Switzerland.

Cooking time: 30 minutes

3 slices lean bacon	½ cup white wine
2 tablespoons flour	2 bouillon cubes
½ pound sliced beef	1 pound macaroni
2 tablespoons oil	6 tablespoons butter
½ pound sliced turkey breast	1 cup grated Parmesan cheese
Salt and white pepper to taste	

Put the thinly sliced bacon in a large-bottomed greased saucepan. In a skillet brown the floured sliced beef in the oil. Arrange on top of the bacon. Brown the sliced turkey breast and lay on top of the beef in the saucepan. Add salt and pepper. Pour in the white wine and cook over a moderate flame. Dilute the bouillon cubes in 1 cup of hot water and add to the saucepan. Continue to cook for 20 minutes over a low flame. In the meantime, cook the macaroni in abundant boiling salted water for 10 minutes. Drain well and put in a serving bowl. Add the butter in dabs and mix. Remove the slices of beef and turkey breast. Pour the sauce over the macaroni and mix together with half of the grated Parmesan. Serve with the rest of the cheese sprinkled on top. The turkey and beef may be served together with the macaroni or as a second course. Serves 4.

MACARONI WITH SUBLIME SAUCE
(*Maccheroni al Sugo Eccelso*)

Cooking time: 30 minutes

½ pound pork (slightly fatty)	Salt and white pepper to taste
¼ pound veal	1 pound macaroni
3 tablespoons oil	4 tablespoons butter
1 medium onion	3 egg yolks
2 tablespoons flour	2 tablespoons lemon juice
½ cup white wine	1 cup grated Parmesan cheese
1 bouillon cube	

Dice the pork and the veal and brown in a saucepan in the oil.
Add the finely chopped onion, and sauté until golden. Add the flour
and mix well. Pour in the white wine, stir, and allow half of it to
evaporate. Dissolve the bouillon cube in 1 cup of hot water and add
to the saucepan. Add salt and pepper. Simmer for 25 minutes over
a low flame. Cook the macaroni in abundant boiling salted water for
10 minutes. While it is cooking melt the butter in a small saucepan
over a very low flame in order that it does not change color. Add
the egg yolks and lemon juice and mix with a fork until well blended.
Remove from the fire. Remove the sauce in the other saucepan from
the fire and cool for 2 minutes. Add the butter, egg, and lemon
mixture, and mix well (this should be done at the last minute—just
as you are draining the macaroni). Put the drained macaroni in a
serving bowl. Add the sauce and the cheese, mix well, and serve immediately. Serves 4.

MACARONI VITERBO STYLE
(Maccheroni alla Viterbese)

Viterbo is a marvelous medieval city 50 miles from Rome. If
you go there, don't forget to visit the Palazzo dei Papi (the Pope's
Palace).

Cooking time: 30 minutes

1 pound ripe tomatoes (3 or 4 medium)
2/3 cup chopped pitted green olives
1 bouillon cube
Salt and pepper to taste
1/2 pound link sausage
1 pound macaroni
3 tablespoons oil
1 cup grated pecorino cheese (or any sharp cheese)
2 cloves garlic
3 basil leaves (or 1/4 teaspoon dried)

Wash and cut up the tomatoes and put in a small saucepan with
1/2 cup of water and the bouillon cube. Boil for 3 minutes. Put
through the fine blade of a food mill. Peel the sausages and put in a
saucepan with the oil. Brown over a moderate flame. In the meantime, chop the garlic and basil leaves very finely. Add to the saucepan when the sausages are well browned. Stir for 1 minute. Quickly

add the tomatoes and stir again. Add the cut-up olives. Add salt and pepper. Cook for 20 minutes over moderate heat. Cook the macaroni in abundant boiling salted water for 10 minutes. Drain well and put in a serving bowl with all of the sauce and the grated cheese. Mix well and serve. Serves 4.

NERO'S MACARONI
(*Maccheroni alla Nerone*)

Cooking time: 50 minutes

3 slices bacon	4 tablespoons flour
4 tablespoons oil	1 cup red wine
½ pound (one large, boneless) chicken breast	¼ cup sugar
	2 chicken bouillon cubes
1 clove garlic	1 pound macaroni
30 to 33 pitted black olives	2 egg yolks
Salt and pepper to taste	Pinch cayenne pepper
1 teaspoon paprika	1 cup grated Parmesan cheese

Dice the bacon, and brown in the oil in a saucepan. Put the chicken breast, the garlic, and the olives through the fine blade of the meat chopper. Add this mixture to the saucepan, add salt and pepper and the paprika, and brown well. Add the flour and stir. Pour in the wine and allow to evaporate. Put the sugar and 2 tablespoons of water in a small saucepan. Caramelize over a moderate flame until it becomes dark brown but not black. Add 1 cup of water and stir until the sugar mixture is completely dissolved. Remove from the fire and add the bouillon cubes. When the wine (in the other saucepan) has evaporated, add the contents of the small saucepan, stir, and simmer covered for 30 minutes over a moderate flame. Stir from time to time. When the sauce is almost ready, cook the macaroni in abundant boiling salted water for 10 minutes. In the meantime, put the egg yolks in a small bowl together with the cayenne and beat. Drain the cooked macaroni and put in a serving bowl together with the sauce and half the cheese. Mix well. Add the egg yolks and toss until well mixed. Serve with the rest of the cheese sprinkled on top. Serves 4.

PROVINCIAL MACARONI
(*Maccheroni alla Provinciale*)

Cooking time: 40 minutes

2½ tablespoons dried mushrooms (or 1 3- or 4-ounce can)

½ pound ground mutton

3 slices bacon

5 tablespoons oil

1 large onion

1 bay leaf

Salt and pepper to taste

2 tablespoons flour

⅓ cup white wine

½ cup tomato paste

1 bouillon cube

1 pound macaroni

1 cup grated Parmesan cheese (or grated Cheddar cheese)

First of all put the dried mushrooms to soak in a cup of warm water. After 5 minutes remove the mushrooms and chop finely together with the mutton. Cut the bacon into julienne strips and sauté in the oil in a saucepan. Add the finely chopped onion and sauté until golden. Now add the mutton and mushrooms, bay leaf, salt, and pepper, and brown well. Add the flour and stir. Pour in the white wine. Allow half of it to evaporate. Dilute the tomato paste in 1 cup of hot water in which you have already dissolved the bouillon cube. Pour into the saucepan, stir, and simmer for 25 minutes over a moderate flame. When the sauce is almost done, cook the macaroni in abundant boiling salted water for 10 minutes. Drain and put in a serving bowl together with all the sauce and half the grated cheese. Mix well and serve with the rest of the cheese sprinkled on top. Serves 4.

MACARONI GENOESE STYLE
(*Maccheroni alla Genovese*)

Cooking time: 40 minutes

1 pound veal

2 tablespoons flour

4 tablespoons oil

1 large onion

2 stalks celery

Salt and pepper to taste

1 chicken bouillon cube

¼ cup tomato paste

½ clove garlic

4 basil leaves (or ¼ teaspoon dried)

2 tablespoons chopped parsley

6 tablespoons butter

⅔ cup grated pecorino cheese (or any sharp cheese)

1 pound macaroni

⅔ cup grated Parmesan cheese

Have the veal thinly sliced. Dust with flour and brown in the oil in a saucepan. Finely chop the onion and add. Chop the celery and add. Continue to sauté. Add salt and pepper. Dissolve the bouillon cube and the tomato paste in 1 cup of hot water and add. Bring to a boil, stirring until well mixed. Simmer for 30 minutes. In the meantime, chop the garlic, the basil, and the parsley *very* finely on a bread board and with a spatula work into the butter together with the pecorino, salt, and pepper in order to form a homogeneous paste. Set aside for use later. When the sauce is almost done, cook the macaroni in abundant boiling salted water for 10 minutes. Drain and put in a preheated serving bowl. Add the paste you have made and mix well. Add the sauce, setting aside a few tablespoons to spoon over the meat later. Toss for 1 minute. Serve with the grated Parmesan sprinkled on top. Serve the veal as a second course accompanied by a green vegetable. Serves 4.

PRIEST'S MACARONI
(*Maccheroni del Prete*)

Cooking time: 40 minutes

1 2½-pound chicken	1 bay leaf
2 tablespoons flour	Salt and pepper to taste
5 tablespoons oil	⅓ cup white wine
1 medium onion	½ cup tomato paste
¼ pound pork (fatty)	1 pound macaroni
1 stalk celery	1⅓ cups grated Parmesan
1 carrot	cheese

Cut the chicken into 8 pieces. Roll in flour and brown in the oil in a saucepan. When well browned, remove from the oil and set aside. Add the finely chopped onion, and sauté. Add the chopped pork and the chopped celery and carrot. Sauté until softened, then add the bay leaf, salt, and pepper. Pour in the white wine and allow half to evaporate. Dilute the tomato paste in 1 cup of hot water, pour into the saucepan, and stir. Return the chicken to the saucepan and cook for 30 minutes more. When almost done, cook the macaroni in abundant boiling salted water for 10 minutes. Drain well and put in a serving bowl. Remove the pieces of chicken from the saucepan and pour the sauce over the macaroni. Add half the grated cheese and mix well. Serve with the rest of the cheese sprinkled on top. Serve the chicken as a second course with whatever vegetable you desire. Serves 4.

MACARONI SALAD
(*Insalata di Maccheroni*)

Cooking time: 20 minutes

1 pound macaroni
⅓ cup sliced pitted green olives
¼ cup sliced pitted black olives
¼ pound mixed pickles
½ clove garlic
1 anchovy fillet
2 basil leaves (or ⅛ teaspoon dried)

2 tablespoons chopped parsley
6 tablespoons oil
3 tablespoons lemon juice
¼ teaspoon cayenne pepper
Salt and pepper
½ cup tuna (packed in olive oil)
¼ pound Gruyère cheese

Break the macaroni into 2-inch pieces and cook in abundant boiling salted water for 10 minutes. Drain and spread out on a serving dish to cool. Stir from time to time to hasten the cooling process. While the macaroni is cooking and cooling, prepare the rest of the ingredients. Slice the pitted olives and the mixed pickles into julienne strips. Crush the garlic on a bread board and chop together with the anchovy, the basil, and the parsley until a very fine paste results. Put the oil in a salad bowl and add the lemon juice. Beat until thickened, then add the anchovy-herb paste, the cayenne, salt, and pepper. Add the cooled macaroni and mix well. Add the olives and the pickles. Also add the tuna and the cheese cut into julienne strips. Toss until well mixed and serve. This is an excellent hot weather dish. Serves 4.

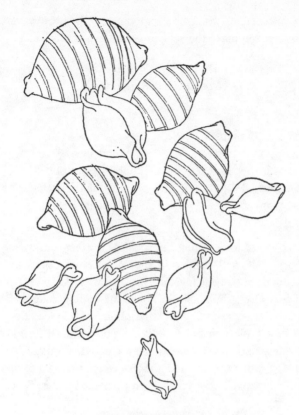

CHAPTER IV
Shells and Family

The shell family is quite large. Among the many varieties that make up this family there is one pasta that is extremely popular in Italy. It is *penne,* a description of which you will find in the Introduction, along with the description of the other major pastas.

For example, the Taverna Flavia in Rome prepares them marvelously well. Another Roman restaurant, Meo Patacca, has made penne one of its great specialities, just as has the restaurant Piccolo Mondo, which serves its famous Penne all'arrabiata. Oddly enough, the other pastas belonging to the shell family are looked down upon by most people. This is a great error, because they are just as delicious as penne. For example, try the Farfalle with Tuna Sauce.

I assure you that you won't be disappointed. Do not always eat the same kind of pasta; make the acquaintance of the shell family.

HEAVENLY SHELLS
(*Conchiglie alla Paradiso*)

A truly heavenly dish . . .

Cooking time: 20 minutes

½ pound ground pork	1 pound shells
Salt and white pepper to taste	2 tablespoons butter
2 tablespoons oil	1 cup grated Dutch cheese (or
½ cup cream	Cheddar cheese)
3 egg yolks	

While the water for cooking the shells is heating, brown the finely ground pork, salt, and pepper in the oil in a saucepan over high heat. In a small bowl beat together the cream, yolks, and a pinch of white pepper. Cook the shells in abundant boiling salted water for 12 minutes. Drain, reserving 3 tablespoons of the cooking water. Put pasta in a preheated bowl. Add the pork and all its juices, the butter in dabs, and the 3 tablespoons of cooking water. Mix. Add the cream-egg yolk mixture and the grated cheese. Toss vigorously until very well mixed. Serve very hot on preheated plates. Serves 6.

SHELLS WITH BEEF SAUCE
(*Conchiglie al Sugo di Manzo*)

The excellent sauce in this recipe may be used for all kinds of pasta, and the meat will serve 4 to 6 persons as a second course.

Cooking time: 80 minutes

3 slices bacon	2 stalks celery
2 cloves garlic	1 bay leaf
6 rosemary needles (or ¼	½ cup white wine
teaspoon dried)	⅓ cup tomato paste
Salt and pepper to taste	¼ pound ripe tomatoes (1
2 pounds beef	medium-large)
4 tablespoons oil	1 pound shells
1 onion	1 cup grated Parmesan cheese
1 carrot	

Slice the bacon *very* thinly and put on a bread board with the crushed cloves of garlic, the rosemary, and salt and pepper. Chop all so finely that a paste is formed. With a sharp-pointed knife, make several deep holes in the meat and fill with this paste. Tie the meat with kitchen twine if needed. Heat the oil in a saucepan and add the meat. Brown well on all sides over high heat. Add the finely chopped onion and continue to brown. Add the cut-up carrot, celery, bay leaf, salt, and pepper. Stir for 1 minute, then add the wine and allow to evaporate. Add the tomato paste diluted in 1 cup of hot water and the cut-up tomatoes. Stir well, cover saucepan, and simmer over low heat for 70 minutes. While it is cooking, test the meat for doneness from time to time. To test, pierce the meat with a large kitchen fork. If it drops from the fork easily it is cooked. Remove the meat from the pan and pass the sauce through the fine blade of a food mill or blend in a blender. If necessary, add a little hot water, but the sauce should be fairly thick. Cook the shells in abundant boiling salted water for 12 minutes. Put in a bowl with the sauce and the cheese and mix well. Serve immediately. The meat may be sliced and served as a second course. Serves 6.

SHELLS WITH OLIVE SAUCE
(*Conchiglie alla Salsa d'Olive*)

Cooking time: 30 minutes

1 medium onion	2 tablespoons flour
5 tablespoons oil	2 bouillon cubes
1 clove garlic	1 cup chopped pitted green
½ pound ripe tomatoes (2 medium)	olives
	1 cup chopped pitted black
1 pinch orégano	olives
Salt and pepper to taste	1 pound shells
4 tablespoons butter	1 cup grated Parmesan cheese

Sauté the finely chopped onion in a saucepan with the oil. Add the unpeeled clove of garlic, the cut-up tomatoes, orégano, salt, and pepper, and cook 20 minutes. In the meantime, melt the butter in a small saucepan, add the flour, and stir over low heat until well blended. Dissolve the 2 bouillon cubes in 1 cup of hot water and add very gradually, stirring continuously. Cook for 5 minutes. Finely chop the pitted olives. Pass the tomato mixture through the fine blade of food mill and return to the saucepan. Add the olives, stir, and continue to simmer for 10 minutes over low heat. Cook the shells in abundant boiling salted water for 12 minutes. Drain and put in a serving bowl. Add all the sauce and the grated cheese, toss until well mixed, and serve. Serves 4.

SHELLS WITH FONDUE
(Conchiglie alla Fonduta)

Cooking time: 30 minutes

½ pound fontina cheese*	6 tablespoons butter
2 cups milk	⅔ cup grated Parmesan cheese
1 pound shells	Cayenne pepper
4 egg yolks	Salt and white pepper to taste

Put the thinly sliced fontina to soak in the milk for 20 minutes. Cook the shells in abundant boiling salted water for 12 minutes. In the meantime, make the fondue. In the top of a double boiler, over medium heat, put the fontina with ⅓ of the milk. Stir continuously, adding the rest of the milk a little at a time until the fontina has melted and the mixture becomes a creamy sauce. Remove from heat and add the egg yolks, mixing gently. When the shells are cooked, drain and put in a serving bowl. Add the butter in dabs and mix. Add the fondue and mix. Serve with the Parmesan and the cayenne dusted on top. Add salt and pepper. Serves 4.

* Fontina is an Italian cheese very similar to American cheese but with a slightly sharper flavor.

SHELLS WITH MOZZARELLA
(Conchiglie alla Mozzarella)

Cooking time: 30 minutes

1 pound shells	Salt and white pepper to taste
¾ pound mozzarella cheese	½ cup milk
½ cup butter	
1⅓ cups grated Parmesan cheese	

Preheat oven to 375° F.

Cook the shells in abundant boiling salted water for 12 minutes. While they are cooking, thinly slice the mozzarella. Drain the cooked shells and put in an ovenproof baking dish, together with the butter in dabs and half the grated Parmesan. Add salt and pepper. Mix well. Level off the pasta and cover with the slices of mozzarella. Pour the milk over all in a thin stream. Dust with the rest of the Parmesan and bake in a 375° oven for 15 minutes. Serve immediately. Serves 4.

SHELLS WITH WALNUTS
(*Conchiglie alle Noci*)

This way of cooking pasta is typical of the northern part of Italy and was given to me by the chef of the restaurant Bagutta of Milan.

Cooking time: 30 minutes

2½ cups shelled walnuts	Salt and white pepper to taste
1 cup milk	1 pound shells
½ cup plus 2 tablespoons butter	1 cup grated Dutch cheese (or
1 tablespoon flour	Cheddar cheese)

Put the nuts in 3 cups of hot water. Remove the brown skin and reduce the nut meats to a paste with a mortar and pestle or put in blender. In small saucepan bring the milk to a full boil. In another saucepan, make a thin Béchamel Sauce (see Index) with half the butter, the flour, and the milk. Add the walnut paste, salt and pepper, and cook over very low heat or in a double boiler while the shells are cooking. Cook the shells in abundant boiling salted water for 12 minutes. Drain and put in a serving bowl with the rest of the butter in dabs. Mix well. Add the walnut sauce and half the grated cheese. Toss until very well mixed and serve dusted with the rest of the cheese. Serves 4.

HOUSEWIFE'S SHELLS
(*Conchiglie della Massaia*)

Cooking time: 20 minutes

1 pound ripe tomatoes (3 or 4 medium)	1 teaspoon potato flour
1 large onion	1 bouillon cube
4 tablespoons oil	Salt and pepper to taste
1 clove garlic	1 pound shells
4 basil leaves (or ¼ teaspoon dried)	¾ cup grated Parmesan

Peel the tomatoes. Sauté the finely chopped onion in the oil in a saucepan and when almost golden add the *very* finely chopped garlic and basil. Stir for 1 minute over low heat. Add the potato flour and the bouillon cube, which has been dissolved in 1 cup hot water. Stir for 1 minute more. Add the cut-up tomatoes, salt and pepper, and mix. Cover the saucepan and simmer until cooked. Cook the shells in abundant boiling salted water for 12 minutes. Drain and put in a serving bowl with the sauce and half the grated Parmesan. Toss until very well mixed. Serve with the rest of the Parmesan sprinkled on top. Serves 4.

SHELLS SAN RAFAELE
(*Conchiglie San Rafaele*)

Cooking time: 40 minutes

⅓ pound (1 large boneless) chicken breast	Salt and white pepper to taste
2 tablespoons flour	2 egg yolks
½ cup butter	1 pound shells
⅓ cup white wine	1⅓ cups grated Parmesan cheese
½ cup milk	½ cup heavy cream

Slice the chicken breast into 2 slices and flatten with a meat mallet. Flour and sauté in a skillet with 2 tablespoons of the butter until barely golden. Remove from the skillet and put on a bread board. Cut into very thin julienne strips. Return to the skillet with the rest of the flour and stir. Add the remaining butter and stir, then add the white wine. Stir again and allow half the wine to evaporate. Add the milk, which you have previously brought to a boil, salt, and pepper, and stir until well blended. Remove from heat and add the egg yolks. Stir. Simmer over very low heat for 25 minutes. In the meantime, cook the shells in abundant boiling salted water for 12 minutes. Drain and put in a preheated serving bowl. Add all the sauce and half the grated cheese. Toss until very well mixed. Add the cream and mix again. Serve dusted with the rest of the cheese. Serves 4.

DUCAL SHELLS
(*Conchiglie Ducale*)

Cooking time: 30 minutes

½ cup pine nuts	Salt and white pepper to taste
1½ cups heavy cream	Nutmeg
½ pound Tilsit cheese	1 pound shells
¼ pound butter	2 egg yolks
1 tablespoon flour	

Put the pine nuts to soak in hot water for 15 minutes. Put the cream in the top of a double boiler over low heat. Add the cheese, thinly sliced, the butter, and the flour. Mix slowly. Do *not* allow to come to a boil. Add the pine nuts (which you have removed from the water), salt, and pepper. Also add a sprinkling of nutmeg. Cook the shells in abundant boiling salted water for 12 minutes. Drain and put in a preheated serving bowl. Beat the egg yolks together with the cheese sauce and add. Mix well and serve. Serves 4.

SHELLS WITH MASCHERPONE CHEESE
(*Conchiglie con Mascarpone*)

Cooking time: 10 minutes

4 fresh Italian sausages	1 pound shells
1 tablespoon oil	1 cup grated Parmesan cheese
½ pound mascherpone cheese*	Salt and pepper to taste

Remove the skins from the sausages (the fat Italian sausages sold in Italian shops). Sauté the sausages in the oil over low heat for 10 minutes. In the meantime, heat the mascherpone in a small sauce-

---

* Mascherpone is a very mild, delicious, creamy Italian cheese that has the texture of stiffly whipped heavy cream.

pan over very low heat. Cook the shells in abundant boiling salted water for 12 minutes. Drain well and mix with the sliced sausages, the mascherpone, and half the grated Parmesan. Add salt and pepper to taste. Mix very well. Serve dusted with the rest of the grated cheese. Serves 4.

MANICHE, GARDENER'S STYLE
(*Maniche all'Ortolana*)

Cooking time: 40 minutes

2 slices bacon	1 tablespoon flour
1 medium onion	Salt and pepper to taste
4 tablespoons oil	½ cup shelled peas
1 ounce dried mushrooms (or	½ cup asparagus tips
1 3- or 4-ounce can)	1 pound maniche
1 stalk celery	2 tablespoons butter
1 carrot	1 cup grated Parmesan cheese

Cut the bacon and onion into julienne strips and sauté in the oil in a saucepan. Put the dried mushrooms in ¾ cup of warm water to soak. Also cut the celery and carrot into julienne strips and sauté in the saucepan. Remove the mushrooms from the water (reserving the water or juice from can, for later use), squeeze them as dry as possible, cut into thin strips, and add to the saucepan. Sauté until all is golden and add the flour, salt, and pepper. Stir until well blended. Add the water in which the mushrooms soaked, cover the saucepan, and cook over low heat for 25 minutes. Boil the peas and asparagus in boiling salted water until cooked, then drain and add to the sauce. Cook the maniche in abundant boiling salted water for 12 minutes, drain, and put in a serving bowl. Add the butter in dabs, all the sauce (which should be fairly thick), and half the grated Parmesan. Toss until well mixed and serve with the rest of the cheese sprinkled on top. Serves 4.

BAKED MANICHE WITH BUTTER SAUCE
(*Maniche alla Salsa di Burro*)

The simplicity of a recipe has nothing to do with its final result; in this case I can assure you that this recipe is delicious and has every right to be served as a party dish.

Cooking time: 20 minutes

1 pound maniche	1⅓ cups grated Cheddar cheese
½ cup heavy cream	Salt and white pepper to taste
2 egg yolks	¾ cup butter

Preheat oven to 400° F.

While the maniche are cooking in abundant boiling salted water for 12 minutes, put the cream and the egg yolks in a small bowl and beat together with 2 tablespoons of grated cheese, salt, and white pepper. Drain the cooked maniche, reserving ¼ cup of the cooking water. Put in an ovenproof casserole. Add dabs of butter, the cooking water, the cream and egg mixture, and half of the remaining grated cheese. Mix well, level off, and dust with the rest of the grated cheese. Bake in a hot oven for 5 minutes. Serves 4.

MANICHE NEAPOLITAN
(*Maniche alla Napolitana*)

Cooking time: 70 minutes

2 tablespoons oil	1 small carrot
1½ pounds beef	Salt and pepper to taste
1 tablespoon flour	½ cup red wine
3 slices bacon	1 pound ripe tomatoes (3 or 4
1 medium onion	medium)
1 clove garlic	1 pound maniche (or rigatoni)
1 stalk celery	1 cup grated Parmesan cheese

Put the oil in a saucepan large enough to hold the piece of meat, which should be lean. Rub the meat with flour and brown on all sides with the bacon in the hot oil. When well browned, add the thinly sliced onion and the unpeeled clove of garlic. Sauté for 3 minutes, then add the coarsely chopped celery and carrot, salt and pepper. Sauté for 5 minutes more. Add the red wine and allow half to evaporate, stirring often. Add the cut-up tomatoes, stir again, and add ½ cup of water. Cover the saucepan and cook for 55 minutes over moderate heat, being careful to turn the meat from time to time. With a fork test the meat for doneness and remove it when it is cooked. Put the sauce through a food mill or blend in a blender. Cook the maniche (or rigatoni) in abundant boiling salted water. Drain and put on a serving dish. Add three fourths of the sauce and half the Parmesan and toss until well mixed. Serve with the rest of the cheese sprinkled on top. Slice the meat, spoon some of the remaining sauce over each slice, and serve as a second course. Serves 4.

MANICHE WITH BUTTER AND TOMATOES
(*Maniche Pomodoro e Burro*)

Cooking time: 20 minutes

1 pound ripe tomatoes (3 or 4 medium)	Salt and pepper to taste
	1 pound maniche (or rigatoni)
1 small onion	6 tablespoons butter
3 tablespoons oil	1 cup grated Parmesan cheese
4 basil leaves (or ¼ teaspoon dried)	

Peel the tomatoes. Finely chop the onion and put in a saucepan with the oil, and sauté until golden. Add the cut-up tomatoes with all their juices, the chopped basil, salt, and pepper. Stir and cook over moderate heat for 10 minutes. Cook the maniche (or rigatoni) in abundant boiling salted water for 12 minutes. Drain well and put in a serving bowl with dabs of butter, the tomato sauce, and half the grated Parmesan. Toss until very well mixed in order to blend the flavors. Serve with the rest of the cheese dusted on top. Serves 4.

MANICHE COUNTRY STYLE
(*Maniche alla Paesana*)

Cooking time: 40 minutes

½ pound pork (fatty)	⅓ cup shelled peas
2 tablespoons oil	2 basil leaves (or ⅛ teaspoon dried)
1 small onion	
1 (3-ounce) can mushrooms	1 pound maniche
Salt and pepper to taste	1 cup grated pecorino cheese (or any sharp cheese)
1 tablespoon flour	
½ pound ripe tomatoes (2 medium)	

Finely dice the pork and brown well in the oil in a saucepan. Add the finely chopped onion and sauté. Thinly slice the drained mushrooms and add, together with salt and pepper. Stir. Add the flour, and stir. Add the cut-up unpeeled tomatoes and stir. Cover and cook over low heat for 30 minutes. Add the cooked peas, chopped basil, and ½ cup of hot water. Cook the maniche in abundant boiling salted water for 12 minutes. Drain and put on a serving plate. Add all the sauce and the cheese. Toss until very well mixed and serve. Serves 4.

RIGATONI WITH ROAST VEAL SAUCE
(*Rigatoni al Sugo di Arrosto*)

If you know that your guests have good appetites, serve this recipe; but if they *mangent comme des oiseaux* (are small eaters) like, say, the French, choose another dish to serve.

Cooking time: 70 minutes

2 pounds roasting veal	Salt and pepper to taste
1 teaspoon flour	1 sprig rosemary (or ½
2 tablespoons oil	teaspoon dried)
1 medium onion	½ cup white wine
1 stalk celery	1 pound rigatoni
1 carrot	6 tablespoons butter
2 cloves garlic	1 cup grated Parmesan cheese

Choose a nice piece of veal, preferably eye of the round, dust with flour, and brown on all sides in the hot oil. When nicely browned, add the cut-up onion, celery, carrot, the unpeeled garlic cloves, salt and pepper, and rosemary. Sauté for a few minutes, then add the white wine, stir, cover the saucepan, and simmer over a low fire for about 1 hour or until the meat is cooked. Turn the meat from time to time, adding a little water when necessary. When the meat is cooked, remove from the saucepan and pour the sauce through a sieve. A brownish sauce should result. Discard all that remains in the sieve and use the sauce to flavor the rigatoni. Cook the rigatoni in abundant boiling salted water for 12 minutes. Drain and put in a preheated serving bowl, add the butter in dabs, half of the grated cheese, and most of the sauce (leave a little for use with the meat). Mix well and serve immediately, dusted with the rest of the cheese. Slice the meat and spoon a little sauce over each slice. Serve as a second course accompanied by a vegetable. Serves 4.

RIGATONI ITALIAN STYLE
(Rigatoni all'Italiana)

Cooking time: 35 minutes

2½ pounds dried mushrooms (or ¼ pound fresh)
½ pound ground pork (fatty)
3 tablespoons oil
1 medium onion
1½ tablespoons flour
½ cup red wine
½ cup tomato paste
1 bouillon cube
Salt and pepper to taste
1 small clove garlic
3 basil leaves (or ¼ teaspoon dried)
1 cup grated Parmesan cheese
2 tablespoons butter
1 pound rigatoni

Put the dried mushrooms to soak in a cup of warm water; reserve the water. Have the pork finely ground, and brown in the oil in a saucepan. Add the finely chopped onion and sauté until golden. Add the flour, and stir. Pour in the red wine, and stir until half evaporated. Add the tomato paste, lower heat, and stir until well blended. Remove the mushrooms from the water, squeeze dry, and chop finely. Add to the saucepan and stir. Pass the mushroom water through a very fine sieve or some cheesecloth in order to remove any grains of sand. Dissolve the bouillon cube in this water (or 1 cup water if using fresh mushrooms) and put in saucepan. Stir again. Raise heat to moderate, add salt and pepper, and cook for 30 minutes. In the meantime, chop together very finely the crushed clove of garlic and the basil leaves. Work this mixture, a pinch of pepper, and ½ tablespoon Parmesan into the butter with a spatula, forming a paste. Add this paste to the sauce about 12 minutes before it is ready; that is, at the moment you start cooking the rigatoni. Cook the rigatoni in boiling salted water for 12 minutes. Drain and put in a serving bowl with all the sauce and half the Parmesan. Mix well and serve with the rest of the Parmesan sprinkled on top. Serves 4.

BUSHMAN'S RIGATONI
(*Rigatoni alla Burina*)

A specialty of Piccolo Mondo . . .

Cooking time: 15 minutes

1 pound rigatoni	Nutmeg
7 tablespoons butter	2 Italian sausages
2 tablespoons flour	¼ pound fresh mushrooms
1 cup milk	1 cup grated Parmesan cheese
Salt and white pepper to taste	

Start cooking the rigatoni in abundant boiling salted water for 12 minutes. In the meantime, prepare a Béchamel Sauce (see Index) with 2 tablespoons of the butter, flour, milk, salt and white pepper, and nutmeg. Chop the sausage and brown in 3 tablespoons of butter in a saucepan. Sauté the mushrooms in 2 tablespoons of butter, add, stir, and continue to cook for a few minutes. Add the white sauce, the cooked drained rigatoni, half the grated Parmesan mixed with a generous pinch of white pepper. Mix well. Put in a serving dish and serve with the rest of the cheese sprinkled on top. Serves 4.

RIGATONI À LA MODE
(*Rigatoni alla Moda*)

A great specialty of Da Gino, a restaurant in Trastevere, the ancient quarter of Rome.

Cooking time: 60 minutes

½ pound veal	1 tablespoon flour
4 tablespoons oil	Salt and white pepper to taste
3 small onions	2 cups milk
3 whole cloves	1 pound rigatoni
1 stalk celery	1 cup grated Parmesan cheese

Thinly slice the meat and brown in the oil in a saucepan. Stud each of the onions with a whole clove and add, together with the coarsely chopped celery. When well browned, add flour, salt, and white pepper, and stir well. Add ½ cup of hot water and stir again.

Bring the milk to a boil and add. Simmer over low heat for 50 minutes. Pass the entire contents of the saucepan through the medium blade of a food mill or blend in a blender. A creamy sauce should result. If it seems too thick, add 2 to 3 tablespoons of hot water. Cook the rigatoni in abundant boiling salted water for 12 minutes. Drain and put in a serving bowl. Pour on the sauce and add the grated cheese. Mix well and serve immediately. Serves 4.

RIGATONI GYPSY
(Rigatoni alla Zingara)

Cooking time: 30 minutes

3 slices lean bacon	¼ cup sliced pitted black olives
2 tablespoons oil	1 pound rigatoni
1 medium onion	4 tablespoons butter
¼ pound fresh mushrooms	1 cup grated Parmesan cheese
½ pound ripe tomatoes (2	(or pecorino cheese) (or
medium)	both mixed)
Salt and pepper to taste	

Sauté the sliced bacon in the oil in a saucepan. Add the finely chopped onion, and sauté. Add the thinly sliced mushrooms and stir over high heat. Add the chopped, unpeeled tomatoes, salt, and pepper, and stir. Lower to moderate heat. Add the sliced olives and stir again. Cover the saucepan and simmer for 20 minutes. Cook the rigatoni in abundant boiling salted water for 12 minutes. Drain and put in a serving bowl. Add the sauce, the butter, and half the grated cheese. Toss until well mixed and serve with the rest of the cheese sprinkled on top. Serves 4.

GRANDMOTHER'S RIGATONI
(Rigatoni alla Moda della Nonna)

This recipe is the dish preferred by Virna Lisi when dining at Hostaria del Orso, the restaurant-night club in Rome known for its marvelous cuisine and beautiful fourteenth-century Roman décor.

Cooking time: 12 minutes

1 pound rigatoni	1 cup heavy cream
6 tablespoons butter	Salt and white pepper to taste
4 egg yolks	1 cup grated Parmesan cheese

Cook the rigatoni in abundant boiling salted water for 12 minutes. In the meantime, in a preheated mixing bowl melt the butter and add the egg yolks, stirring gently with a wooden spoon. Add the cream, a pinch of salt, and a pinch of white pepper. Also add half the grated Parmesan, continuing to stir gently until the ingredients are mixed. Add the cooked drained rigatoni to the bowl, making sure, however, that you put the rigatoni in the bowl with one hand and with the other hand immediately start mixing rapidly so that the heat of the rigatoni will blend the sauce and the rigatoni will be completely coated with this deliciously delicate sauce. Serve on preheated plates, dusted with the rest of the Parmesan. Serves 4.

RIGATONI WITH SAUSAGES AND EGGS
(*Rigatoni alle Salsicce e Uova*)

Cooking time: 30 minutes

½ pound Italian sausages	1 bouillon cube
4 tablespoons oil	Salt and pepper to taste
2 cloves garlic	1 pound rigatoni
2 basil leaves (or ⅛ teaspoon dried)	3 eggs
	1 cup grated Parmesan cheese

Remove the skins from the sausages and brown in the oil in a saucepan, pressing down on the sausages with a wooden spoon in order to crumble them while they are browning. Very finely chop the garlic and the basil, and add when the sausages are well browned. Stir for 1 minute. Add the bouillon cube dissolved in 1 cup of hot water, salt and pepper and stir again. Cook for 20 minutes. Cook the rigatoni in abundant boiling salted water for 12 minutes. In the meantime, in a small bowl beat together the eggs, a pinch of pepper, and 1 tablespoon of the grated Parmesan. Drain the rigatoni and put in a preheated serving bowl. Add the sausages with all their juices and half the remaining grated Parmesan and mix well. Add the beaten eggs and toss vigorously until well mixed. Serve with the rest of the Parmesan sprinkled on top. Serves 4.

DITALONI WITH ONIONS, ARGENTINE STYLE
(*Ditaloni alle Cipolle all'Argentina*)

Alfredo, who collaborated with me on this book, told me that this way to prepare ditaloni is very well known in Buenos Aires.

Cooking time: 20 minutes

½ pound onions (2 medium)	1 bay leaf
2 tablespoons oil	Salt and white pepper to taste
3 basil leaves (or ¼ teaspoon dried)	1 pound ditaloni
1 tablespoon chopped parsley	6 tablespoons butter
	1 cup grated Parmesan cheese

Put a large pot of salted water on to heat for cooking the pasta. Cut the onions into strips and sauté in the oil in a skillet. When it barely begins to color, add the coarsely chopped basil and parsley, the whole bay leaf, salt, and pepper. Continue to cook over low heat. By this time, the water has come to a boil. Add the ditaloni and cook for 10 minutes, stirring from time to time. Drain and put in a serving bowl. Add the butter and half the Parmesan. Mix well. Add the contents of the skillet in which the onions were sautéed. Mix well and serve with the rest of the Parmesan dusted on top. Serves 4.

DITALONI WITH TOMATOES
(*Ditaloni al Pomodoro*)

Cooking time: 20 minutes

1½ pounds ripe tomatoes (5 medium)	Salt and pepper to taste
1 large onion	1 pound ditaloni
4 tablespoons oil	1 cup grated Gruyère cheese
4 basil leaves (or ¼ teaspoon dried)	

Put a large pot of salted water on to boil for cooking the pasta. Peel the tomatoes and reserve for later use. Sauté the finely chopped onion in the oil in a saucepan. Add the cut-up tomatoes, the basil, salt, and pepper, and stir. Cook over moderate heat for 20 minutes.

As soon as the water begins to boil, add the ditaloni and cook for 10 minutes. Drain and put in a serving bowl with the sauce and the grated Gruyère. Mix well and serve. These are good even several hours after they've been cooked. Serves 4.

BUTTERED DITALONI
(*Ditaloni Imburrati*)

Cooking time: 15 minutes

1 pound ditaloni	Salt and white pepper to taste
⅔ cup butter	1 cup grated Parmesan cheese

Put a large pot of salted water on the fire and bring to a boil. Add the ditaloni and cook for 10 minutes. Drain, taking care to reserve ½ cup of the cooking water. Put the drained ditaloni in a serving bowl with dabs of butter and a generous pinch of salt and white pepper. Mix thoroughly, adding 2 tablespoons of the cooking water at a time until all the ingredients are well blended and the ditaloni are covered with a creamy sauce. Add the grated Parmesan, mix, and serve at once. Serves 4 to 6.

DITALONI VILLA D'ESTE
(*Ditaloni alla Villa d'Este*)

Cooking time: 40 minutes

¼ pound veal	1 chicken bouillon cube
¼ pound pork	1 pound ditaloni
3 tablespoons oil	4 tablespoons butter
1 small onion	1 cup grated Parmesan cheese
Salt and pepper to taste	3 egg yolks
1 teaspoon flour	2 tablespoons cognac

Finely chop the 2 meats, and brown in a saucepan with the oil. Sauté the finely chopped onion with the meat. Add salt and pepper and cook for 5 minutes. Add the flour and stir for 1 minute. Add the bouillon cube dissolved in 2 cups of hot water, stir, cover the saucepan, and cook over a low flame for 20 minutes. Cook the ditaloni in abundant boiling salted water for 10 minutes. Drain the pasta and put in a preheated serving bowl with dabs of butter, the entire contents of the saucepan, and half the grated Parmesan. Mix well. Add the beaten yolks and cognac, and toss until well mixed. Serve at once dusted with the rest of the Parmesan. Serves 4 to 6.

DITALI WITH CHEESE
(*Ditali al Formaggio*)

Cooking time: 20 minutes

2 medium onions	White pepper to taste
1 tablespoon oil	1 cup grated Parmesan cheese
¼ pound butter	1 pound ditali
3 eggs	

Put a pot of salted water to heat for cooking the ditali. In the meantime, cut the onions into thin strips and sauté in the oil and 2 tablespoons of the butter in a saucepan. In a small mixing bowl beat together the eggs, a pinch of white pepper, and half the grated Parmesan. As soon as the water begins to boil, start cooking the ditali (10 minutes). Drain and put in a preheated serving bowl with dabs of the remaining butter. Toss until well mixed. Add the onion and the remaining grated cheese and mix again. Add the beaten egg mixture and mix once again. Cover the bowl and allow to rest for 2 minutes before serving. Serves 4.

DITALI WITH PURÉED BEANS
(*Ditali con Fagioli Passati*)

Cooking time: 20 minutes

1 large onion	1 (16-ounce) can white navy
4 tablespoons oil	beans
2 stalks celery	¾ cup uncooked ditali
1 small ripe tomato	⅔ cup grated pecorino cheese
1 leaf sage	(or any sharp cheese)
Salt and pepper to taste	

Finely chop the onion and sauté in the oil in a saucepan. When golden, add the cut-up celery and unpeeled tomato, which has been cut in fourths and seeded, the sage, salt, and pepper. Cook for 3 minutes, then add the beans and 4 cups of hot water. Taste for salt. Boil for 10 minutes. Put the entire contents of the saucepan through a food mill. Return to the saucepan and bring to a boil again. Add the ditali and cook for 10 minutes. Serve dusted with the grated pecorino. Serves 4.

DITALI À LA TOSCA
(*Ditali alla Tosca*)

Cooking time: 60 minutes

2 ounces dried mushrooms (or 1 6-ounce can)
3 slices bacon
2 tablespoons oil
½ pound lamb
1 medium onion
1 teaspoon flour
½ cup white wine
Salt and pepper to taste
1 pound ripe tomatoes (3 or 4 medium)
1 pound ditali
1 cup grated Parmesan cheese

Put the dried mushrooms to soak in warm water (reserve the water). Cut the bacon into spaghetti-like strips and brown in the oil in a saucepan. Cut the lamb in the same manner and brown with the bacon for 5 minutes. Finely chop the onion, and add. Sauté until barely golden. Add the flour and stir for 1 minute, then add the white wine, salt, and pepper, and stir continuously. When most of the wine has evaporated, add the cut-up peeled tomatoes. Stir. Squeeze the mushrooms dry and chop coarsely, add. Add 4 tablespoons of the water in which they have soaked. Cook for 40 minutes over moderate heat. Ten minutes before the sauce is done, start cooking the ditali in abundant boiling salted water. Drain and put in a serving bowl. Add the entire contents of the saucepan and half the grated cheese. Mix well and serve dusted with the rest of the cheese. Serves 4.

DITALI PASHA
(*Ditali alla Pascia*)

Cooking time: 70 minutes

1 medium onion	½ cup white wine
4 tablespoons oil	½ pound ripe tomatoes (2
1 stalk celery	medium)
½ pound stewing veal	1 pound ditali
1 tablespoon flour	1 cup grated Parmesan cheese
Salt and pepper to taste	

Sauté the finely chopped onion in the oil in a saucepan. Add the finely chopped celery and the veal cut in small cubes and rolled in flour. Brown for 10 minutes very slowly. Add salt and pepper. Add the wine and allow half to evaporate, stirring constantly. Add the cut-up, peeled tomatoes and ½ cup hot water. Stir and cover. Simmer for 60 minutes. Cook the ditali in abundant boiling salted water for 10 minutes. Drain well and put in a serving bowl. Add all the sauce (including the meat) and half the grated Parmesan. Toss until well mixed. Serve dusted with the rest of the cheese.
Serves 4.

DITALI WITH RAGÙ
(*Ditali Raguttati*)

Cooking time: 70 minutes

1 medium onion	½ cup red wine
4 tablespoons oil	½ cup tomato paste
¼ pound beef, diced	¼ pound mortadella, diced
1 carrot	2 tablespoons diced salami
1 stalk celery	1 pound ditali
1 bay leaf	1 cup grated Parmesan cheese
Salt and pepper to taste	

Sauté the finely chopped onion in the oil in a saucepan until golden. Add the diced beef, stirring until browned. Add the finely chopped carrot and celery, bay leaf, salt, and pepper, and continue to sauté for 5 minutes. Add the red wine. Evaporate for 2 minutes over a moderate flame. Dilute the tomato paste in 1½ cups of hot water and add. Stir. Add the diced mortadella and salami, and simmer over low heat for 50 minutes. Cook the ditali in boiling water for 10 minutes. Drain and put in a serving bowl. Pour on entire contents of the saucepan and half the grated cheese. Mix well. Serve dusted with the rest of the cheese. Serves 4.

DITALI WITH CORNED TONGUE AND CREAM
(Ditali alla Lingua e Crema)

Cooking time: 50 minutes

4 tablespoons dried mushrooms (or 6 ounces canned)	Salt and white pepper to taste
2 slices bacon or salt pork	2 tablespoons potato flour
1 tablespoon oil	3 tablespoons butter
¼ pound corned tongue	1 bouillon cube
1 medium onion	1 pound ditali
¼ cup white wine	1 cup grated Parmesan cheese

Put the dried mushrooms to soak in 1 cup of warm water (reserve this water). Finely dice the bacon (or salt pork), and sauté in the oil in a saucepan over low heat. Also finely dice the tongue, and add. Brown for 3 minutes. Sauté the finely chopped onion over a slightly higher flame until it becomes softened. Pour in the wine and allow to evaporate. Remove the dried mushrooms from the water and squeeze dry. (If using canned mushrooms, reserve juice.) Chop finely and add. Add salt and pepper. Add 4 tablespoons of the mushroom water, stir, and allow to simmer for 30 minutes. In a small saucepan make a creamy sauce by adding the potato flour to the melted butter and gradually adding 1 cup of broth made with the bouillon cube, and 1 cup of water. Simmer very slowly until the ditali are cooked. Cook the ditali in abundant boiling salted water for 10 minutes. Drain well and put in a serving bowl with the tongue sauce and mix well. Add the cream sauce and half the Parmesan and toss until well mixed. Serve with the rest of the cheese sprinkled on top. Serves 4.

FARFALLE À LA LUGANEGA
(*Farfalle alla Luganega*)

Remember, to make a good wine sauce, you should always use a quality wine.

Cooking time: 20 minutes

½ pound sausages
1 tablespoon oil
1 cup white wine
1 pound farfalle

¼ pound butter
1 cup grated Parmesan cheese
Salt and white pepper to taste

Peel and crumble the sausages, and brown well in the oil in a saucepan over low heat. Add the white wine, cover the saucepan, and cook for 12 minutes, very slowly. Cook the farfalle in abundant boiling salted water for 8 minutes. Drain and put in a serving bowl. Add dabs of butter, half the Parmesan, and a generous pinch of salt and white pepper. Mix well. Add the sausages with their juices and mix again. Serve dusted with the rest of the Parmesan.
Serves 4.

FARFALLE ABRUZZI STYLE
(*Farfalle all'Abruzzese*)

Cooking time: 10 minutes

1 pound small farfalle
3 slices bacon
2 tablespoons oil

1 cup ricotta cheese
1 cup grated Parmesan cheese
Salt and pepper to taste

Start to cook the small farfalle in abundant boiling salted water. In the meantime, brown the bacon in the oil in a skillet for 8 minutes. Drain the cooked pasta, reserving ½ cup of the water. Dilute the ricotta in the water and add. Also add the bacon and half the grated cheese. Add salt and pepper. Mix well. Serve with rest of cheese sprinkled on top. Serves 5.

DRUNKEN FARFALLE
(*Farfalle alla Sbronza*)

A quick delicious dish, perfect for midnight suppers . . .

Cooking time: 10 minutes

1 pound farfalle	Salt and white pepper to taste
2 tablespoons oil	1 clove garlic
6 tablespoons butter	1⅓ cups grated Parmesan
½ cup cognac	cheese

Cook the farfalle for 8 minutes in abundant boiling salted water
to which the oil has been added. In a small bowl work together
the butter and the cognac so that a soft cream results. Add salt
and pepper. Rub a wooden bowl with the clove of garlic. Put the
cooked drained farfalle in this bowl, quickly add the grated cheese
and toss until very well mixed. Add the butter-cognac mixture and
mix again. Dust with freshly ground white pepper and serve immediately. Serves 4.

FARFALLE WITH TUNA SAUCE
(*Farfalle al Sugo di Tonno*)

Cooking time: 25 minutes

1½ pounds ripe tomatoes (5 medium)	½ cup canned tuna (packed in olive oil)
2 cloves garlic	Salt and pepper to taste
4 tablespoons oil	1 pound farfalle
¼ dried red pepper	2 tablespoons chopped parsley

Peel the tomatoes first and reserve for later use. Sauté the finely
chopped garlic in oil with the red pepper and the crumbled tuna.
Mix for a minute or so. Add salt and pepper, then add the chopped
tomatoes and all their juice. Stir and bring to a boil over a high
flame. Lower the flame to moderate and cook for 25 minutes
(the sauce is ready when the oil floats to the surface). In the
meantime, cook the farfalle in abundant boiling salted water for 8
minutes. Drain well and put in a serving bowl. Add the parsley
and mix well. Taste the sauce for salt and add some if necessary.
Pour over the farfalle. Mix thoroughly and serve immediately.
Serves 4.

FARFALLE AND PEAS
(*Farfalle e Piselli*)

Here is an extremely copious dish. I suggest that you serve it alone with a dessert.

Cooking time: 30 minutes

1 medium onion	½ pound peas (1 cup shelled)
¼ pound butter	Salt and white pepper to taste
½ cup white wine	1 pound farfalle
1 stalk celery	1 cup grated Parmesan cheese
1 carrot	

Sauté the thinly sliced onion in the butter in a saucepan until barely golden. Add the white wine and the sliced celery and carrot. Also add the peas, salt and white pepper, and 3 tablespoons of hot water. Cook for 20 minutes. Cook the farfalle in abundant boiling salted water for 8 minutes. Drain and put in a serving bowl with all the sauce, including the vegetables. Mix well, adding the Parmesan a little at a time until it is all absorbed. Serve immediately. Serves 4.

FARFALLE COUNTRY STYLE
(*Farfalle alla Paesana*)

Cooking time: 30 minutes

½ cup shelled green peas	2 basil leaves (or ⅛ teaspoon dried)
3 slices lean bacon	
3 tablespoons oil	Pepper
1 small onion	½ cup asparagus tips
Salt to taste	1 pound farfalle
½ cup tomato paste	2 tablespoons butter
1 bouillon cube	1 cup grated Parmesan cheese

First of all cook the peas. Coarsely chop the bacon and put in a saucepan with the oil. Sauté for a few minutes. Add the finely chopped onion, and sauté until almost golden. Add ½ cup of hot water. Bring to a rapid boil. Add the peas and salt. Boil for 15 minutes. Dilute the tomato paste in ¾ cup of hot water in which you have already dissolved the bouillon cube. Add to the peas. Also add the chopped basil and the pepper. Add more salt if needed. Add the asparagus tips and bring to a boil over moderate heat. Cook the farfalle in abundant boiling salted water for 8 minutes. Drain and put in a serving dish. Add the butter in dabs, the entire contents of the saucepan, and half the grated cheese. Mix well. Serve dusted with the rest of the Parmesan. Be sure that each portion gets an equal share of the vegetables. Serves 4.

FARFALLE IN TASTY SAUCE
(*Farfalle in Salsa Gustosa*)

Cooking time: 30 minutes

½ pound ripe tomatoes (2 medium)
1 chicken bouillon cube
½ pound turkey breast
3 tablespoons oil
1 small onion
1 clove garlic
3 basil leaves (or ¼ teaspoon dried)

2 tablespoons tomato paste
Salt and pepper to taste
2 tablespoons pine nuts
4 tablespoons butter
½ cup grated Gruyère cheese
½ cup grated Parmesan cheese
1 pound farfalle

Coarsely cut up the tomatoes and put in a saucepan with ¼ cup water and the bouillon cube. Boil for 3 minutes, then pass through the fine blade of a food mill. Set aside for use later. Thinly slice the turkey breast and put in a saucepan with the oil and the finely chopped onion. Sauté until browned. Chop very finely the crushed clove of garlic and the basil leaves, and add. Stir over high heat for 1 minute, then add the tomato paste, salt, and pepper. Make a paste of the pine nuts, using the flat side of the blade of a knife. Work these crushed pine nuts together with the butter and 1 tablespoon of the mixed grated cheeses to form a paste. Cook the farfalle in boiling salted water for 8 minutes. Drain and put in a preheated serving bowl. Add the paste you have made, putting little dabs here and there over the pasta. Also add all the sauce with the turkey and half of the remaining mixed grated cheeses. Toss until very well mixed and serve dusted with the rest of the cheese. Serves 4.

PENNE IN HOT SAUCE
(*Penne in Salsa Forte*)

In the south of Italy, the hot dishes are particularly appreciated. But not everyone likes spicy dishes, so I suggest that you ask your guests before preparing this dish for a party.

Cooking time: 20 minutes

2 cloves garlic	1 basil leaf (or ⅛ teaspoon
1 dried red pepper	dried)
5 tablespoons oil	½ teaspoon paprika
1½ pounds ripe tomatoes (5	Salt and pepper to taste
medium)	1 pound penne
2 tablespoons chopped parsley	

Sauté the very finely chopped garlic and the red pepper, broken into 3 pieces, in the oil in a fairly large saucepan. When golden, add the peeled, cut-up tomatoes, the parsley, the basil, and the paprika, and cook over high heat. Add salt and pepper. In the meantime, cook the penne in abundant boiling salted water for 10 minutes. When the penne are cooked, the sauce should be ready—it should be fairly thick and oily. Drain the penne and put in the saucepan with the sauce. Mix well and serve. This dish may also be served cold. Serves 4.

PENNE WITH CREAM
(*Penne con Panna*)

Cooking time: 20 minutes

6 tablespoons butter	1 pound penne
4 tablespoons potato flour	1 cup heavy cream
1 cup milk	⅔ cup grated Gruyère cheese
Salt and white pepper to taste	⅓ cup grated Parmesan cheese

Put a large pot of salted water on to boil for cooking the penne. In the meantime, prepare the sauce. Melt the butter in a small saucepan and add the potato flour. Stir over low heat until well blended. Gradually add the hot milk, stirring continuously. A thin white (béchamel) sauce results. Season with salt and white pepper. Cook the penne in the boiling water for 10 minutes. Drain and put in a preheated serving bowl. Pour on the white sauce. Mix. Add the cream and half the grated Gruyère and Parmesan mixed together. Toss until very well mixed and dust with the rest of the grated cheese. Serves 4.

PENNE LAZIO STYLE
(*Penne alla Laziale*)

Cooking time: 40 minutes

3 slices bacon	1 pound ripe tomatoes (3
3 tablespoons oil	medium)
1 large onion	3 basil leaves (or ¼ teaspoon
¼ pound chicken giblets	dried)
1 stalk celery	1 pound penne
Salt and pepper to taste	1 cup grated Parmesan cheese
¼ cup white wine	(or pecorino cheese)

Cut the bacon into small pieces and sauté in the oil in a saucepan until golden. Add the finely chopped onion and continue to sauté until golden. Add the cut-up chicken giblets, thinly sliced celery, salt, and pepper, and brown for 3 minutes. Add the white wine and allow half of it to evaporate. Add the finely chopped tomatoes and the basil leaves. Stir. Cover the saucepan and simmer slowly for 30 minutes. Cook the penne in abundant boiling salted water for 10 minutes. Drain well and put in a serving dish. Add the sauce and the grated cheese, mix well, and serve. Serves 4.

PENNE HUNTER STYLE
(*Penne alla Cacciatora*)

Cooking time: 55 minutes

1 ounce dried mushrooms (or	1 basil leaf (or ⅛ teaspoon
1 4-ounce can)	dried)
6 tablespoons butter	1 whole clove
¼ pound veal	1 pinch cinnamon
2 slices ham (or lean bacon)	1 pinch nutmeg
1 small onion	Salt and pepper to taste
1 carrot	1 pound penne
½ stalk celery	1 cup grated Parmesan cheese
1 clove garlic	(optional)
2 cups red wine	

Before beginning your sauce, chop the dried mushrooms and put them to soak for 15 minutes. Now sauté together in the butter in a saucepan the cut-up veal, ham (or bacon), onion, carrot, celery, and finely chopped garlic. Sauté until barely colored, then add the red wine and the coarsely chopped mushrooms. Stir. Add the finely chopped basil leaf, the whole clove, the cinnamon, the nutmeg, and salt and pepper. Cook slowly for about 40 minutes. In the meantime, cook the penne in abundant boiling salted water for 10 minutes. Drain and put in a serving bowl. Add all the sauce and, if desired, the grated Parmesan. Mix well and serve immediately. Serves 4.

PENNE ARABIAN STYLE or MAD PENNE
(Penne all'Arrabbiata)

The restaurant Piccolo Mondo kindly gave me this recipe, for which it is famous. If you come to Rome, you will realize how very inexpensive it is to eat at a good restaurant.

Cooking time: 25 minutes

1½ pounds ripe tomatoes (5 medium)	1 pound penne
	Salt to taste
2 cloves garlic	2 tablespoons chopped parsley
1 dried red pepper whole	Paprika (if desired)
5 tablespoons oil	

Peel the tomatoes and reserve for later use. Sauté the garlic and the red pepper in the oil in a skillet. Add the tomatoes and cook over moderate heat until the sauce becomes concentrated and the oil rises to the surface. Cook the penne in abundant boiling salted water for 10 minutes. Drain and add to the skillet. Add salt. Mix well. Put on a heated platter. Sprinkle the parsley on top and serve immediately. If you like a very hot sauce, add ½ teaspoon paprika to the sauce. Serves 4.

SHELLS AND FAMILY

PENNE WITH COGNAC
(*Penne al Cognac*)

A great specialty of Taverna Flavia in Rome . . .

Cooking time: 30 minutes

2 slices bacon	1 bay leaf
3 tablespoons oil	1 pound penne
1 medium onion	⅓ cup cognac
1 pound tomatoes (3 medium)	1 cup grated Cheddar cheese
Salt and pepper to taste	½ cup heavy cream

Finely dice the bacon and sauté in the oil in a saucepan with the coarsely chopped onion. Add the cut-up tomatoes, salt and pepper, and the bay leaf. Stir and cook for 30 minutes. When the sauce has cooked for about 20 minutes, cook the penne in abundant boiling salted water for 10 minutes. In the meantime, pass the sauce through a food mill, remove from fire, and pour in the cognac. Drain the cooked penne and put in a preheated serving bowl. Add all the sauce and half the grated cheese. Toss until well mixed. Add the cream and toss again. Serve dusted with the rest of the Cheddar. Serves 4.

PENNE COUNTRY STYLE
(*Penne alla Paesana*)

Cooking time: 30 minutes

2 cloves garlic	Salt and pepper to taste
4 tablespoons oil	2 basil leaves (or ⅛ teaspoon
1½ pounds ripe tomatoes (5	dried)
medium)	¼ cup shelled green peas
2 stalks celery	1 pound penne
1 (4-ounce) can mushrooms	1 cup grated Parmesan cheese

Sauté the finely chopped garlic in the oil in a saucepan. When it is golden in color add the cut-up, peeled tomatoes. Add the sliced celery and mushrooms and cook over moderate heat. Add salt and pepper. Add the basil and the peas. Cover the saucepan and cook for 30 minutes. Cook the penne in abundant boiling salted water for

10 minutes. Drain and put in a serving bowl with all the sauce and the grated Parmesan. Toss until very well mixed and serve.
Serves 4.

PENNE WITH SALAMI
(*Penne al Salame*)

This recipe was given to me by the chef of the hotel Le Dune in Sabaudia, 50 miles from Rome. Sabaudia is one of the most beautiful beaches in Italy.

Cooking time: 20 minutes

¼ pound salami, sliced	2 tablespoons flour
1 medium onion	½ cup white wine
3 tablespoons oil	1 bouillon cube
2 cloves garlic	Salt and pepper to taste
2 basil leaves (or ⅛ teaspoon dried)	1 pound penne
4 tablespoons butter	1 cup grated Parmesan cheese

The salami should not be sliced too thickly. Put it in a skillet with 1 cup water. Bring to a boil and simmer over low heat for 1 minute. Remove the salami from the water and cut it into spaghetti-like strips. Sauté the finely chopped onion in the oil in a saucepan until golden. Add the salami, and sauté, stirring slowly over low heat. Chop *very* finely the cloves of garlic and the basil, and add to the saucepan, stirring for 1 minute more. Add the butter and, when it is melted, add the flour. Stir until it has blended with the other ingredients. Slowly pour in the wine in order to prevent lumps, stirring continuously. Dissolve the bouillon cube in 1 cup of hot water and add. Add salt and pepper. Stir. Cook over moderate heat for 15 minutes. In the meantime, cook the penne in abundant boiling salted water for 10 minutes. Drain and put in a serving bowl with all the sauce and half the grated cheese. Mix well and serve dusted with the rest of the Parmesan. Serves 4.

PENNE WITH SALMON
(*Penne al Salmone*)

This dish may be served hot or cold.

Cooking time: 30 minutes

1 pound ripe tomatoes (3 medium)	½ cup white wine
2 cloves garlic	2 tablespoons chopped parsley
5 tablespoons oil	¼ dried red pepper
½ pound smoked salmon	Salt and pepper to taste
1 tablespoon flour	1 pound penne
	½ cup heavy cream

Peel the tomatoes and reserve for later use. Sauté the finely chopped garlic in the oil in a saucepan until almost golden. Add the salmon, cut up in small pieces, and sauté for a few minutes more. Add the flour and stir until blended. Add the wine, stirring continuously. Allow half of it to evaporate, then add the cut-up tomatoes and the parsley. Also add the red pepper, salt, and pepper. Stir again and cook over medium-low heat for 20 minutes, stirring from time to time. Ten minutes before the sauce is ready, start cooking the penne in abundant boiling salted water for 10 minutes. Drain and put in a serving bowl with all the sauce. Toss until well mixed. Add the cream and mix again. Serves 4.

PENNE WITH CREAM SAUCE
(*Penne alla Crema*)

This recipe is a specialty of the restaurant Rugantina in Naples.

Cooking time: 20 minutes

2 cups milk	3 egg yolks
¾ cup butter	1 pound penne
6 tablespoons flour	1⅓ cups grated Gruyère cheese
Salt and white pepper to taste	1 small wedge cheese spread
1 chicken bouillon cube	

Put the water for cooking the penne on to boil. Bring the milk to a full boil and set aside for use later. Prepare the cream sauce: melt the butter in a saucepan and add the flour, stirring to blend. Gradually add the milk, stirring continuously in order not to form lumps. Add salt and pepper, and cook very slowly over very low heat for 10 minutes. Stir often. Put the saucepan with this white sauce in another, larger saucepan with hot water or a double boiler. Continue to cook over low heat. Dissolve the bouillon cube in ¼ cup hot water. Add to a bowl containing the beaten egg yolks and mix. Add this mixture to the white sauce and stir. Remove the sauce from the fire. In the meantime the water has come to a boil. Cook the penne in abundant boiling salted water for 10 minutes. Drain and put in a serving bowl with all the cream sauce, half the grated cheese, and the wedge of cheese spread cut in pieces. Toss until very well mixed. Serve with the rest of the cheese sprinkled on top. Serves 4.

PENNE WITH HAM
(*Penne al Prosciutto*)

Cooking time: 30 minutes

4 slices lean bacon	Salt and pepper to taste
3 tablespoons oil	1 bouillon cube
1 medium onion	1 pound penne
2 tablespoons flour	6 thin slices cooked ham
⅓ cup white wine	1 cup grated Cheddar cheese
6 tablespoons tomato paste	

Cut the lean bacon into small cubes. Sauté in the oil in a saucepan until brown. Add the finely chopped onion, and sauté until golden. Add the flour and stir. Pour in the white wine and allow half of it to evaporate. Add the tomato paste and stir for 2 minutes. Add the salt and pepper. Dissolve the bouillon cube in 1½ cups of hot water and add. Stir and simmer over moderate heat for 20 minutes. Ten minutes before the sauce is ready, cook the penne in abundant boiling salted water for 10 minutes. In the meantime, cut the sliced ham into thin spaghetti-like strips and add to the sauce. Drain the penne and put in a serving bowl with all the sauce and half the grated cheese. Toss until well mixed and serve with the rest of the cheese dusted on top. Serves 4.

PENNE ABRUZZI STYLE
(*Penne all'Abruzzese*)

Cooking time: 25 minutes

4 slices lean bacon	2 tablespoons chopped parsley
6 tablespoons butter	2 eggs
1 pound penne	Salt and white pepper to taste
¾ cup ricotta	¾ cup grated Cheddar cheese

Cut the bacon into spaghetti-like strips and put in a saucepan with the butter. Sauté over low flame for 5 minutes. Remove from fire. Cook the penne in abundant boiling salted water for 10 minutes. In the meantime, in a serving bowl put the ricotta, the parsley, and the eggs. Mix well. Add salt and white pepper. Work these ingredients with a wooden spoon until they become a blended cream. Gradually add ¼ cup of the water in which the penne are cooking, stirring continuously until a very soft cream results. Drain the cooked penne and add to the bowl with the ricotta. Toss vigorously until well mixed. Add the contents of the saucepan in which the bacon was cooked. Mix again. Add the grated cheese, toss once more, and serve immediately. Serves 4.

PENNE WITH DRIED MUSHROOMS
(*Penne ai Funghi Secchi*)

Carrara is known throughout the world for its beautiful marble. Not only did I acquire a beautiful marble statue while I was there, but I was given this recipe by the chef of the town's best restaurant, Soldaini.

Cooking time: 30 minutes

4 ounces dried mushrooms	1 pound penne
¾ cup butter	1⅓ cups grated Parmesan
Salt and pepper to taste	cheese
7 tablespoons tomato paste	

Wash the dried mushrooms *very* well in order to remove any grains of sand. Put them in 2 cups of warm water to soak for 10 minutes. Remove from the water, squeeze dry, and chop. Sauté in the butter in a saucepan over low heat. Add salt and pepper. Pass the mushroom water through a very fine sieve or cheesecloth. Dilute the tomato paste in this water and add to the saucepan. Cook for 20 minutes. In the meantime, cook the penne in abundant boiling salted water for 10 minutes. Drain and put in a serving bowl. Add the sauce and the grated Parmesan and toss until well mixed. Serve immediately. Serves 4.

PENNE ST. ANTHONY
(*Penne alla Maniera di Sant'Antonio*)

Cooking time: 30 minutes

5 slices bacon	Salt to taste
6 tablespoons butter	Pinch of paprika
¼ dried red pepper	1 pound penne
½ cup white wine	1 cup grated pecorino cheese
½ cup tomato paste	(or any sharp cheese)

Cut the bacon into small cubes and brown in the butter in a fairly large saucepan. Add the dried red pepper and the white wine and stir. When half has evaporated, add the tomato paste diluted in 2 cups of warm water. Add salt and paprika to taste. Stir and cook for 25 minutes over moderate heat. In the meantime, cook the penne in abundant boiling salted water for 10 minutes. Drain and put in the saucepan with the grated cheese. Mix with a wooden spoon. Remove from heat, cover, and allow to rest for 3 minutes before serving. Serves 4.

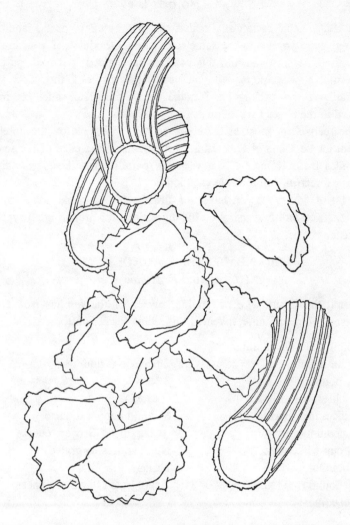

CHAPTER V

Stuffed Pasta

Stuffed pasta is served in practically all Italian restaurants, elegant or not. Tortellini, ravioli, agnolotti, cannelloni, rigatoni—all these types of pasta are considered much more delicate than spaghetti or macaroni by gourmets and for this reason are more costly.

In Italy each restaurant makes its own stuffed pasta, and I strongly urge you to do the same if possible. Of course, if you don't have the time, you can find this pasta in specialized Italian shops or in certain supermarkets. All you need do is to cook the pasta as directed on the package and make the appropriate sauce as indicated in the pages that follow.

The recipes for most of these sauces were given me by the hotel-restaurant Le Dune of Sabaudia, a little town on the edge of the sea, 50 miles from Rome. It is a veritable paradise for those who are seeking a restful, comfortable vacation.

A bit of advice: if you have not already done so, read my Introduction. You will find many useful suggestions for preparing all types of pasta.

GRANDMOTHER'S AGNOLOTTI
(*Agnolotti della Nonna*)

Nona, the lovely wife of Tonino, owner of the famous *trattoria* in Sacrofano near Rome, invented this recipe for her customers.

Cooking time: 70 minutes

Pasta dough	2 teaspoons flour
½ pound sausages	3 basil leaves (or ¼ teaspoon
3 tablespoons oil	dried)
3 slices lean bacon	Salt and pepper to taste
1 medium onion	¾ cup diced Gruyère cheese
⅓ cup white wine	Nutmeg, freshly grated
1 bouillon cube	2 eggs
¾ pound ripe tomatoes (2 or 3	1 cup grated Parmesan cheese
medium)	

Prepare the pasta dough, using the same procedure as for Spinach Ravioli (see Index). Peel the sausages and put in a saucepan with the oil and the sliced bacon and onion. Sauté. Add the white wine and stir. When wine is half evaporated, add the bouillon cube dissolved in 1 cup of hot water. Cook over moderate heat for 35 minutes. Peel the tomatoes and set aside. As soon as the sausages are cooked, remove them and all the other ingredients from the saucepan with a slotted spoon. Continue to simmer the juices remaining in the saucepan until partially evaporated. Add the flour and stir well. Cut up the tomatoes and add to the saucepan with all their juice. Chop the basil and add. Add salt and pepper. Cook over moderate heat for 25 minutes. In the meantime, put the sausage, bacon, and onion through the meat chopper. To this mixture add the finely diced Gruyère, a generous grating of nutmeg, 1 egg, and half the Parmesan. Pass all these ingredients through the meat chopper again. Make the agnolotti in the same manner you make spinach ravioli. Beat 1 egg together with ½ cup water and moisten the pasta with a pastry brush dipped in this mixture. As soon as the agnolotti are made and the sauce is thick enough, cook them in abundant boiling salted water for 8 minutes. Drain carefully in order not to break them, and put in a preheated serving dish. Add the sauce and the rest of the grated Parmesan. Mix carefully and serve immediately. Serves 4.

GNOCCHI, ITALIAN STYLE
(*Gnocchi all'Italiana*)

Cooking time: 90 minutes

1¼ pounds potatoes (4 medium)	1 stalk celery
	⅔ cup tomato paste
1 medium onion	4 basil leaves (or ¼ teaspoon dried)
½ pound pork (fatty)	
¼ pound beef	3 cups flour for pasta
4 tablespoons oil	1 egg for pasta
Salt and pepper to taste	1 cup grated Parmesan cheese
1 carrot	

Put the potatoes (unpeeled) on to boil. In the meantime, prepare the sauce. Sauté the thinly sliced onion, pork, and beef in the oil in a saucepan until browned. Add salt and pepper and the thinly sliced carrot and celery, and continue to sauté. Dissolve the tomato paste in 1½ cups hot water and pour into saucepan. Add the basil, stir, and cover the saucepan. Cook slowly over low heat for 70 minutes. When the potatoes are cooked, peel them and put them through a potato ricer or the fine blade of a food mill. Put on a board with half the flour and the egg. Mix until the mixture is crumbly, then start kneading and working the dough until it is blended. If it seems too soft, add more flour. Cut the dough in pieces and roll each piece until it has a diameter of about ½ inch. Cut into ¾-inch pieces. Roll each piece in flour and, pressing down on each piece with your index and middle fingers, make a slight rolling motion so that a shell-like shape results. When the sauce is ready, pass it through the fine blade of a food mill or blend in a blender. Drop the gnocchi in a pot of boiling salted water. Stir gently. Allow to boil for 1 minute after rising to the surface. Drain and put in a bowl with half the sauce and half the Parmesan. Divide into the individual dishes. Spoon the rest of the sauce over each portion and dust with the rest of the Parmesan. Serve at once. Serves 4.

GNOCCHI, PIEDMONT STYLE
(*Gnocchi alla Piemontese*)

Cooking time: 90 minutes

1¼ pounds potatoes (4 medium)	¼ cup white wine
	Salt and pepper to taste
1 ounce dried mushrooms (1 4-ounce can)	1 chicken bouillon cube
	3 cups flour for pasta
1 small onion	1 egg for pasta
2 cloves garlic	½ tablespoon flour
4 tablespoons oil	2 tablespoons butter
2 slices bacon	1 cup grated Parmesan cheese
½ pound ground beef	

Put the unpeeled potatoes on to boil. In the meantime, prepare the sauce. Put the dried mushrooms in ¾ cup warm water to soak. Sauté the finely chopped onion and garlic in the oil in a saucepan. Add the finely chopped bacon and beef, and brown. Pour in the white wine, salt, and pepper. Dissolve the bouillon cube in the mushroom water (or ¾ cup juice from can) and add, together with the mushrooms. Cook over moderate heat for 70 minutes. In the meantime, using 3 cups of flour and the egg, prepare the gnocchi as instructed in the recipe Gnocchi Italian Style (see Index). Put a little of the sauce in a small cup and add ½ tablespoon of flour to it, mixing well. Add to the saucepan, stir and pass the entire contents of the saucepan through the fine blade of the food mill or blend in a blender. Return to heat. Cook the gnocchi in a large pot of boiling salted water. Stir slowly with a wooden spoon. The gnocchi should cook for 1 minute after rising to the surface. Drain carefully and put in a serving bowl with the sauce, the butter in dabs, and half the Parmesan. Mix and serve with the rest of the Parmesan sprinkled on top. Serves 4.

AGNOLOTTI ROMAN STYLE
(*Agnolotti alla Romana*)

Cooking time: 70 minutes

Pasta dough

2½ pounds dried mushrooms (or 1 3-ounce can chopped)

4 slices lean bacon

1 medium onion

3 tablespoons oil

½ pound lamb

Salt and pepper to taste

1 bouillon cube

1 small clove garlic

2 basil leaves (or ⅛ teaspoon dried)

3 tablespoons butter

3 or 4 chicken livers

1 tablespoon flour

⅓ cup white wine

⅓ cup tomato paste

3 ounces mortadella sausage

½ cup diced dried mozzarella cheese

1⅓ cups grated Parmesan cheese

2 eggs

Nutmeg to taste

Prepare and roll out the pasta as instructed for Lasagne Bolognese Style (see Index), but roll it a little thinner. Put the dried mushrooms to soak in ½ cup of hot water and reserve ¾ of this water for later use. Sauté the thinly sliced bacon and onion in the oil in a saucepan. Add the thinly sliced lamb, salt, and pepper, and brown well. Add 1½ cups hot water in which you have dissolved the bouillon cube. Stir, cover, and cook over moderate heat for 40 minutes. Finely chop together the crushed clove of garlic and the basil. Put in a small skillet with the butter, and sauté over low heat. When barely golden, add the coarsely chopped chicken livers and continue to sauté, stirring often. Add the flour, salt and pepper if needed, and stir again. Add the white wine and allow half to evaporate. Add the mushrooms, which you have squeezed dry and chopped, and the reserved ¾ of the water in which they have soaked (if canned, use liquid plus water to make ½ cup). Stir and simmer very slowly for 15 minutes. Remove the cooked meat, the bacon, and all the other ingredients from the saucepan with a slotted spoon. To the juices left in the pan add the tomato paste, and stir for 1 minute over moderate heat. Add the entire contents of the skillet, including the fat in which the chicken livers were sautéed. Stir until well mixed and simmer slowly for 15 minutes more. Put the cooked lamb, bacon, mortadella, and dried mozzarella through a meat chopper. Add half the grated Parmesan, 1 egg, and a generous pinch of nutmeg. Mix and pass through the meat chopper once more so that a smooth paste results. Mix the two sauces. Prepare the beaten egg and ¼ cup water with which to brush the pasta and prepare the agnolotti as described in the recipe Spinach Ravioli (see Index.) Cook the agnolotti in a large pot of boiling salted water for 8 minutes. Drain carefully in order not to break them, and put in a preheated platter. Pour on the sauce and the rest of the grated cheese, mix well, and serve immediately. Serves 4.

AGNOLOTTI PIEDMONT STYLE
(*Agnolotti alla Piemontese*)

La Grotta of Asti is considered one of the best restaurants of Piedmont. This recipe was given to me by its chef, Angelo.

Cooking time: 80 minutes

Pasta dough	2 or 3 medium-size ripe
4 slices lean bacon	tomatoes
¼ pound turkey breast	2 basil leaves (or ⅛ teaspoon
1 medium onion	dried)
Salt and pepper to taste	2 thin slices cooked ham
3 tablespoons oil	3 slices fontina cheese (or
½ cup red wine	American cheese)
1 chicken bouillon cube	2 eggs
1 stalk celery	1 cup grated Parmesan cheese
1 carrot	Nutmeg to taste
1 tablespoon flour	

Make the pasta dough as instructed for Spinach Ravioli (see Index), but roll it slightly thinner. Put the sliced bacon, sliced turkey breast, chopped onion, salt, and pepper in the oil in a saucepan and brown. When well browned, add the red wine. When half evaporated add the bouillon cube diluted in 1 cup of hot water. Stir and simmer over moderate heat for 35 minutes. As soon as all is cooked and the juices have almost completely evaporated, remove the turkey and bacon and reserve for later use. Put the sliced celery and carrot in the same saucepan and sauté. Add the flour and stir. Add the cut-up tomatoes, basil, salt, and pepper, and cook over moderate heat for 30 minutes. In the meantime, pass through the meat chopper the bacon, the turkey, the ham, and the fontina cheese. To this mixture add 1 egg, half the grated Parmesan, and a generous pinch of nutmeg, and mix well. Pass the whole mixture through the meat chopper again so that a smooth paste results. Prepare a beaten egg and ¼ cup water mixture with which to brush the rolled pasta dough and proceed to make the agnolotti as described in Spinach Ravioli. Put the tomato sauce through a food mill or blend in a blender. Cook the agnolotti in abundant boiling salted water for 8 minutes, taking care to put them in the water very gently in order not to break them. Drain carefully and put in a preheated serving dish. Add the sauce and the grated Parmesan, mix, and serve immediately. Serves 4.

DUCAL AGNOLOTTI
(*Agnolotti Ducale*)

Cooking time: 90 minutes

Pasta dough
2 slices bacon
4 tablespoons oil
½ pound pork
¼ pound chicken breast
Salt and pepper to taste
1 onion
⅓ cup white wine
1 bouillon cube
1 small clove garlic

3 basil leaves (or ¼ teaspoon dried)
¼ pound fresh mushrooms
2 tablespoons flour
2 medium-size ripe tomatoes
2 eggs
1⅓ cups grated Parmesan cheese
Nutmeg to taste

Make and roll dough as for Spinach Ravioli (see Index). Brown the sliced bacon in 3 tablespoons of the oil in a saucepan. Also add the sliced pork and chicken breast, salt and pepper, and the finely chopped onion. Brown well and add the white wine. When half evaporated, dissolve the bouillon cube in 1 cup of hot water and add. Stir, cover, and cook over moderate heat for 40 minutes. In the meantime, finely chop the garlic and the basil leaves together and in the remaining oil sauté in a small skillet with the thinly sliced mushrooms. Sauté for 10 minutes over moderate heat. Remove the cooked meats from the saucepan with a slotted spoon and set aside. Add the flour to the juices in the saucepan and stir. Add the cut-up tomatoes, ½ cup hot water, salt, and pepper. Cook over moderate heat for 20 minutes. Grind the meats in the meat chopper. Mix with 1 egg, half the grated Parmesan, and the nutmeg. Put through the meat chopper again in order to have a smooth paste. Prepare an egg and ¼ cup water mixture with which to brush the dough and prepare the agnolotti, following the same procedure described in the recipe for Spinach Ravioli. Pass the tomato sauce through a food mill or blend in a blender and return to the saucepan. Add the entire contents of the skillet in which the mushrooms were cooked. Stir and cook for 10 minutes more over very low heat. Cook the agnolotti in abundant boiling salted water for 8 minutes. Drain and put in a preheated serving dish. Add the sauce and half the remaining grated cheese. Mix carefully in order not to break the agnolotti. Sprinkle with the rest of the cheese and serve immediately. Serves 4.

AGNOLOTTI WITH BEEF
(*Agnolotti alla Carne di Manzo*)

I often prepare this recipe during my travels but it is always in America that I have the most success. The reason for this is that in the United States the beef is often of better quality than in its neighboring countries.

Cooking time: 2 hours

Pasta dough	1 bouillon cube
1 ounce dried mushrooms (or 1 3-ounce can, chopped)	⅓ cup tomato paste
	4 large tomatoes
2 slices lean bacon	¼ pound mortadella sausage
1 medium onion	⅛ pound Gruyère cheese
3 tablespoons oil	2 eggs
½ pound beef	1 cup grated Parmesan cheese
Salt and pepper to taste	Nutmeg
½ cup white wine	

Prepare the pasta dough as for Lasagne Bolognese Style (see Index), but roll it slightly thinner. Put the dried mushrooms to soak in ½ cup hot water and reserve water. Sauté the sliced bacon and the finely chopped onion in the oil in a saucepan. Add the thinly sliced beef, and brown together with the bacon and onion. Add salt and pepper and the white wine. When half the wine has evaporated, add the bouillon cube dissolved in 1½ cups of hot water. Stir, cover, and simmer over moderate heat for 1 hour. Remove the mushrooms from the water, squeeze dry, and chop finely. Pass the water they have been soaking in through cheesecloth or a very fine sieve. Return the mushrooms to the water and add tomato paste. (If using canned mushrooms, add liquid plus water to make ½ cup.) As soon as the meat is cooked, remove it, the bacon, and all the other ingredients with a slotted spoon and set aside. Add the cut-up peeled tomatoes to the juices left in the pan. Add the mushrooms with their water and the tomato paste, salt and pepper, and ½ cup hot water. Cook for 30 minutes over low heat. Pass the meat, the mortadella, and the Gruyère through the finest blade of a meat chopper. Mix with 1 egg, 1 tablespoon of grated Parmesan, and a generous grating of nutmeg. Put through the chopper again in order to obtain a smooth paste. Prepare an egg and water mixture by mixing the egg together with ¼ cup water with which to brush the dough, and make the agnolotti following the same procedure used in Spinach Ravioli (see Index). Carefully put the agnolotti in boiling salted water and boil for 8 minutes. Drain carefully in order not to break them, and put in a preheated serving dish. Add the sauce (which should be fairly thick), mix well, and serve with the remaining Parmesan sprinkled on top. Serves 4.

CANNELLONI WITH MUSHROOMS
(*Cannelloni ai Funghi*)

Cooking time: 50 minutes

Pasta dough	Salt and pepper to taste
1½ pounds flour for pasta	6 tablespoons butter
4 eggs	½ cup flour
4 large tomatoes	3 cups milk
1 pound mushrooms	Nutmeg to taste
1 clove garlic	½ pound cooked ham
4 tablespoons oil	2 cups grated Parmesan cheese
1 tablespoon lemon juice	

Preheat over to 350° F.

Prepare the pasta dough with 1½ pounds of flour and 4 eggs and follow the directions given for Homemade Pasta (see Index) but roll the dough a little thinner than for Lasagne Bolognese Style. Cut the dough into 2″×4″ rectangles. Put the tomatoes in boiling water and peel. Wash the mushrooms and slice thinly. In a saucepan sauté the finely chopped garlic in the oil until barely golden. Add the mushrooms and lemon juice. Stir over high heat for a few minutes. Add salt and pepper. Add the cut-up tomatoes and continue to cook for 10 minutes. In the meantime, prepare a Béchamel Sauce (see Index) with the butter, ½ cup of flour, 3 cups of milk, nutmeg, salt, and pepper. When the mushrooms are cooked, remove from saucepan with a slotted spoon, draining well. Chop them coarsely together with the cooked ham and put in a dish with 2 tablespoons of sauce, 1 cup grated Parmesan, and a generous grating of nutmeg. Mix well. If the mixture seems too loose, add 1 tablespoon of dried bread crumbs to bind the mixture together. Cook the pasta rectangles in boiling salted water in a very large pot. Cook about 6 at a time, 2 minutes each time. Remove the pasta from the water with a sieve and put immediately in a pot of cold water. Repeat until all the rectangles are cooked. Remove them from the cold water and spread out on clean dish towels. Put a little mushroom filling on each rectangle and roll, beginning from the narrow end. Add the remaining mushroom filling to the white sauce and stir until well mixed. Spread a little of this sauce on the bottom of an ovenproof dish. Arrange the cannelloni side by side on the sauce and cover with the rest of the sauce. Sprinkle the remaining Parmesan generously on top. Put in a moderate oven (350°) for 20 minutes. When you remove them from the oven allow them to cool for 3 minutes before serving. Serve with a wide cake server or a pancake turner in order not to break them.
Serves 4.
NOTE: After putting the filling in the roll, there should be some left. Add this remaining filling to the white sauce and then pour over the cannelloni.

PRINCE'S CANNELLONI
(*Cannelloni del Principe*)

Cooking time: 80 minutes

10 ounces pasta dough	¾ cup diced Gruyère cheese
1 2-pound chicken	2 medium-size ripe tomatoes
1 medium onion	3 basil leaves (or ¼ teaspoon
Salt and pepper to taste	dried)
3 tablespoons oil	¼ pound cooked ham
1 chicken bouillon cube	¼ teaspoon nutmeg
6 tablespoons butter	2 eggs
½ cup flour	1⅓ cups grated Parmesan
5 cups milk	cheese

Preheat oven to 375° F.

Prepare the pasta dough as directed in the recipe Lasagne Bolognese Style (see Index), and cut into 2"×4" rectangles. Cut up the chicken and brown with the chopped onion and salt and pepper in the oil in a saucepan. When well browned, add the bouillon cube dissolved in 1 cup of hot water. Cover the saucepan and cook over moderate heat for 40 minutes. Stir from time to time. In the meantime, make a Béchamel Sauce with the butter, flour, and milk (see Index). The sauce should be fairly thin. Finely dice the Gruyère. When the chicken is cooked, remove from the saucepan. To the juices left in the saucepan, add the peeled, chopped tomatoes, the basil, salt, and pepper, and cook for 20 minutes. Debone the chicken and put the meat through the fine blade of meat chopper together with the ham. Put in a mixing bowl. Add a generous grating of nutmeg, 2 eggs, ⅔ cup of grated Parmesan, 2 tablespoons of white sauce, and mix well, forming a smooth paste. Cook and fill the pasta rectangles as described in the recipe Cannelloni with Mushrooms (see Index). Pass the tomato sauce through a food mill or blend in a blender and mix with the white sauce. Spread half of this sauce on the bottom of an ovenproof dish. Arrange the cannelloni in the dish. Sprinkle the tiny cubes of Gruyère here and there over the cannelloni and spread the rest of the sauce evenly on top. Sprinkle with the rest of the grated Parmesan and put in a 375°

oven for 15 minutes. Allow to cool for 3 minutes after removing
from the oven and serve. Serves 4.

CANNELLONI MILANESE STYLE
(*Cannelloni alla Milanese*)

Georgio, owner of one of the best restaurants of Milan, on via
Abricci, is known for this specialty.

Cooking time: 80 minutes

1½ pounds flour for pasta	¼ pound butter
4 eggs for pasta	4 tablespoons flour
1 medium onion	5 cups milk
3 tablespoons oil	Salt and pepper to taste
½ pound pork (fatty)	¼ teaspoon nutmeg
½ pound turkey breast	¼ pound mortadella sausage
Salt and pepper to taste	2 eggs
1 bouillon cube	1⅔ cups grated Parmesan
2 medium-size ripe tomatoes	cheese

Preheat oven to 375° F.

Make the pasta dough with 1½ pounds of flour and 4 eggs and
follow the directions given for Homemade Pasta (see Index), but
be sure to roll the dough a little thinner than for Lasagne Bolognese
Style. Thinly slice the onion, and sauté in oil in a saucepan until
barely golden. Brown the thinly sliced pork. Also brown the coarsely
chopped turkey. Add salt and pepper. Dissolve the bouillon cube in
1 cup of hot water, and add. Cook for 40 minutes. In the meantime,
peel the tomatoes. Make a Béchamel Sauce (see Index) with the
butter, flour, and milk, salt and pepper, and nutmeg. Remove the
meat from the saucepan with a slotted spoon, leaving the juices in
the pan. Add the peeled, chopped tomatoes to the saucepan with
salt and pepper to taste. Cook for 20 minutes over moderate heat.
Pass the cooked meat and the mortadella through the finest blade
of a meat chopper. Add the eggs, 1 cup grated Parmesan, 2 tablespoons of white sauce, a lttle nutmeg, and mix. Pass through the
meat chopper again so that a smooth paste results. Make the
cannelloni, using the same procedure described in Cannelloni with
Mushrooms (see Index). Spread half of the white sauce evenly on

the bottom of an ovenproof baking dish. Lay the cannelloni side by side on the layer of white sauce. Pour half of the tomato sauce over them and sprinkle with half the remaining grated cheese. Spread on the rest of the white sauce and drizzle the rest of the tomato sauce over all. Dust with the rest of the Parmesan and put in a 375° oven for 15 minutes. Serves 4.

CANNELLONI ROMAN STYLE
(Cannelloni alla Romana)

Cooking time: 40 minutes

Pasta dough
3 slices lean bacon
3 tablespoons oil
½ pound lean pork or veal
⅛ pound Italian sausage
Salt and pepper to taste
¼ pound mortadella sausage

¼ pound Gruyère or other mild cheese
1 egg
1⅓ cups grated Parmesan cheese
Nutmeg to taste

Preheat oven to 375° F.

Prepare the pasta dough as instructed for Lasagna Bolognese Style (see Index), but roll it a little thinner. Brown the thinly sliced bacon in the oil in a saucepan. Also add the thinly sliced meat and sausage, and brown for 10 minutes over moderate heat. Add salt and pepper and stir often. Add 3 or 4 tablespoons hot water, the coarsely chopped mortadella, and cover the saucepan. Cook over low heat for 20 minutes. Check from time to time and add water when necessary. When the meat is well cooked, there should be no juices left in the saucepan. Allow the meat to cool, then pass through the fine blade of the meat chopper together with the Gruyère (or other mild cheese). Put in a small bowl. Add the egg, half the grated Parmesan, and nutmeg to taste. Mix well so that a blended paste results. Cut the pasta into 2½"×4" rectangles. Cook a few at a time and proceed to make the cannelloni as instructed in the Cannelloni with Mushrooms recipe (see Index). Spread a half-inch layer of Béchamel Sauce (see Index) on the bottom of an ovenproof baking dish and lay the cannelloni side by side thereon. Spread on the rest of the béchamel, sprinkle with the remaining Parmesan and put in a 375° oven for 15 minutes.

Variation: A good meat Ragù (see Index) may be used instead of (or together with) the béchamel. Serves 4.

CANNELLONI BÉARNAISE
(*Cannelloni alla Bearnese*)

Cooking time: 80 minutes

Pasta dough	5 cups milk
4 slices lean bacon	1½ cups diced cooked ham
3 tablespoons oil	1½ cups diced Gruyère cheese
Generous ½ pound sliced veal	1 egg
Salt and pepper to taste	1⅓ cups grated Parmesan
1 bouillon cube	cheese
½ pound mushrooms	Nutmeg to taste
8 tablespoons flour	2 medium-size ripe tomatoes
6 tablespoons butter	1 medium onion

Preheat oven to 375° F.

Prepare the pasta as directed in Lasagne Bolognese Style (see Index), but roll it a little thinner. Brown the thinly sliced bacon in the oil in a saucepan. Also add the sliced veal, salt, and pepper, and continue to brown over moderate heat for 5 minutes. Dissolve the bouillon cube in 1 cup of hot water, stir, cover the saucepan, and simmer. Wash and clean the mushrooms and add whole to the saucepan. Cook for 30 minutes over moderate heat. Make a Béchamel Sauce (see Index) with the flour, butter, and milk, and cook very slowly for 20 minutes. As soon as the meat is cooked, remove it from the saucepan, leaving the juices therein. Put the meat through the fine blade of the meat grinder together with half the ham and half the Gruyère. Put this ground mixture in a small mixing bowl and mix together with the egg, half the grated Parmesan, 2 tablespoons of white sauce, and a generous grating of nutmeg. Remove the mushrooms from the saucepan. Add the cut-up, peeled tomatoes, sliced onion, salt, and pepper to the juices left in the saucepan and cook over low heat for 20 minutes, stirring from time to time. Make the cannelloni, following the same procedure as for Cannelloni with Mushrooms (see Index). Finely dice the mushrooms, the ham, and the Gruyère, and mix with a generous pinch of pepper and 1 tablespoon grated Parmesan. Mix well and reserve for later use. Pass the tomato sauce through a food mill or blend in a blender and mix with the white sauce. Spread a half-inch layer of this sauce on the bottom of an ovenproof dish. Arrange the cannelloni side by side in the dish. Sprinkle the diced ham-mushroom-cheese mixture over all and cover with the rest of the sauce. Dust with the rest of the grated Parmesan and bake in a 375° oven for 15 to 20 minutes. Allow to cool for 5 minutes after removing from the oven and serve on preheated plates. Serves 4.

CANNELLONI SUPREME
(Cannelloni Supremi)

One evening in 1972 my wife and I dined at Gigi Fazi, one of the better known hosteria of Rome. After dinner Gigi chatted with us and gave me this recipe to pass on to you.

Cooking time: 60 minutes

Pasta dough	½ cup cottage cheese
10 tablespoons butter	1 cup diced Swiss cheese
10 tablespoons flour	4 eggs
5 cups milk	Nutmeg to taste
2 chicken bouillon cubes	⅔ cup grated Cheddar cheese
Salt and white pepper to taste	1⅓ cups grated Parmesan
2½ cups chopped cooked ham	cheese
1½ cups chopped mortadella sausage	2 egg yolks

Make the pasta as instructed in the recipe for Lasagne Bolognese Style (see Index). Make a Béchamel Sauce (see Index) with the butter, the flour, and the milk. Add to the white sauce 2 bouillon cubes dissolved in 1 cup of hot water, salt, and pepper. Stir well and simmer over very low heat (or in a double boiler) for 25 minutes, stirring often. In the meantime, finely chop the ham, the mortadella, the cottage cheese, and the Swiss cheese. Put in a mixing bowl with 2 eggs, a generous grating of nutmeg, and salt and pepper. Also add half the grated Cheddar and Parmesan and 4 tablespoons of white sauce. Mix well. Add 1 or 2 more tablespoons white sauce if you find the mixture is not soft enough. Cut the pasta

into 2½"×4" rectangles and make the cannelloni as instructed in the recipe Cannelloni with Mushrooms (see Index). Remove the white sauce from the fire. Allow to cool. In a small bowl, beat the 2 whole eggs and the 2 egg yolks with a wire whisk. Add a little at a time to the cooled white sauce, beating continuously until almost stiff. Pour half of this sauce into a well-buttered ovenproof dish. Even it off and lay the cannelloni side by side in the dish. Sprinkle with half the remaining grated Cheddar and Parmesan mixed together. Cover with the rest of the white sauce and spread the rest of the cheese on top. Bake in a 375° oven for 15 to 20 minutes. Allow to cool for 2 minutes before serving. Serve on preheated plates.
Variation: Ricotta may be substituted for the cottage cheese.
Serves 4.

CANNELLONI WITH SAUSAGE
(*Cannelloni alle Salcicce*)

Cooking time: 80 minutes

Pasta dough	Salt and pepper to taste
¾ pound Italian sausages	Nutmeg to taste
4 slices lean bacon	2 large ripe tomatoes
1 medium onion	2 bay leaves
4 tablespoons oil	¼ pound cooked salami
½ cup white wine	½ cup cottage cheese
1 bouillon cube	1 egg
6 tablespoons butter	1⅓ cups grated Parmesan
8 tablespoons flour	cheese
5 cups milk	

Preheat oven to 375° F.

Make the pasta as instructed in the recipe for Lasagne Bolognese Style (see Index). Boil the sausages in water for 5 minutes. Remove from fire. Slice the bacon and the onion, and sauté in the oil in a saucepan. Remove skins from sausages and add to the saucepan. Sauté until well browned. Add the white wine and allow to evaporate. Dissolve the bouillon cube in 1 cup of hot water, cover the saucepan, and simmer over moderate heat for 30 minutes. In the meantime, in a small saucepan, make a Béchamel Sauce (see Index) with the butter, flour, milk, salt and pepper, and nutmeg. Cook over very

low heat for 20 minutes, stirring often. As soon as the sausages
are cooked and the juices in the saucepan almost completely evaporated, remove the sausages and the bacon with a slotted spoon
and set aside. Add the cut-up tomatoes, salt and pepper, and bay
leaves to the saucepan, and cook for 25 minutes over moderate heat.
Set aside 2 sausages for use later and pass the other sausages, the
bacon, the cooked salami and the cottage cheese through the finest
blade of a meat chopper. To this ground mixture add the egg,
2 tablespoons of white sauce, and half the grated Parmesan and
mix well. Pass the whole mixture through the meat chopper again so
as to form a blended paste. Proceed to make the cannelloni as
described in Cannelloni with Mushrooms (see Index). Pass the
tomato sauce through a food mill or blend in a blender. Thinly slice
the 2 remaining sausages and add to the puréed tomato sauce. Mix
with the white sauce. Spread half of this sauce evenly in a buttered
ovenproof baking dish. Arrange the cannelloni side by side on the
sauce. Sprinkle half the remaining grated Parmesan over all. Cover
with the rest of the sauce and dust with the rest of the grated
Parmesan. Bake in a moderate oven for 15 minutes. Allow to cool
for 5 minutes before serving. Serves 4.

CANNELLONI FLORENTINE STYLE
(*Cannelloni alla Florentina*)

Cooking time: 70 minutes

Pasta dough	5 cups milk
½ pound pork (fatty)	Nutmeg to taste
2 tablespoons oil	2 large ripe tomatoes
¼ pound turkey breast	¼ pound mushrooms
Salt and pepper to taste	⅓ cup cottage cheese
1 chicken bouillon cube	¼ pound soft mild cheese
½ cup butter	1 egg
8 tablespoons flour	1 cup grated Parmesan cheese

Preheat oven to 375° F.

Prepare the pasta dough as instructed for Lasagne Bolognese
Style (see Index). Sauté the sliced pork in the oil in a saucepan
until brown. Add the sliced turkey breast and continue to brown.
Add salt and pepper. Dissolve the chicken bouillon cube in 1 cup

of hot water and add. Cover and simmer for 30 minutes. In the meantime, make a Béchamel Sauce (see Index) with the butter, flour, milk, salt and pepper, and nutmeg, and cook for 20 minutes over very low heat, stirring often. As soon as the meats are cooked and their juices have almost completely evaporated, remove the meats with a slotted spoon and to the same saucepan add the cut-up tomatoes, salt and pepper, and the whole mushrooms. Cook for 20 minutes over moderate heat. Put the meats through the meat chopper together with the cottage cheese and the soft mild cheese. Put this mixture in a mixing bowl and add the egg, half the grated Parmesan and a generous grating of nutmeg. Mix everything well and pass through the meat chopper again so that a smooth paste results. Put the tomato sauce through a food mill or blend in a blender, after having removed the mushrooms and set them aside for use later. Make the cannelloni with the same procedures described in Cannelloni with Mushrooms (see Index). Spread half the white sauce on the bottom of a buttered ovenproof baking dish. Lay the cannelloni carefully side by side on the white sauce. Slice the mushrooms and scatter evenly over the cannelloni. Spoon half the tomato sauce here and there over the cannelloni and cover with the rest of the white sauce. Drizzle the rest of the tomato sauce over the white sauce, forming stripes. Sprinkle with the rest of the Parmesan and bake in a 375° oven for 15 to 20 minutes. Cool for 3 minutes before serving on heated plates. Serves 4.

TRICOLOR CANNELLONI
(*Cannelloni Tri-colore*)

Cooking time: 80 minutes

Pasta dough	8 tablespoons flour
4 slices lean bacon	5 cups milk
1 medium onion	Nutmeg to taste
2 tablespoons oil	2 medium-size ripe tomatoes
½ pound turkey breast	¼ pound Edam cheese
Salt and pepper to taste	¼ pound mortadella sausage
1 chicken bouillon cube	1⅓ cups grated Parmesan
1 pound fresh spinach	cheese
⅔ cup butter	2 eggs

Preheat oven to 375° F.

Make and roll the pasta as instructed for Lasagne Bolognese Style (see Index). Sauté the thinly sliced bacon and onion together in the oil in a saucepan until well browned. Add the sliced turkey breast, salt, and pepper, and brown. Add the chicken bouillon cube dissolved in 1 cup of hot water, cover the saucepan, and cook for 25 minutes over moderate heat. In the meantime, wash the spinach and cook in very little boiling water for about 8 minutes. Drain very well and squeeze out as much moisture as possible by pressing down in a sieve or colander. Make a Béchamel Sauce (see Index) with the butter, flour, milk, salt and pepper, and nutmeg, and cook over very low heat for 20 minutes. Put the spinach through the fine blade of a food mill or blend in a blender. As soon as the turkey breast and bacon are cooked, remove from the saucepan with a slotted spoon and to the juices remaining in the saucepan add the cut-up tomatoes, salt and pepper, and ½ cup water. Cook for 25 minutes. Through the finest blade of the meat grinder pass the cooked turkey and bacon, the Edam cheese, the mortadella, and 2 tablespoons of grated Parmesan. Mix these ground ingredients with 2 eggs and 1 tablespoon of white sauce. Put through the meat grinder again. Make the cannelloni with the same procedure described in Cannelloni with Mushrooms (see Index). Put the puréed spinach in a dish with salt and pepper, 1 tablespoon of white sauce and ½ tablespoon of grated Parmesan. Mix well. Pass the tomato sauce through the food mill or blend in a blender. Spread half the white sauce evenly on the bottom of a buttered ovenproof dish. Arrange the cannelloni side by side on the white sauce. Spread half the spinach mixture along the right side of the row of cannelloni and half the tomato sauce along the left side, leaving the center white. Very carefully pour the rest of the white sauce over all, being very careful not to spread the colors. Spread the rest of the spinach mixture on the right side very carefully and the rest of the tomato sauce on the left side, leaving the center white. Sprinkle with the rest of the grated Parmesan and bake for 12 minutes in a 375° oven. Cool for 4 minutes before serving on heated plates. Serves 4.

CANNELLONI VENETIAN STYLE
(*Cannelloni alla Veneziana*)

This is a specialty of the restaurant La caravella of Venice.

Cooking time: 80 minutes

Pasta dough	3 tablespoons chopped parsley
4 slices lean bacon	1⅔ cups grated Parmesan
1 small onion	cheese
4 tablespoons oil	¼ pound cooked ham
¼ cup tomato paste	5 tablespoons butter
1 bouillon cube	5 tablespoons flour
Salt and pepper to taste	5 cups milk
6 eggs	Nutmeg to taste

Preheat oven to 375° F.

Make the pasta dough and roll it as instructed for Lasagne Bolognese Style (see Index). Sauté the thinly sliced bacon and the finely chopped onion in 2 tablespoons of oil in a saucepan until golden. Add the tomato paste and stir. Add the bouillon cube dissolved in 1 cup of hot water. Add salt and pepper. Simmer for 25 minutes. In the meantime, beat well together in a mixing bowl 5 eggs, salt and pepper, parsley, and 2 tablespoons of grated Parmesan. Make a thin omelet by cooking in a large skillet with the remaining 2 tablespoons of oil. If you don't have a large skillet make 2 or 3 smaller omelets. Put the omelet on a bread board and chop finely. Also finely chop the ham and the bacon, which you have removed from the saucepan. Put all these chopped ingredients in a mixing bowl. Add 1 egg and half the remaining grated Parmesan. Make a Béchamel Sauce (see Index) with the butter, flour, milk, salt and pepper, and nutmeg, and cook very slowly for 15 minutes, stirring often. Add 2 tablespoons of white sauce to the chopped ingredients, and mix. If the mixture does not seem to hold together enough, add a little more white sauce. Mix very well. Make the cannelloni using the same procedure described in Cannelloni with Mushrooms (see Index). Spread half the white sauce evenly on the bottom of a buttered baking dish. Arrange the cannelloni side by side on the white sauce. Sprinkle half the remaining grated

Parmesan over all. Pour on the rest of the white sauce and spread evenly. Dust with the rest of the Parmesan and bake in a 375° oven for 15 minutes. Serves 4.

RAVIOLI WITH RICOTTA
(*Ravioli di Ricotta*)

Cooking time: 20 minutes

Pasta dough	2 tablespoons chopped parsley
1 cup ricotta cheese (or cottage cheese)	Salt and white pepper to taste
	Nutmeg
2 cups grated Parmesan cheese	½ cup heavy cream
3 eggs	¼ pound butter

Prepare the pasta dough as directed in Lasagne Bolognese Style (see Index). Pass the ricotta through the fine blade of a food mill into a mixing bowl. Mix with half the grated Parmesan, 2 eggs, parsley, salt and pepper, nutmeg, and ¼ cup of cream. Mix well until a smooth paste results. In a cup beat together 1 egg and ¼ cup water. Using a pastry brush, moisten the dough with this mixture and make the ravioli in the same manner described in Spinach Ravioli (see Index). Cook the ravioli in abundant boiling salted water for 8 minutes. Drain well and put in a preheated serving dish. Add all the butter and the rest of the cream. Mix carefully in order not to break the ravioli. Sprinkle generously with the rest of the Parmesan. Serves 4.

MEAT RAVIOLI TORTONESE
(*Ravioli di Carne alla Tortonese*)

Cooking time: 50 minutes

Pasta dough	1 bouillon cube
2 slices bacon	¼ pound mortadella sausage
2 tablespoons oil	2 eggs
½ pound veal	2 cups grated Parmesan cheese
Salt and pepper to taste	6 tablespoons butter
¼ cup white wine	

Prepare the pasta dough as directed in Lasagne Bolognese Style (see Index). Sauté the thinly sliced bacon in the oil in a saucepan. When slightly golden, add the thinly sliced veal, salt, and pepper. Brown over a high flame for 5 minutes, then add the white wine. Stir for 2 minutes, allowing the wine to evaporate. Add the bouillon cube dissolved in 1 cup of hot water. Simmer for 40 minutes over low heat. When the meat and bacon are cooked and the juices almost completely evaporated, remove the meat from the saucepan. Cool the meat a little, then pass through the meat chopper together with the mortadella. Mix with 1 egg and half the grated Parmesan and put through the meat chopper again. Beat 1 egg with ¼ cup water and with a pastry brush moisten the dough you have prepared. Make the ravioli, following the same procedure described in Spinach Ravioli (see Index). Cook in abundant boiling salted water for 8 minutes. Drain well and put in a preheated serving dish. Add the butter and remaining Parmesan, mix carefully, and serve.

Variation: These ravioli are excellent with Italian Ragù (see Index) substituted for the butter. Serves 4.

HOLIDAY RAVIOLI
(*Ravioli per Giorni di Festa*)

Cooking time: 40 minutes

Pasta dough	¼ pound mortadella sausage
4 slices lean bacon	¼ pound (or slightly less)
¼ pound chicken breast	Gruyère cheese
1 small onion	2 eggs
3 tablespoons oil	1⅓ cups grated Parmesan
Salt and pepper to taste	cheese
1 chicken bouillon cube	4 tablespoons butter
2 large ripe tomatoes	
3 basil leaves (or ¼ teaspoon dried)	

Make the pasta dough as directed in Lasagne Bolognese Style (see Index). Sauté the sliced bacon and chicken breast with the finely chopped onion in the oil in a saucepan. Add salt and pepper. When barely golden add 1 cup water in which you have dissolved the bouillon cube. Cook over high heat for 10 minutes. When the juices are almost completely evaporated, remove the bacon and the chicken and set aside for use later. To the same saucepan add the cut-up, peeled tomatoes, the basil, salt and pepper, and ½ cup of hot water. Stir. Cook over moderate heat for 30 minutes. Pass the cooked bacon and chicken, the mortadella, and the Gruyère cheese through the finest blade of the meat chopper. Mix with 1 egg and half the grated Parmesan. Put through the meat chopper again. Beat 1 egg with ¼ cup water and moisten the dough with a pastry brush dipped in this mixture. Make the ravioli following the same procedure described in Spinach Ravioli (see Index). Put the tomato sauce through a food mill or blend in a blender. Cook the ravioli in abundant boiling salted water for 8 minutes. Drain carefully and put in a preheated serving dish. Add the butter in dabs, half the remaining grated Parmesan, and all the tomato sauce. Mix carefully in order not to break the ravioli. Serve with the rest of the Parmesan sprinkled on top. Serves 4.

RAVIOLI WITH CREAM
(*Ravioli alla Crema*)

Cooking time: 70 minutes

Pasta dough	3 tablespoons flour
½ pound turkey breast	⅓ cup milk
4 slices lean bacon	¼ pound Gruyère cheese
1 small onion	2 eggs
3 tablespoons oil	Nutmeg
Salt and white pepper to taste	1⅓ cups grated Parmesan
2 bouillon cubes	cheese
4 tablespoons butter	½ cup heavy cream

Make and roll the pasta dough as directed in Lasagne Bolognese Style (see Index). Thinly slice the turkey. Sauté the sliced bacon and thinly sliced onion in the oil in a saucepan. When golden add the turkey and brown. Add salt and pepper. Add the bouillon cubes dissolved in ½ cup of hot water. Cover the saucepan and simmer for 25 minutes over moderate heat. In the meantime, in a small saucepan, make a Béchamel Sauce (see Index) with the butter, flour, milk, salt, and white pepper. Cook very slowly for 10 minutes, stirring often. Remove the turkey and bacon from the other saucepan. Put them through a meat chopper together with the Gruyère cheese. Mix with 1 egg, nutmeg, and 1 tablespoon of grated Parmesan. Put the whole mixture through a meat chopper again in order to have a smooth paste. Beat 1 egg with 1 tablespoon of water and moisten the rolled-out dough with a pastry brush dipped in this mixture. Make the ravioli following the procedure described in Spinach Ravioli (see Index). Add the white sauce to the juices remaining in the saucepan and stir until well mixed. Cook the ravioli in abundant boiling salted water for 8 minutes. Drain and put in a preheated serving dish. Add the white sauce and half the remaining grated Parmesan. Mix carefully in order not to break the ravioli. Add the cream and mix again. Serve with the rest of the cheese sprinkled on top. Serves 4.

SPINACH RAVIOLI
(*Ravioli di Spinaci*)

This recipe was given to me by the Italian actor Marcello Mastroiani. It is one of his favorites.

Cooking time: 40 minutes

Pasta dough
1 pound spinach
1¼ cups ricotta cheese (or cottage cheese)
2 eggs
½ cup heavy cream

1⅔ cups grated Parmesan cheese
Salt and white pepper to taste
Nutmeg to taste
6 tablespoons butter

Prepare the pasta dough as instructed in Lasagne Bolognese Style (see Index), but roll it just a little thinner. Wash the spinach and cook in very little water for 10 minutes. Remove from pot with a sieve (in order that any possible grains of sand remain in the bottom of the pot) and squeeze as dry as possible. Put the spinach through the fine blade of a food mill or blend in a blender. Put in a bowl. Put the ricotta through the same food mill and add to the bowl. Add 1 egg, cream, half the grated Parmesan, salt and white pepper, and nutmeg. Beat the other egg in a cup with 1 tablespoon of water. Brush this mixture on the rolled-out dough with a pastry brush. With the ricotta-spinach mixture make little balls about the size of a small walnut and arrange in a row, an inch apart, on a strip of dough. Cover with another strip of dough. Press down on all sides of the little mounds with your fingers. Cut with a pastry cutter or a sharp knife, making sure each of the ravioli is firmly sealed on all sides. Boil in abundant boiling salted water for 8 minutes. Drain and serve with butter and the rest of the Parmesan sprinkled on top.

Variation: These ravioli are also delicious with Italian Ragù (see Index). Serves 4.

TORTELLINI WITH PEAS AND MUSHROOMS
(*Tortellini ai Funghi e Piselli*)

Cooking time: 40 minutes

3 slices lean bacon	1 clove garlic
1 small onion	1 tablespoon flour
3 tablespoons oil	1 tablespoon chopped parsley
Salt and pepper to taste	1 bouillon cube
¾ cup shelled green peas	1 pound tortellini
¼ pound mushrooms	4 tablespoons butter
1 tablespoon lemon juice	1 cup grated Parmesan cheese

Cut the bacon and the onion into julienne strips and sauté in half the oil in a saucepan. When barely golden add 1 cup of hot water, salt, and pepper, and bring to a boil. Add the peas and continue cooking until tender. In the meantime, wash, clean, and thinly slice the mushrooms and put in a dish with the lemon juice. Mix. In another saucepan, sauté the finely chopped garlic in the rest of the oil. When almost golden, add the mushrooms and lemon juice, salt and pepper. Stir and cook over moderate heat until the liquids have evaporated. Add the flour and parsley, and stir. Add the bouillon cube dissolved in ¾ cup of hot water and bring to a boil. Cook for 15 minutes over moderate heat. Cook the tortellini in abundant boiling salted water for 10 to 12 minutes. Drain and put in a preheated serving dish in which you have already put the peas and bacon and their juices. Add the butter in dabs and mix. Add the mushroom sauce and half the grated Parmesan and mix again. Serve with the rest of the Parmesan dusted on top. Serves 4.

TORTELLINI WITH CREAM
(*Tortellini alla Panna*)

Cooking time: 20 minutes

1 pound tortellini	Salt and white pepper to taste
4 tablespoons butter	1 egg yolk
1 tablespoon flour	1 cup grated Cheddar cheese
1 chicken bouillon cube	½ cup heavy cream

Put the tortellini in a large pot of boiling salted water. When the water comes to a boil again regulate the heat so that the tortellini do not boil too rapidly. Cook until done, approximately 10 to 12 minutes. In the meantime, melt the butter in a small saucepan. Add the flour and stir. Add ½ cup of hot water in which the bouillon cube has been dissolved, salt and pepper. Cook continuously over very low heat for 5 minutes. Just before draining the tortellini, remove this sauce from the fire and when it has cooled a little add the egg yolk and stir until well mixed. Drain the tortellini and put in a preheated serving dish. Add the white sauce, half the grated cheese and mix. Add the cream and mix again. Serve with the rest of the cheese dusted on top. Serves 4.

TORTELLINI WITH BUTTER AND TOMATO SAUCE
(*Tortellini con Burro e Pomodoro*)

Cooking time: 30 minutes

2 large ripe tomatoes	½ bouillon cube
1 medium onion	Salt and pepper to taste
3 tablespoons oil	1 pound tortellini
1 tablespoon flour	4 tablespoons butter
4 basil leaves (or ¼ teaspoon dried)	1 cup grated Parmesan cheese

Peel the tomatoes and reserve for later use. Finely chop the onion and sauté in the oil in a saucepan until almost golden. Add the flour and stir. Add the finely chopped tomato with the chopped basil, and cook over high heat for 2 minutes, stirring constantly. Add the half bouillon cube dissolved in ½ cup of hot water, salt, and pepper, and cook over moderate heat for 25 minutes more. When the sauce is almost ready, cook the tortellini in boiling salted water for 10 minutes. Water must not boil too rapidly or tortellini will break. Drain and put in a preheated serving dish. Add the butter in dabs, all the sauce, and half the grated cheese. Mix thoroughly but carefully in order not to break the pasta. Serve with the rest of the cheese sprinkled on top. Serves 4.

TORTELLINI WITH CHICKEN SAUCE
(*Tortellini al Sugo di Pollo*)

Cooking time: 50 minutes

2 slices bacon	2 or 3 medium ripe tomatoes
3 tablespoons oil	Salt and pepper to taste
1 medium onion	3 basil leaves
1 2½-pound chicken	1 chicken bouillon cube
2 tablespoons flour	1 pound tortellini
1 clove garlic	1 cup grated Cheddar cheese
½ cup white wine	

Cut the bacon into very thin spaghetti-like strips and sauté in the oil in a saucepan with the thinly sliced onion. Cut the chicken into 8 pieces. Also use the neck. Flour each piece and brown in the saucepan with the bacon and the onion. Be careful not to allow the onion to brown too much and be sure to stir often. If there is any flour left, add it together with the unpeeled clove of garlic. Add the wine and stir. When half has evaporated, add the cut-up tomatoes, salt and pepper, and the basil. Stir and cook over high heat for 3 minutes. Add the bouillon cube dissolved in 1 cup of hot water and bring to a boil. Lower heat and cook over moderate heat for 40 minutes more. Test the chicken for doneness from time to time. When it is cooked, remove from the saucepan with a fork, but continue to cook the sauce. When the 40 minutes are almost up, cook the tortellini in abundant boiling salted water for 10 to 12 minutes. Remove the skin and meat from the neck and return to the sauce. Pass the entire contents of the saucepan through a food mill or blend in a blender. Drain the tortellini and put in a preheated serving dish. Add three fourths of the sauce and half the grated cheese. Mix and serve with the rest of the cheese dusted on top. Serve the chicken as a second course with a little sauce spooned over each piece and accompanied by whatever vegetable you desire. Serves 4.

TORTELLINI ITALIAN STYLE
(*Tortellini all'Italiana*)

Cooking time: 60 minutes

3 slices bacon	Salt and pepper to taste
½ pound (or slightly less) veal	1 bay leaf
1 medium onion	2 medium-size ripe tomatoes
3 tablespoons oil	1 bouillon cube
1 stalk celery	1 pound tortellini
1 carrot	1 cup grated Parmesan cheese

Thinly slice the bacon, the veal, and the onion, and sauté in the oil in a saucepan. Add the thinly sliced celery, carrot, salt and pepper, and bay leaf, and continue to brown for 2 minutes. Add the cut-up tomatoes and cook over high heat for 5 minutes. Add the bouillon cube dissolved in 1 cup of hot water, stir, and bring to a boil. Lower heat, cover, and simmer for 50 minutes more. Ten minutes before the sauce is ready, cook the tortellini in boiling salted water for 10 to 12 minutes. In the meantime, pass the sauce (including the meats) through the medium blade of a food mill or blend in a blender. Drain the cooked tortellini and put in a preheated serving bowl. Add all the sauce and half the grated Parmesan and mix. Serve with the rest of the cheese sprinkled on top.
Serves 4.

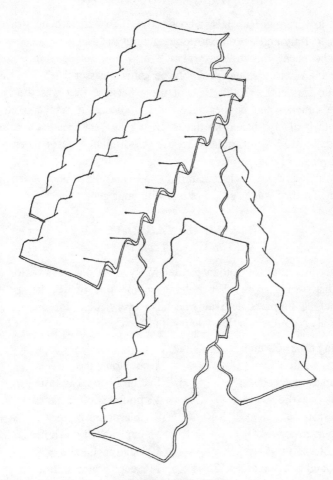

CHAPTER VI
Oven Pasta

Practically all types of pasta may be baked in the oven; that is why in this chapter you will find recipes for baked rigatoni, ditali, farfalle, macaroni, and, of course, lasagne, which is the pasta par excellence for cooking in this manner.

The French writer François Rabelais (1494–1553) invented a character whom he called Gargantua, a giant and a great eater of pasta, just as was Rabelais, who discovered baked lasagne while on a visit to Italy and ate an enormous quantity of it.

In the pages that follow you will also find recipes for timballi, which in America would probably be called "casseroles." The name timballo was given to this type of pasta because that was the name of the cone-shaped copper receptacle in which it was cooked. A timballo is always baked so that a crust may be formed. Of course, nowadays you are not obliged to use the original type of receptacle. Any ovenproof dish or pan may be used.

If you follow the recipes carefully, you may have no doubt whatsoever that they will be sure-fire hits with your guests.

TIMBALE OF TAGLIATELLE
(*Timballo di Tagliatelle*)

I met in Rome the Italian painter Maryini, who is a bachelor and does his own cooking. When he gave me this recipe, he assured me that he prepared and ate this dish every night for one month. He highly recommends that you try it at least once.

Cooking time: 60 minutes

1 large onion	1 bouillon cube
4 tablespoons oil	Salt and pepper to taste
1 clove garlic	½ pound cooked ham
1 carrot	4 tablespoons butter
1 stalk celery	½ cup shelled green peas
4 tablespoons flour	1 pound tagliatelle
1 pound ripe tomatoes (3 medium)	1¼ cups grated Parmesan cheese
3 basil leaves (or ¼ teaspoon dried)	

Preheat oven to 350° F.

Sauté the coarsely chopped onion in the oil in a saucepan. Add the unpeeled clove of garlic, the sliced carrot, and celery, and sauté for 1 minute more. Add the flour and stir until well blended. Add the cut-up tomatoes and the basil leaves. Dissolve the bouillon cube in 1 cup of hot water and add to the saucepan. Add salt and pepper. Stir. Cook over moderate heat for 40 minutes. Cut the ham into julienne strips and sauté in the butter in a small skillet. Add the cooked, drained peas, add very little salt (the ham is salty) and pepper, and sauté for 1 minute more. When the sauce has cooked for almost 60 minutes, cook the tagliatelle in abundant boiling salted water for 6 minutes. In the meantime, put the sauce through the medium blade of a food mill or blend in a blender. Add the ham and peas to the sauce and return to the heat, bringing to a boil again. Drain the cooked pasta and put in a buttered ovenproof dish. Add all the sauce and half the Parmesan. Mix well and spread evenly. Dust with the rest of the Parmesan and bake in a moderate oven for 8 minutes. Allow to cool for 4 minutes before serving. Serves 6.

TIMBALE OF FETTUCCINE
(*Timballo di Fettuccine*)

Cooking time: 80 minutes

2½ tablespoons dried mushrooms (or 1 3-ounce can chopped)	2 bouillon cubes
	Salt and pepper to taste
	¾ cup shelled green peas
1 large onion	4 tablespoons butter
3 tablespoons oil	3 eggs
½ pound pork (fatty)	1¼ cups grated Parmesan
3 tablespoons flour	cheese
½ cup white wine	1 pound fettuccine
¼ cup tomato paste	

Preheat oven to 350° F.

Put the dried mushrooms to soak in 1 cup of hot water. Slice the onion very thinly and sauté in the oil in a saucepan over low heat. Add the chopped pork and brown over moderate heat until golden. Add the flour and stir until blended. Pour in the white wine and allow half to evaporate. Add the tomato paste, stir for 1 minute, and add the mushrooms, which have been squeezed as dry as possible and chopped. Stir. Dissolve the bouillon cubes in 2 cups of hot water and add. Add salt and pepper. Cook over moderate heat for 60 minutes. In a small saucepan sauté the cooked (or canned) peas in the butter with salt and pepper. Beat the eggs in a small bowl with a pinch of pepper and 2 teaspoons of grated Parmesan. When the sauce is almost ready, cook the fettuccine in boiling salted water for 6 minutes. Taste the sauce for salt and add the peas to it, together with all the melted butter. Drain the fettuccine and put in a buttered baking dish. Add all the sauce and half the remaining Parmesan and mix. Add the beaten eggs and mix well. Spread evenly and dust with the rest of the Parmesan. Bake in a moderate oven for 8 minutes. Allow to cool a few minutes before serving. Serves 4.

PENNE ALLA BARZINI, OVEN-BAKED
(Penne alla Barzini)

This dish is a favorite of the famous author-journalist Luigi Barzini, who wrote the best-seller *The Italians.*

Cooking time: 50 minutes

8 small tomatoes	3 tablespoons olive oil
½ pound mozzarella cheese	1 pound penne
Salt and pepper to taste	6 tablespoons butter
4 basil leaves (or ¼ teaspoon dried)	1 cup grated Parmesan cheese

Preheat oven to 350° F.

Plunge the tomatoes into boiling water for 1 minute. Peel and put immediately in ice water. Remove from the water and, starting from the stem end, remove the pulp with a knife or small scoop, being careful not to break them. Fill with the mozzarella, which has been chopped and mixed with salt and pepper and the chopped basil leaves. Put in a baking dish, drizzle the olive oil evenly over them, and bake in a 350° oven for 20 minutes. In the meantime, cook the penne in abundant boiling salted water for 10 minutes, drain, and turn onto a greased baking dish. Mix with the butter and the grated cheese. Arrange the cooked tomatoes over the pasta and bake for a few minutes. Serve very hot. Serves 4.

TIMBALE OF LASAGNETTE WITH EGGS
(*Timballo di Lasagnette alle Uova*)

Cooking time: 20 minutes

1 pound lasagnette	2 chicken bouillon cubes
¼ pound butter	4 eggs
Salt and pepper to taste	1 cup grated Parmesan cheese

Preheat oven to 350° F.

Cook the lasagnette in boiling salted water for 8 minutes. Drain and put in a buttered baking dish. Add the butter in dabs and a pinch of pepper and salt and mix. Dissolve the bouillon cubes in 1 cup of hot water and pour over the pasta. Move the dish around a bit in order to distribute the liquid evenly. Break an egg in each corner of the dish and sprinkle the grated cheese over all. Bake in a 350° oven for 8 minutes. If the pasta seems too moist, allow it to rest a few minutes, then serve. Serves 4.

TIMBALE OF MEZZEZITE, FLORENTINE STYLE
(*Timballo di Mezzezite alla Fiorentina*)

Cooking time: 40 minutes

1 medium onion	6 tablespoons butter
4 tablespoons oil	5 tablespoons flour
1½ pounds peeled tomatoes	2 cups milk
(5 medium)	1 pound mezzezite
3 basil leaves (or ¼ teaspoon	1 cup grated Parmesan cheese
dried)	¼ pound fontina cheese (or
Salt and pepper to taste	American cheese)

Preheat oven to 350° F.

Sauté the finely chopped onion in the oil in a saucepan. Add the chopped tomatoes with all their juice, the basil, salt and pepper. Stir and cook over moderate heat until the rest of the timballo is ready. Make a Béchamel Sauce (see Index) with the butter, flour, milk, salt and pepper. Cook the mezzezite in boiling salted water for 10 minutes. Drain and put back into the pot in which they were cooked. Add all the tomato sauce, the béchamel, and half the

Parmesan. Mix well and put in a buttered baking dish. Spread evenly and top with thin slices of fontina. Dust with the rest of the Parmesan. Bake in a 350° oven for 15 minutes. Allow to cool for 5 minutes before serving. Serves 4.

TIMBALE OF SWEET BUCATINI
(*Timballo di Bucatini Dolci*)

This recipe may surprise you because of the sugar and cinnamon called for in the ingredients. My wife often prepares this dish for dinner when we are in the mood for something delicate and light tasting. She suggests that you serve grated carrots with lemon dressing following the bucatini.

Cooking time: 70 minutes

Meat Ragù, white (see Index)	½ cup sugar
1 pound bucatini	¼ teaspoon cinnamon
4 tablespoons butter	⅔ cup grated Gruyère cheese
1 cup grated Parmesan cheese	

Preheat oven to 350° F.

Prepare the ragù as instructed. Cook the bucatini in abundant boiling salted water for 6 minutes. Drain and mix with dabs of butter and half the grated Parmesan. Combine the sugar and cinnamon and add to the pasta. Grease an ovenproof dish and spread half the bucatini evenly in it. Dust with the rest of the Parmesan and the Gruyère, leaving a tablespoon or two to sprinkle on top later. Remove the meat from the ragù with a slotted spoon and spread over the bucatini. Cover with the rest of the bucatini, spread evenly, and drizzle the sauce (ragù) over all. Dust with the remaining grated cheese and bake in a 350° oven for 5 minutes. Allow to cool for 5 minutes before serving. Serves 6.

TIMBALE OF DITALONI
(*Timballo di Ditaloni*)

Cooking time: 20 minutes

2 cups milk

1 pound ditaloni

6 tablespoons butter

1¼ cups grated Gruyère cheese

2 eggs

Salt and white pepper to taste

Preheat oven to 350° F.

Boil the milk and set aside to cool. Cook the ditaloni in abundant boiling salted water for 10 minutes. Drain and put in a buttered baking dish. Add dabs of butter and half the grated cheese. Mix well. Beat the eggs together with salt and a generous pinch of white pepper, mix with the milk, and pour over all. Mix again. Spread the pasta evenly and dust with the rest of the cheese. Bake in a 350° oven for 5 minutes. Serves 6.

TIMBALE OF MEZZEZITE
(*Timballo di Mezzezite*)

Cooking time: 80 minutes

Ragù, Italian style (see Index)

4 tablespoons butter

2 tablespoons flour

2 cups milk

2 tablespoons butter

¼ cup dry bread crumbs

1 pound mezzezite

1½ cups grated Parmesan cheese

Preheat oven to 350° F.

Prepare the ragù as instructed. Prepare a white (béchamel) sauce, using the 4 tablespoons of butter, the flour, and the milk (see Index). Grease an ovenproof baking dish with 2 tablespoons of butter, making sure to use all of it. Dust with the bread crumbs, shaking the pan continuously until all the bread is absorbed, forming a kind of thin crust. Cook the mezzezite in boiling salted water for 10 minutes. Drain and put back in the pot in which they were cooked. Add the ragù, the béchamel, and half the Parmesan. Toss until well mixed. Add to the baking dish by ladlefuls, taking care not to break the "crust." Even off and dust with the rest of the Parmesan. Bake in a moderate oven for 10 minutes. Allow to cool for 3 minutes. With a blade of a knife very carefully loosen the timballo from the sides of the dish. Put a large tray over the dish and turn upside down. Remove dish and you have a lovely crusty timballo to bring to the table. Serves 6.

FARFALLE PIEDMONTESE, OVEN-BAKED
(*Farfalle Piemontese*)

Cooking time: 20 minutes

½ pound (or slightly less) fontina cheese sliced (or American cheese)	2 egg yolks
	¼ pound butter
	Salt and pepper to taste
2 cups milk	½ cup grated Parmesan cheese
1 pound farfalle	1 small truffle (optional)

Preheat oven to 400° F.

Put the sliced cheese in a bowl with the milk and allow to soak for 1 hour before beginning to prepare this dish. Start cooking the farfalle in abundant boiling salted water. While the pasta is cooking, put the fontina in the top of a double boiler with a little of the milk in which it soaked. Add the egg yolks and the butter. Cook over simmering water until the mixture is creamy. Be sure to stir often. Add salt and pepper. Drain the cooked farfalle and mix with the creamy cheese mixture. Put into a buttered ovenproof casserole, dust with the grated Parmesan, and bake in a 400° oven for 10 minutes. If you care to, just before serving sprinkle with a very thinly sliced truffle.

Variation: Arrange the casserole with alternate layers of pasta and mushrooms (6 ounces) sautéed in butter. Serves 6.

FARFALLE BAVARIAN
(*Farfalle alla Bavarese*)

Via Laurina in Rome, located between Piazza di Spagna and Piazza del Popolo, is one of the city's unique streets because you can find every kind of food-shop proprietor from butcher to fresh-pasta maker. I was given this recipe by the owner of the pasta shop where my wife shopped daily for her fresh pasta.

Cooking time: 30 minutes

½ pound Emmentaler cheese	1 cup heavy cream
4 tablespoons butter	⅔ cup grated Gruyère cheese
¼ pound cooked spinach	3 egg yolks
1 pound farfalle	Salt and white pepper to taste

Preheat oven to 400 ° F.

Have the Emmentaler sliced into very thin slices. Butter an oven-proof dish and cover the bottom with a layer of spinach, squeezed as dry as possible. Arrange the slices of cheese on top of the spinach. Cook the farfalle in abundant boiling salted water for 10 minutes. Drain and mix with the cream. Lay over the cheese in the baking dish. Dust with the grated Gruyère. Beat together the egg yolks, salt and white pepper, and pour over all. Bake in a 400° oven for 15 minutes. For an especially attractive presentation, cover the bottom of a round-bottomed casserole with foil. Grease the foil and add the ingredients as described above. When cooked, turn the casserole upside down onto a platter so that you will have a silver half sphere. With scissors, make a crosslike cut in the top and pull back the corners so that they will look like four petals of a flower. Serves 6.

TIMBALE OF WIDE FETTUCCINE
(*Timballo di Fettuccine Larghe*)

Cooking time: 80 minutes

3 tablespoons oil	3 basil leaves (or ¼ teaspoon
3 slices bacon	dried)
1 medium onion	1 bouillon cube
Generous ½ pound lamb	4 tablespoons butter
1 clove garlic	4 tablespoons flour
1 stalk celery	1½ cups milk
2 carrots	1 pound wide fettuccine
Salt and pepper to taste	1¼ cups grated Parmesan
½ cup red wine	cheese
¼ cup tomato paste	
½ pound ripe tomatoes (2	
medium)	

Preheat oven to 350° F.

Sauté in the oil in a saucepan the thinly sliced bacon and onion, the thinly sliced meat, and the unpeeled clove of garlic. When brown, add the thinly sliced celery and carrots, the salt and pepper, and continue to sauté for 2 minutes. Add the red wine, stir, and allow half of it to evaporate. Add the tomato paste and stir for 1 minute, then add the cut-up tomatoes, the basil, and the bouillon cube dissolved in 1½ cups of hot water. Stir well and cook over moderate heat for 60 minutes. In the meantime, make a Béchamel Sauce (see Index) with the butter, flour, and milk and cook over very low heat for 20 minutes. Cook the fettuccine in abundant boiling salted water for 6 minutes. Put the meat and tomato sauce through the medium blade of a food mill or blend in a blender. Drain the fettuccine and return to the pot in which they cooked. Add the two sauces combined together and half the Parmesan. Spread the fettuccine evenly in a buttered baking dish. If there is any sauce left in the bottom of the pot, spoon it up and spread over the fettuccine. Dust with the rest of the Parmesan and bake in a moderate oven for 10 minutes. Allow to cool for 4 minutes before serving. Serves 6.

MACARONI TIMBALE NO. 1
(*Timballo di Maccheroni No. 1*)

Cooking time: 70 minutes

2½ tablespoons dried mushrooms (or ¼ pound fresh)

1 pound ripe tomatoes (3 medium)

½ pound pork (fatty)

1 medium onion

3 tablespoons oil

2 bay leaves

Salt and pepper to taste

1 stalk celery

1 bouillon cube

6 tablespoons butter

4 tablespoons flour

2 cups milk

1 pound macaroni

¼ cup dry bread crumbs

1¼ cups grated Parmesan cheese

Preheat oven to 350° F.

Put the mushrooms to soak in 1 cup of hot water. Pass the peeled tomatoes through the fine blade of a food mill or blend in a blender. Finely grind the pork. Sauté the finely chopped onion in the oil in a saucepan until golden. Add the ground pork, bay leaves, salt

and pepper, and continue to sauté until the meat is browned. Add
the mushrooms, which have been squeezed as dry as possible and
chopped. Also add the chopped celery. Stir for a few minutes, then
add the tomatoes and the bouillon cube dissolved in 1 cup of hot
water. Stir and cook over moderate heat for 50 minutes. In the meantime, make a Béchamel Sauce (see Index) with 4 tablespoons of the
butter, the flour, and the milk. Cook the béchamel for 10 minutes.
When the meat sauce is almost ready, cook the macaroni in abundant
boiling salted water for 10 minutes. Grease an ovenproof baking dish
with the remaining 2 tablespoons butter and dust with the bread
crumbs, making sure to completely coat the sides and bottom of the
dish. Drain the cooked macaroni, add the 2 sauces mixed together
and half the Parmesan. Mix well. Spread evenly in the baking dish,
taking care not to ruin the butter and bread crumb coating. Dust
with the rest of the cheese and bake in a moderate oven for 10
minutes. Allow to cool for 4 minutes before serving. Cut in squares
and serve with a cake server. Serves 6.

MACARONI TIMBALE NO. 2
(Timballo di Maccheroni No. 2)

Cooking time: 70 minutes

1 pound ripe tomatoes (3 medium)
2 cloves garlic
2 basil leaves (or ⅛ teaspoon dried)
1 chicken bouillon cube
½ pound turkey breast
4 tablespoons oil
1 medium onion
¼ pound mushrooms

Salt and pepper to taste
6 tablespoons butter
½ cup flour
2 cups milk
1 pound macaroni
3 tablespoons dry bread crumbs
2 tablespoons chopped parsley
1¼ cups grated Parmesan cheese

Preheat oven to 350° F.

Cut up the tomatoes and put in a saucepan with the garlic and the
basil. Dissolve the bouillon cube in 1 cup of hot water and add.
Bring to a boil and cook for 15 minutes over moderate heat. In the
meantime, slice the turkey breast. Use a meat mallet to pound the
slices as thin as possible. Flour the turkey slices. In another sauce-

pan, brown the floured slices of turkey in hot oil. When browned on both sides, remove from the oil and set aside for use later. Finely chop the onion and sauté it in the oil in the saucepan. Pass the tomatoes through the fine blade of a food mill or blend in a blender. Cut the turkey breasts into julienne strips and add to the saucepan. Stir for 1 minute. Wash and slice the mushrooms, then cut each slice into thin strips and add. Add the blended tomato sauce and salt and pepper, stir and cook over moderate heat for 35 minutes. Make a Béchamel Sauce (see Index) with 4 tablespoons of butter, 4 tablespoons of flour, and the milk. Cook the béchamel for 20 minutes over very low heat. Cook the macaroni in abundant boiling salted water for 10 minutes. In the meantime, butter and dust with bread crumbs an ovenproof baking dish (using the remaining 2 tablespoons of butter). Mix the 2 sauces together with the chopped parsley. Drain the cooked macaroni, mix with the combined sauces and half the Parmesan, and spread out evenly in the baking dish. Dust with the rest of the Parmesan and bake in a moderate oven for 10 minutes. Allow to cool for 4 minutes after removing from the oven. Cut into squares and serve with a pancake turner or cake server. Serves 6.

OVEN-BAKED BUCATINI
(*Bucatini al Forno*)

Cooking time: 50 minutes

Bolognese Sauce (see Index)	4 tablespoons butter
Béchamel (white) Sauce	1 cup heavy cream
1 pound bucatini	1 cup grated Parmesan cheese

Preheat oven to 350° F.

Prepare the Bolognese Sauce as instructed. Also prepare the béchamel sauce (see Index). When the sauce is almost ready, cook the bucatini in abundant boiling salted water for 10 minutes. Drain and mix with the sauce (from which you have removed the bay leaf), the white sauce, the butter, the cream, and half the grated cheese. Toss until well mixed. Put in a buttered baking dish, spread it evenly, and dust with the rest of the cheese. Bake in a moderate oven for 10 minutes. Allow to cool for a few minutes and serve. Serves 6.

TIMBALE, PERUGIA STYLE
(*Timballo alla Perugina*)

Cooking time: 40 minutes

5 tablespoons dried mushrooms (or 1 3- or 4- ounce can chopped)	½ cup tomato paste
	Salt and pepper to taste
	2 tablespoons butter
1 pound pork	4 tablespoons flour
1 small onion	1½ cups milk
4 tablespoons oil	1 pound large bucatini
1 clove garlic	1¼ cups grated Parmesan
3 basil leaves (or ¼ teaspoon dried)	cheese

Preheat oven to 350° F.

Wash the mushrooms well and put in 2 cups of warm water to soak. Reserve this water for later use. Coarsely chop the pork and brown with the finely chopped onion in the oil in a saucepan. Chop very finely the crushed clove of garlic and the basil leaves. Add to the saucepan. Remove the mushrooms from the water and squeeze as dry as possible. (If using canned, reserve liquid and add water to make 1 cup.) Chop and add to the saucepan. Pass the mushroom water through a very fine sieve or cheesecloth to remove any particles of sand. Dilute the tomato paste in this water and add to the sauce. Add salt and pepper. Cook over moderate heat for 25 minutes. Prepare a Béchamel Sauce (see Index) with the butter, flour, and milk. Cook the large bucatini in boiling salted water for 10 minutes. Drain and return to the pot in which they cooked. Add the sauce and the béchamel and half the grated Parmesan. Toss until well mixed. Spread evenly in a buttered ovenproof dish. Dust with the rest of the Parmesan and put in a moderate oven for 12 minutes. Allow to cool for 5 minutes before serving. Serves 6.

BAKED MACARONI ALLA DE ALBA
(*Maccheroni alla de Alba*)

Contessa Anna de Alba of Spain, my sister-in-law, who has been living in Rome for the past seven years, loves Italian food and usually does all of her own cooking. She invented this recipe, which has been a great success with all of her friends, and she was delighted to share it with us.

Cooking time: 45 minutes

3 tablespoons butter	¼ pound ham
1 tablespoon flour	¼ pound chicken breast,
1½ cups milk	cooked
Salt and pepper to taste	1 pound macaroni
¼ pound mushrooms	1 cup grated Parmesan cheese
1 tablespoon chopped truffles	

Preheat oven to 350° F.

Melt 1 tablespoon of the butter in a saucepan over low heat. Add the flour and stir for a minute or so without browning. Remove the saucepan from the fire and add boiling milk gradually, stirring all the time. Add salt and pepper and return to the fire. Cook for 5 minutes. In another saucepan melt 1 tablespoon of butter over low heat. Add the mushrooms, cut into julienne strips, and the chopped truffles, also cut into tiny julienne strips. Add the coarsely chopped ham and chicken breast. Cook for about 20 minutes. Mix the 2 sauces. Cook the macaroni in abundant boiling salted water for 10 minutes. Drain. Butter an ovenproof dish with some of remaining butter. Put in the macaroni and the sauce. Mix. Dust with the grated Parmesan and dot with dabs of butter. Put in a 350° oven for 20 minutes. Serves 6.

DITALONI CASSEROLE
(*Ditaloni al Forno*)

Cooking time: 60 minutes

1 small onion	Salt and white pepper to taste
2 tablespoons oil	1 pound ditaloni
½ pound veal	4 tablespoons butter
1 small carrot	1 cup grated Parmesan cheese
½ stalk celery	
2 basil leaves (or ⅛ teaspoon dried)	

Preheat oven to 350° F.

Thinly slice the onion and sauté in the oil in a saucepan. Add the diced veal and brown for a few minutes. Finely chop together the carrot, celery, and basil. Add to the saucepan together with salt and white pepper. Stir over moderate heat for 3 minutes. Add 2 cups of hot water, stir, and cover the saucepan. Simmer over low heat for 50 minutes. Cook the ditaloni in abundant boiling salted water for 10 minutes. Drain and put in an ovenproof baking dish in which you have put the butter. Mix well. Add the contents of the saucepan and half the grated Parmesan. Mix well. Spread evenly in the dish and dust with the rest of the Parmesan. Bake in a moderate oven until it begins to brown—about 10 minutes. Serves 4.

OVEN-BAKED RIGATONI
(*Rigatoni al Forno*)

Cooking time: 40 minutes

1 medium onion	1 chicken bouillon cube
3 tablespoons oil	1 pound rigatoni
½ pound turkey breast	6 tablespoons butter
Salt and pepper to taste	1⅓ cups grated Parmesan
2 tablespoons flour	cheese
¾ cup tomato paste	

Preheat oven to 350° F.

Finely chop the onion and sauté in the oil in a saucepan. Chop the turkey breast and add when the onion is golden. Add salt and pepper and stir for 3 minutes or until browned. Add the flour and stir for 1 minute. Add the tomato paste and stir for 1 minute more over moderate heat. Dissolve the bouillon cube in 1½ cups of hot water and pour into the saucepan. Stir and cook over moderate heat for 20 minutes. Cook the rigatoni in abundant boiling salted water for 12 minutes. Drain and put in an ovenproof dish. Add the butter in dabs and mix. Add all the sauce and half the grated cheese. Toss until well mixed. Even off and dust with the rest of the grated cheese. Bake in a 350° oven for 10 minutes. Serves 4.

OVEN-BAKED LASAGNE NO. 1
(Pasticcio di Lasagne No. 1)

Cooking time: 50 minutes

1 medium onion	2 tablespoons flour
4 tablespoons oil	⅓ cup white wine
¼ pound pork	⅓ cup tomato paste
¼ pound veal	1 bouillon cube
Salt and pepper to taste	1 pound lasagne
1 bay leaf	4 tablespoons butter
1 stalk celery	1 cup grated Parmesan cheese

Preheat oven to 350° F.

Sauté the finely chopped onion in the oil in a saucepan. Add the finely chopped meats, salt and pepper, and the bay leaf, and brown. When well browned, add the chopped celery and stir. Add the flour and mix well with the other ingredients. Add the white wine, stirring while half of it evaporates. Add the tomato paste. Stir. Dissolve the bouillon cube in 1½ cups of boiling water and pour into the saucepan. Bring to a boil again, then lower the flame to moderate and cook for 25 minutes, stirring from time to time. Cook the lasagne in abundant boiling salted water, being careful to slide the pasta into the water a little at a time in order to prevent the pieces from sticking together. Cook for 10 minutes and drain. Put into an oven-proof baking dish in which you have already melted the butter. Mix well. Add all the sauce and half the cheese and mix again. Dust with the rest of the Parmesan and bake in a moderate oven for 10 minutes. Serves 4.

OVEN-BAKED LASAGNE NO. 2
(*Pasticcio di Lasagne No. 2*)

Cooking time: 30 minutes

5 tablespoons dried mushrooms (or 1 4-ounce can chopped)	Salt and pepper to taste
3 slices bacon	6 eggs
1 medium onion	2 tablespoons chopped parsley
5 tablespoons oil	1⅓ cups grated Parmesan cheese
1 stalk celery	1 pound lasagne
½ cup tomato paste	4 tablespoons butter

Preheat oven to 350° F.

Put the mushrooms to soak in 1½ cups of warm water (making sure to wash them first) and reserve this water for later use. Dice the bacon and sauté the chopped onion in half the oil in a saucepan. Add the chopped celery and stir for 1 minute. Add the tomato paste and stir for 2 minutes over low heat. Remove the mushrooms from the water, squeeze dry, and chop coarsely. (If using canned mushrooms, reserve liquid.) Add to saucepan and stir. Add the water in which the mushrooms were soaking. (Add enough water to liquid from can to make 1 cup.) Add salt and pepper. Stir and cover. Cook over moderate heat for 20 minutes. In the meantime, beat together in a bowl the 6 eggs, the parsley, and 1 tablespoon of the grated Parmesan. With this mixture and the rest of the oil, make some thin omelets in a skillet. Put the omelets on a bread board and cut into half-inch squares. Cook the lasagne in abundant boiling salted water for 10 minutes, slipping them into the water a little at a time. While they are cooking, put the omelet squares in the sauce and stir well, continuing to cook the sauce for a few minutes. Drain the cooked lasagne and put in an ovenproof baking dish in which you have previously melted the butter. Mix. Add the sauce and half the remaining cheese and mix again. Even off the pasta and dust wth the rest of the Parmesan. Bake in a moderate oven for 5 minutes. Serves 4.

STUFFED TAGLIATELLE, BIELLA STYLE
(*Tagliatelle Imbottite alla Biellese*)

Cooking time: 40 minutes

4 eggs
2 slices day-old bread
¼ cup milk
¼ pound ground veal
1 cup grated Parmesan cheese
Salt and white pepper to taste
1 tablespoon flour

2 tablespoons oil
1 pound tagliatelle
6 tablespoons butter
Generous ½ pound mozzarella
cheese
¼ pound dried Italian sausage

Preheat oven to 350° F.

Hard-cook the eggs and set aside. Soak the bread in the milk for a few minutes. Mix the ground veal, the bread, which has been squeezed as dry as possible, ⅓ cup of the Parmesan, salt and pepper. Mix these ingredients until well blended and make meat balls the size of an olive. Roll them in the flour and fry in oil in a skillet over moderate heat until barely golden. Cook the tagliatelle in abundant boiling salted water for 6 minutes. Drain and mix with the butter until well coated. Add half of the remaining Parmesan and mix again. Put half of the tagliatelle in a buttered baking dish, making sure to spread them evenly. Slice the mozzarella, the eggs, and the sausage. Set aside half the mozzarella. Arrange the rest of the mozzarella, the sliced eggs, the sausage, and the meat balls over the tagliatelle. Add the rest of the tagliatelle and spread evenly. Cover with the rest of the mozzarella and the rest of the grated cheese. Bake in a 350° oven for 20 minutes. Serve hot. Serves 6.

TAGLIATELLE PUDDING
(*Dolce di Tagliatelle*)

This recipe is a favorite dish of the Italian boxer Benvenuti, because it's delicious and packed full of energy. So if you or your children seem a little tired lately, why not try this dish.

Cooking time: 20 minutes

6 cups milk	2 tablespoons honey
¼ pound butter	¼ teaspoon salt
2 tablespoons flour	1 pound tagliatelle
½ cup sugar (scant)	¼ teaspoon cinnamon

Preheat oven to 450° F.

Bring the milk to a full boil and allow to cool. Melt the butter in a large saucepan, add the flour, and stir until well blended over a low flame. Add the sugar, honey, and salt. Add the milk gradually, stirring constantly. Bring to a boil. Lower flame to moderate. Add the tagliatelle and cook in this mixture for 7 minutes, stirring constantly. A creamy mixture should result. Spread evenly in a buttered baking dish or casserole. Dust with the cinnamon and bake in a hot (450°) oven for 5 minutes. Allow to cool for a few minutes before serving. This is excellent as a warm or cold dessert.
Serves 6.

BAKED TAGLIATELLE À LA TRAGLIA
(*Tagliatelle Pasticciate alla Traglia*)

Cooking time: 80 minutes

Bolognese Sauce (see Index)	6 tablespoons butter
¼ pound mushrooms	2 eggs, hard-cooked
Salt and pepper to taste	1 cup grated Parmesan cheese
1 pound tagliatelle	

Preheat oven to 350° F.

First of all, prepare the Bolognese sauce. Wash and thinly slice the mushrooms. Cook them in ¼ cup water and 2 tablespoons of sauce, salt and pepper. Cook the tagliatelle in abundant boiling salted water for 6 minutes. Butter an ovenproof dish. Drain the cooked tagliatelle and mix with the butter. Cover the bottom of the baking dish with a ladleful of sauce. Spread one third of the tagliatelle evenly in the dish and sprinkle half of the mushrooms on top. Arrange slices of hard-cooked egg over all this and dust with some of the Parmesan. Repeat this procedure a second time. Cover with the remaining third of the tagliatelle. Spoon the rest of the sauce evenly over all and dust with the remaining Parmesan. Bake in a 350° oven for 15 minutes. It may be served hot or cold. Serves 6.

BAKED TAGLIATELLE PIEDMONT
(*Tagliatelle Pasticciate alla Piemontese*)

Cooking time: 90 minutes
Ragù Piedmont (see Index)   1 cup grated Parmesan cheese
1 pound tagliatelle   Salt and white pepper to taste
2 tablespoons butter
¼ pound chicken livers, sautéed
   in butter

Preheat oven to 350° F.

When the ragù is almost done, cook the tagliatelle in abundant boiling salted water for 6 minutes. Drain and put in an ovenproof dish. Mix with the ragù, the butter, and the coarsely chopped chicken livers. Add half the grated Parmesan, salt and pepper, and mix again. Spread evenly in the baking dish and dust with the rest of the Parmesan. Bake in a 350° oven for 5 minutes. Serves 6.

MACARONI WITH CHEESE AU GRATIN
(*Maccheroni Gratinati al Formaggio*)

Cooking time: 20 minutes
1 pound macaroni   White pepper to taste
½ pound Gruyère cheese   ¼ pound butter
½ pound Parmesan cheese   1 cup milk

Preheat oven to 350° F.

Cook the macaroni in abundant boiling salted water for 10 minutes. In the meantime, finely dice the Gruyère and the Parmesan.

Put in a bowl together with a pinch of white pepper. Butter an ovenproof baking dish. Drain the cooked macaroni and mix together with the butter. Spread half the macaroni evenly in the baking dish. Sprinkle with half the cheese mixture. Cover with the rest of the macaroni, making sure to spread it evenly. Sprinkle the rest of the cheese on top. Drizzle the milk evenly over all and put in a 350° oven for 10 minutes. Serves 6.

SHEPHERD'S BAKED MACARONI
(Maccheroni dei Pastori)

Cooking time: 25 minutes

1 pound macaroni	6 tablespoons butter
1¼ cups fresh ricotta (or cottage cheese)	1½ cups grated Gruyère cheese
	Salt and white pepper to taste

Preheat oven to 350° F.

Cook the macaroni in abundant boiling salted water for 10 minutes. In the meantime, put into a large serving bowl the ricotta, the butter, the grated Gruyère, a pinch of salt, and a pinch of white pepper. Mix together very well, adding from time to time a tablespoon of the water in which the macaroni is cooking. Do this until a soft, creamy mixture results. Drain the cooked macaroni and add to the contents in the bowl. Toss until well mixed. Spread this mixture evenly in a buttered baking dish and put in a 350° oven for 8 to 10 minutes, or until a golden crust begins to form. Serves 8.

MACARONI AU GRATIN WITH GRUYÈRE
(Maccheroni Gratinati al Gruyiera)

Cooking time: 20 minutes

1 pound macaroni	¾ cup diced fontina (or Cheddar) cheese
2 tablespoons flour	2 eggs
7 tablespoons butter	Salt and white pepper to taste
2 cups milk	⅔ cup grated Parmesan cheese
1½ cups diced Gruyère cheese	

Preheat oven to 350° F.

Cook the macaroni in abundant boiling salted water for 10 minutes. In the meantime, prepare a Béchamel Sauce (see Index) with the flour, 4 tablespoons of butter, and 2 cups of milk. Drain the cooked macaroni and mix with the finely diced Gruyère and the fontina (or Cheddar), also finely diced. Beat the eggs together with a pinch of salt and some white pepper and add to the macaroni, together with the rest of the butter. Mix well and spread evenly in a buttered baking dish. Pour on the white sauce and dust with the grated Parmesan. Bake in the oven for about 10 minutes or until a golden crust begins to form. Serves 6.

BAKED MACARONI WITH WHITE SAUCE
(*Maccheroni in Bianco*)

Cooking time: 30 minutes

2 or 3 medium onions	2 cups milk
8 tablespoons butter	Pepper to taste
Salt	2 egg yolks
Nutmeg	1¼ cups diced Gruyère cheese
2 tablespoons flour	1 pound macaroni

Preheat oven to 350° F.

Thinly slice the onions and cook in boiling water until softened. Drain well and put in a saucepan with 4 tablespoons of butter. Sauté over moderate heat. Add salt, a sprinkling of nutmeg, and continue to sauté over very low heat until very soft but not colored. Set aside. In another small saucepan make a Béchamel (white) Sauce (see Index) with 2 tablespoons of butter, the flour, and the milk. Add salt and pepper and remove from the fire. Add the egg yolks and the Gruyère, finely diced. Add this sauce to the saucepan in which you have cooked the onions. Mix well. Cook the macaroni in rapidly boiling salted water for 10 minutes. Drain and mix with the remaining 2 tablespoons of the butter. Spread evenly in a buttered baking dish and pour the sauce over all. Bake in a 350° oven until a golden crust has formed. Serves 6.

CHEF'S BAKED ELBOW MACARONI
(*Elbow Maccheroni del Cuoco*)

Here is another magnificent dish invented for you by Alfredo, my collaborator on this book.

Cooking time: 40 minutes

3 slices bacon
3 tablespoons oil
1 medium onion
¼ pound veal
Salt and pepper to taste
1 bay leaf
2 tablespoons flour
⅓ cup white wine
⅓ cup tomato paste

1 bouillon cube
1 clove garlic
2 basil leaves (or ⅛ teaspoon
   dried)
1 pound elbow macaroni
1 cup grated Parmesan cheese
¼ pound fontina cheese
   (similar to American cheese)

Preheat oven to 400° F.

Cut up the bacon into small pieces and sauté in the oil in a saucepan. Add the finely chopped onion and sauté until golden. Add the finely chopped veal, salt and pepper, and the bay leaf. Stir and brown over high heat. Add the flour and stir until blended. Pour in the white wine and allow half of it to evaporate, stirring continuously. Dilute the tomato paste and the bouillon cube in 1½ cups of hot water and add. Stir. Chop together very finely the clove of garlic and the basil leaves. Add and stir. Cover the saucepan and cook for 30 minutes over moderately low heat. Cook the macaroni in abundant boiling salted water for 12 minutes. Drain and put in an ovenproof dish. Mix together with the sauce and half the grated Parmesan. Spread the pasta evenly and dust with the rest of the grated cheese. Arrange thin slices of fontina on top and bake in a 350° oven for 5 minutes. Serve hot. Serves 6.

SWEET LASAGNE AU GRATIN
(*Lasagne Zuccherate e Gratinate*)

Cooking time: 30 minutes

2 cups milk	2 eggs
¾ cup seedless raisins	3 tablespoons dry bread crumbs
1 pound lasagne	½ teaspoon cinnamon
3 tablespoons sugar	6 tablespoons butter

Preheat oven to 350° F.

Bring the milk to a full boil and allow to cool. Put the raisins in 1 cup of water to soak. Cook the lasagne in abundant boiling salted water for 8 minutes. Drain and put in a large bowl. Add the sugar, the milk, the raisins (which have been well drained), and the well-beaten eggs. Mix well. Butter an ovenproof baking dish and dust with 2 tablespoons of bread crumbs. Add the pasta mixture and even off. Mix the remaining tablespoon of bread crumbs with the cinnamon and sprinkle on top. Dot the surface with dabs of butter. Bake in a 350° oven for 20 minutes. Allow to cool for 5 minutes before serving. Serves 6.

LASAGNE BOLOGNA STYLE
(*Lasagne alla Bolognese*)

Cooking time: 70 minutes

Bolognese Sauce (see Index)	4 eggs
5 tablespoons butter	1⅓ cups grated Parmesan cheese
Salt to taste	
5 tablespoons flour	1¼ cups diced mozzarella cheese
4 cups milk	
1¼ pounds flour	

Preheat oven to 400° F.

Make the Bolognese sauce as directed. Make a Béchamel (white) Sauce (see Index) with the butter, salt, 5 tablespoons of flour, and the milk. Now make the pasta. Make a well in the 1¼ pounds of flour in the center of the kitchen table. Put the beaten eggs in the well together with an eggshell full of water. Gradually work the flour into the egg mixture with a fork, then start working the dough with your hands until a smooth, consistent dough results. Roll the dough as instructed for Homemade Pasta (see Index). The dough should be paper thin. Cut the rolled dough into rather wide strips. Cook a few at a time in abundant boiling salted water for 3 minutes. Remove from the pot of boiling water with a large sieve and plunge into another pot with cold water. Remove from the cold water and put on clean dish towels to dry. Mix together the Bolognese sauce and the béchamel. Cover the bottom of a greased baking dish with a ladleful of this sauce, then proceed as follows: put in a layer of the cooked pasta, spread with the Bolognese-béchamel mixture, dust with grated Parmesan, and sprinkle with finely diced mozzarella. Bake in a hot oven (400°) for 15 minutes. Allow to cool for 5 minutes after removing from the oven. Cut in squares to serve. Serve with a pancake turner. Serves 6.

RIGATONI STUFFED WITH MUSHROOMS
(*Rigatoni Ripieni di Funghi*)

This is one of the most delicious recipes in this book. It is well worth the time it takes to prepare it.

Cooking time: 70 minutes

1 pound mushrooms	½ pound ripe tomatoes (2 medium)
2 tablespoons lemon juice	2 cloves garlic
3 slices lean bacon	1 egg
3 tablespoons oil	1 cup grated Gruyère cheese
Salt and pepper to taste	1⅓ cups grated Parmesan cheese
6 tablespoons butter	4 tablespoons dry bread crumbs
8 tablespoons flour	¾ pound large rigatoni
4 cups milk	
Nutmeg	

Preheat oven to 350° F.

Wash, clean, and thinly slice the mushrooms. Put in a bowl with the lemon juice and mix. Set aside for use later. Sauté the thinly sliced bacon in the oil in a saucepan. When golden, add the mushrooms, salt and pepper, stir, and cook over moderate heat for 30 minutes until their liquid has evaporated. In the meantime, in a small saucepan make a Béchamel (white) Sauce (see Index) with the butter, flour, milk, salt, pepper, and nutmeg, cooking over very low heat for 20 minutes and stirring often. Remove the bacon and the mushrooms with a slotted spoon so that all the oil remains in the saucepan. Into the saucepan put the cut-up tomatoes, chopped garlic, salt and pepper, and ½ cup of hot water. Cook for 30 minutes over moderate heat. In the meantime, chop the mushrooms and bacon and put in a mixing bowl with the egg, half the grated cheeses mixed together, 1 tablespoon white sauce, and the dry bread crumbs. Mix until a smooth paste results. Cook the rigatoni in abundant boiling salted water for 8 minutes. Drain very carefully in order not to break them. Put immediately into another pot containing cold water. Pass the tomato sauce through the fine blade of a food mill or blend in a blender. Remove the rigatoni from the cold water and drain well. Fill with the mushroom mixture. Spread half the white sauce evenly on the bottom of a buttered baking dish. Arrange the stuffed rigatoni side by side on the white sauce. Spoon half the tomato sauce over the rigatoni. Cover with the rest of the white sauce. Drizzle the rest of the tomato sauce over this and dust with the rest of the grated cheeses. Put in a moderate oven (350°) for 15 minutes. Serves 4.

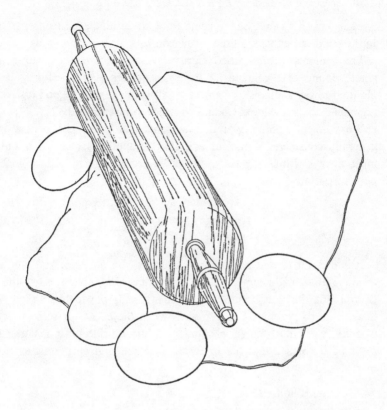

CHAPTER VII

Homemade Pasta

In this chapter you will learn how to prepare the pasta for fettuccine and tagliatelle.*

You will realize that it is not difficult to make your own pasta. All you need is a little time. I can assure you that the results are well worth the trouble.

Of course, you may use the fresh pasta that one finds in specialized stores, or, as I mentioned in the chapter "Noodles and Family," you may use the commercially packed egg noodles that one finds on the

---

* The difference between fettuccine and tagliatelle: fettuccine are slightly wider (about ⅛ inch) than tagliatelle.

market, but this won't be the same thing at all as the pasta prepared in the manner I explain a little further on.

The famous singer Enrico Caruso was accustomed to eating a whole pound of tagliatelle all by himself after every performance. He used to say smilingly, "Remember all your life that a good dish of tagliatelle and some good Chianti wine never hurt anybody."

We wish to remind you that 3 ounces of pasta per person is generally considered sufficient and that Neapolitans claim that one must always drink a glass of water after having enjoyed a good plate of pasta.

HOMEMADE PASTA
(Sfoglia di Pasta al Uovo)

It is difficult to find an Italian housewife who does not know how to make homemade egg pasta and *tirare la sfoglia,* as they say—that is, roll out the dough into a perfectly round, paper-thin sheet. It takes a lot of practice, but it is well worth the effort. In some parts of Italy, particularly in farm country, a future bride must make egg pasta in the presence of her in-laws before she is given permission to marry!

1½ pounds flour (6 cups),   4 eggs
   preferably semolina flour

Put the flour on a board and make a well in the center of the flour. Break the eggs into the well. Break up the eggs with a fork and beat slightly. Gradually start mixing the flour with the eggs until most of it is absorbed, leaving just a little aside in case you need it later. Work the dough on the board until you have a smooth, consistent dough. Divide the dough into balls about the size of a large orange. Flatten a ball of dough with your hand and start rolling. The secret of obtaining a round, uniform sheet of pasta is to be sure to start in the center and roll outward in all directions, always returning to the center after every roll outward. When the dough, or *sfoglia,* is fairly thin, sprinkle the surface with flour and roll it over itself on a rolling pin or stick, starting at the edge of the circle. When the pasta is thus wound around the rolling pin, with the heels of the palms of your hands, starting at the center and working outward, start smoothing out the dough with a fair amount of pressure, rolling the rolling pin back and forth all the time on the floured board. Unroll and repeat until you have obtained the desired thickness. Repeat for each ball of dough. This dough may be used for lasagne, ravioli, tortellini, fettuccine, tagliatelle, etc. For lasagne, cannelloni, ravioli, and tortellini, simply cut the pieces in the size required. For fettuccine or tagliatelle, sprinkle the surface of the *sfoglia* with flour and fold. Cut into strips of the desired width with a sharp large knife. Shake out and spread out on the board. This pasta may be used immediately, in which case it will cook in a few minutes. Or, if desired, it may be dried, uncooked, and kept indefinitely. Caution: fresh pasta cooks more quickly than dry pasta.

This recipe is for 4 generous servings. The 1½ pounds of flour should make about 3 balls the size of an orange. You are to use all of the dough to serve 4 people—whether it's 2 or 3 or 4 balls.

GREEN PASTA
(*Sfoglia Verde*)

This is the recipe for green pasta, which, depending on how it is cut, is used for fettuccine, tagliatelle, baked lasagne, etc.

½ pound spinach	4 eggs
1½ cups flour	

Wash the spinach and cook in 2 tablespoons of water until tender. Squeeze very dry and pass through the fine blade of a food mill 2 times. Put the flour on a board and make a well in the center. Put the eggs and the spinach in the center and beat together with a fork, working in the flour a little at a time. When all the flour has been absorbed, start kneading the dough until it is smooth and of medium consistency. Add flour if necessary. Roll out the pasta with a rolling pin as directed in recipe for Homemade Pasta (see Index) or with a pasta machine. Allow to dry for a few minutes before cutting in desired width. Serves 4.

FETTUCCINE WITH BOLOGNESE SAUCE
(*Fettuccine alla Bolognese*)

Cooking time: 50 minutes

2½ tablespoons dried mushrooms (or 1 3- or 4-ounce can chopped)

3 slices raw ham (prosciutto) or bacon

1 onion

1 carrot

1 stalk celery

Small bunch parsley

2 tablespoons butter

3 tablespoons oil

1 clove garlic

1 whole clove

1 bay leaf

Pinch of marjoram

Salt and pepper to taste

½ pound beef (preferably sirloin)

1 cup dry red wine

1 tablespoon flour

1 pound ripe tomatoes (3 medium)

½ bouillon cube

1 pound fettuccine

1 cup grated Parmesan cheese

Put the mushrooms in 1 cup warm water to soak. Put the ham or bacon through the meat grinder. Also grind the onion, the carrot, the celery, and the parsley. Put all in a saucepan with the butter and oil. Add the clove of garlic, the clove, the bay leaf, the marjoram, salt and pepper, and sauté for 5 minutes. Add the coarsely ground beef and the mushrooms, which have been squeezed dry and coarsely chopped. (If using canned mushrooms, drain thoroughly.) Cook for 5 minutes. Pour in the red wine and allow to evaporate. Thicken the sauce with a tablespoon of flour diluted in a little warm water. Stir until it begins to turn yellow, then add the mashed tomatoes. Taste and, if needed, add ½ bouillon cube. Cover the saucepan and simmer over a very low flame, stirring frequently, for 40 minutes. If the sauce becomes too thick, add a little boiling water. When the sauce is done, remove the garlic, the whole clove, and the bay leaf. Cook the fettuccine in abundant boiling salted water for 6 minutes if fresh (8 minutes if dry). Drain and put in serving dish. Add the sauce and half the cheese. Mix well and serve with rest of the cheese sprinkled on top. Serves 4.

FETTUCCINE WITH RICOTTA
(*Fettuccine con Ricotta*)

Alberto Sordi, one of the most famous Italian actors, and Frederico Fellini, the emperor of the international movie directors, told me that right after the war they were so poor that they ate this dish at least three times a week because it was inexpensive, filling, and tasty.

Cooking time: 10 minutes

½ medium onion	7 tablespoons ricotta
2 tablespoons olive oil	2 egg yolks
4 tablespoons butter	1 pound fettuccine
1 8-ounce can peas, drained	½ cup grated Parmesan cheese
Salt to taste	
1 leaf fresh sage (or ⅛ teaspoon dried)	

Sauté the chopped onion in the oil and 2 tablespoons of butter in a saucepan until barely golden. Add the peas, salt, and sage and cook for 8 or 10 minutes. In a serving bowl mix together the ricotta with the egg yolks. Cook the fettuccine in abundant boiling salted water for 6 minutes if fresh (8 minutes if dry). Put the drained fettuccine in the bowl with the egg yolk-ricotta mixture. Add 1 tablespoon of the boiling water in which the pasta was cooked and the grated cheese. Toss until well mixed. Add the sauce and the rest of the butter in dabs. Mix again and serve. Serves 4.

FETTUCCINE PICCOLO MONDO
(*Fettuccine alla Piccolo Mondo*)

This is another recipe given to us by the famous Roman restaurant Piccolo Mondo.

Cooking time: 15 minutes

½ cup shelled peas	Salt to taste
3 tablespoons butter	Pinch nutmeg
¼ pound mushrooms	1 medium-size ripe tomato
4 tablespoons oil	3 slices ham or bacon
2 tablespoons flour	1 pound green fettuccine
2 cups milk	1 cup grated Parmesan cheese

Cook the peas in 1 tablespoon of the butter for 15 minutes. Wash the mushrooms carefully, slice thinly, and cook in 3 tablespoons of the oil for 15 minutes. Prepare a Béchamel (white) Sauce (see Index) with the 2 tablespoons of butter, 2 tablespoons of flour, and 2 cups of boiling milk. Season with salt and a little nutmeg. Continue to cook everything for 5 minutes more, continuing always to stir the sauce. Peel the tomato and cut in quarters. Cook in a saucepan with 1 tablespoon of oil for 10 minutes. Cut the ham or bacon into thin strips and sauté in remaining oil for 5 minutes. Cook the fettuccine in abundant boiling salted water for 6 minutes if fresh (8 minutes if dry). Mix the peas and the mushrooms with all the other ingredients and pour over the fettuccine. Mix well with the grated cheese and serve immediately. Serves 4.

OVIDIO'S FETTUCCINE
(*Fettuccine d'Ovidio*)

One evening my wife and I had the pleasure of eating at the home of Ovidio Scocchera, one of Italy's finest chefs. He personally prepared all of the dishes served, and this recipe was his invention for that evening. Also, try his recipe for Spaghetti with Ragù, Italian style, given in Chapter I.

Cooking time: 40 minutes

5 tablespoons dried mushrooms (or 1 3- or 4-ounce can)	1 bay leaf
3 slices bacon	2 tablespoons flour
3 tablespoons oil	1 chicken bouillon cube
1 medium onion	1 pound fettuccine
¼ pound turkey breast	4 tablespoons butter
¼ pound veal	Pinch cayenne pepper
Salt and pepper to taste	1 cup grated Parmesan cheese

Put the dried mushrooms to soak in 1 cup of hot water (reserve this water for later use). Cut the bacon into spaghetti-like strips and sauté in the oil with the finely chopped onion in a saucepan over a moderate fire. When barely golden, add the turkey and the veal (both also cut into thin strips like the bacon), salt and pepper, and the bay leaf. Stir and brown for 5 minutes. Remove the mushrooms from the water, squeeze dry, and cut in strips. (If using canned, reserve juice.) Add to the saucepan. Add the flour and stir until well blended. Dissolve the bouillon cube in the mushroom water and pour into the saucepan. Bring to a boil and, if necessary, add another half cup of hot water. Cover and simmer for 30 minutes. In the meantime, when the time is almost up, cook the fettuccine in abundant boiling salted water for 8 minutes if dry, 6 minutes if fresh. Drain and put on a platter together with dabs of butter and the cayenne mixed with half the grated Parmesan. Mix, then add all the sauce, including the meat. Mix again and serve with the rest of the cheese sprinkled on top. Serves 4.

TOSSED FETTUCCINE
(*Fettuccine Montate*)

Cooking time: 30 minutes

¼ pound butter	1 pound fettuccine
3 tablespoons flour	2 eggs
1½ cups milk	2 egg yolks
¼ teaspoon cayenne pepper	½ cup heavy cream
White pepper to taste	1 cup grated Gruyère cheese

While the water for cooking the fettuccine is heating, melt the butter in a small saucepan, add the flour, stir for a minute or so, and gradually add the milk (preferably hot), stirring continuously. Add the cayenne and white pepper. Simmer slowly for 10 minutes. Remove from fire and cool for 10 minutes. By this time the water should be boiling. Cook the fettuccine for 6 minutes if fresh (8 minutes if dry). Add the eggs one at a time to the creamy sauce, beating with a whisk after each addition. Do the same with each yolk. When well blended, add the cream and whip vigorously until stiff. Drain the cooked fettuccine and put on a preheated platter. Add the whipped sauce and half the grated cheese. Mix well. Serve with the rest of the cheese sprinkled on top. Serves 4.

FETTUCCINE DELICIOUS
(Fettuccine Deliziose)

Cooking time: 50 minutes

½ pound lamb	4 tablespoons butter
¼ pound chicken breast	2 tablespoons flour
4 tablespoons oil	Salt and pepper to taste
1 medium onion	6 tablespoons tomato paste
1 small clove garlic	¾ cup seedless raisins
3 basil leaves (or ¼ teaspoon dried)	1 pound fettuccine
	1 cup grated Parmesan cheese

Slice the lamb and chicken breast rather thickly. Brown in the hot oil in a saucepan over a high flame for 3 minutes. Remove from the oil and put on a bread board. Add the finely chopped onion to the saucepan and sauté, stirring constantly. Cut the meat into long, thin strips and add to the saucepan as soon as the onion becomes golden. Sauté for 3 minutes more. Chop the garlic and the basil very finely and add. Stir for 1 minute, then add the butter and flour and stir until well blended. Add salt and pepper. Dilute the tomato paste in 1½ cups of hot water, add, and stir. Wash the raisins, chop coarsely, and add. Simmer for 35 minutes over a low flame. When almost done, cook the fettuccine in abundant boiling salted water for 6 minutes if fresh (8 if fettuccine are dry). Drain and put on a platter. Add all the sauce and half the grated Parmesan. Mix well and serve with the rest of the cheese sprinkled on top. Serves 4.

KING'S FETTUCCINE
(*Fettuccine del Re*)

Cooking time: 50 minutes

2 ounces dried mushrooms (or 1 3- or 4-ounce can chopped)
¼ pound pork (fatty)
4 tablespoons oil
1 small onion
½ stalk celery
4 tablespoons flour
½ cup white wine
1 pound ripe tomatoes (3 medium)
½ pound turkey breast
4 tablespoons butter
Salt and pepper to taste
½ cup Marsala (or cooking sherry)
1 pound fettuccine
1⅓ cups grated Cheddar cheese

Wash the dried mushrooms and put in a cup of warm water to soak. Slice the pork and put in a saucepan with the oil, sliced onion, and sliced celery, and sauté for 10 minutes. Brown well. Add 2 tablespoons of flour and stir. Add the white wine and allow to evaporate. Peel and cut up the tomatoes and add, stirring well. Remove the mushrooms from the water, squeeze dry, and chop, setting aside for use later. (If using canned, add water to make ¾ cup juice.) Add half of the mushroom water to the saucepan and stir. Cover and simmer for 40 minutes. In the meantime, remove tendons from the turkey breast and slice into 8 fillets. Flatten with a meat mallet. Dust with the remaining flour and sauté in a skillet in which you have melted the butter. When golden on both sides, add salt and pepper and the Marsala. Simmer for 5 minutes. Add the chopped mushrooms and one half of the remaining water in which they soaked. Simmer slowly for 10 minutes. When the sauce is almost ready, cook the fettuccine in abundant boiling salted water for 6 minutes if fresh (8 minutes if dry). While they are cooking, pass the contents of the saucepan through the fine blade of a food mill (taking care to pass all the meat through) or, better still, blend in a blender. Drain the cooked fettuccine and put on a platter. Add the sauce and half the grated cheese. Mix well and sprinkle the rest of the cheese on top. Arrange the turkey fillets on top. Spoon a little of the mushroom sauce over each fillet or, if you prefer, make up individual servings and put 2 fillets with mushroom sauce over each serving. Serves 4.

TASTY FETTUCCINE
(*Fettuccine Buon Gusto*)

Cooking time: 20 minutes

2 ounces dried mushrooms	1 teaspoon flour
(or 1 4-ounce can chopped)	2 bouillon cubes
3 slices ham or bacon	Salt and pepper to taste
1 tablespoon oil	1 pound fettuccine
3 tablespoons butter	1 cup grated Parmesan cheese

Put a large pot of salted water on the fire to heat for cooking the fettuccine. Put the dried mushrooms in 1 cup of hot water to soak. Cut the ham (or bacon) into strips and brown in the oil and the butter in a saucepan. Add the flour and stir. Dissolve the bouillon cubes in 1½ cups hot water and add with salt and pepper. Remove the mushrooms from the water, squeeze dry, and chop coarsely. Add. Simmer slowly until the fettuccine are cooked. Cook the fettuccine in the boiling water for 6 minutes if fresh (8 minutes if dry), drain, and put on a serving platter. Add the sauce and the grated cheese, tossing for 2 minutes in order to mix well. Serve immediately. Serves 4.

FETTUCCINE ROMAN STYLE
(*Fettuccine alla Romana*)

Cooking time: 40 minutes

½ pound chicken giblets	2 basil leaves (or ⅛ teaspoon
1 medium onion	dried)
5 tablespoons oil	4 tablespoons butter
½ cup white wine	1 pound fettuccine
Salt and pepper to taste	1 cup grated pecorino or
1 bay leaf	Parmesan cheese
½ cup tomato paste	

Clean the giblets. Coarsely chop the hearts and gizzards. Set aside the livers for use later. Finely chop the onion and sauté in the oil in a saucepan. When barely golden, add the gizzards and hearts.

Sauté until browned. Add the wine, salt and pepper, and the bay leaf. As soon as the wine has evaporated, add the tomato paste, diluted in 2 cups of hot water, and the basil. Simmer slowly for 30 minutes. In the meantime, melt 3 tablespoons of the butter in a small skillet. Add the cut-up livers and sauté until browned. Add to the sauce and continue to simmer. Cook the fettuccine for 6 minutes if fresh (8 minutes if dry), drain, and put on a serving dish. Add the sauce, the rest of the butter, and the cheese. Toss until very well mixed and serve immediately. Serves 4.

FETTUCCINE WITH ARTICHOKES
(*Fettuccine con Carciofi*)

Artichokes play a big role in Italian cooking. They are more often served as an appetizer, but this delicate vegetable when mixed with fresh pasta, as called for in this recipe, makes a marvelous dish.

Cooking time: 30 minutes

4 artichokes	4 tablespoons butter
2 tablespoons oil	1 cup grated Parmesan cheese
1 tablespoon lemon juice	Salt and pepper to taste
1 pound fettuccine	

Clean the artichokes well, making sure that no tough leaves or thorny fuzz remains. Cut in thin spaghetti-like strips. Put in an enamel or porcelainized saucepan with the oil and lemon juice and sauté for 20 minutes. Add a little water from time to time in order to allow them to become tender. Cook the fettuccine in abundant boiling salted water for 6 minutes if fresh (8 minutes if dry). Drain and put in a serving bowl. Add the butter, the artichokes, and half the grated Parmesan mixed with salt and pepper. Toss until well mixed and serve with the rest of the cheese sprinkled on top. Serves 4.

FETTUCCINE WITH BUTTER AND ANCHOVIES
(*Fettuccine con Burro e Acciughe*)

Cooking time: 10 minutes

8 tablespoons butter	1 tablespoon chopped parsley
¼ pound (2 2-ounce cans) anchovy fillets	Salt and pepper to taste
	1 pound fettuccine

Put a pot of salted water on the fire for cooking the fettuccine. Melt the butter in a small saucepan over a very low flame. Add the anchovies and, stirring, press down with a wooden spoon in order to mash them to a creamy consistency. Add 2 tablespoons of hot water. Add the parsley, salt and pepper. Cook the fettuccine for 6 minutes if fresh (8 minutes if dry) and drain. Put on a serving dish with the entire contents of the saucepan. Mix well and serve immediately. Serves 4.

GREEN FETTUCCINE ITALIAN STYLE
(Fettuccine Verdi all'Italiana)

Cooking time: 40 minutes

1 pound green fettuccine	1 stalk celery
3 slices bacon	1 carrot
1 medium onion	¼ cup white wine
3 tablespoons oil	½ cup tomato paste
¼ pound ground beef	1 bouillon cube
Salt and pepper to taste	1 cup grated Parmesan cheese
1 bay leaf	

Prepare the green noodles as in the recipe Green Pasta (see Index). Finely chop the bacon and the onion and sauté in the oil in a saucepan. Add the ground beef, salt and pepper, bay leaf, finely chopped celery and carrot, and brown over a high flame. Add the wine and allow to evaporate. Add the tomato paste and the bouillon cube diluted in 1½ cups of hot water. Stir and allow to come to a boil. Lower the flame, cover, and simmer slowly for 30 minutes. Stir from time to time. Cook the green fettuccine in abundant boiling salted water for 6 minutes if fresh (8 minutes if dry). Drain and put in a serving bowl together with all the sauce and half the grated cheese. Mix carefully in order not to break the fettuccine, and serve with the rest of the cheese sprinkled on top. Serves 4.

RED FETTUCCINE WITH BRAISED BEEF
(*Fettuccine Rosse allo Stufato*)

Cooking time: 70 minutes

1 medium onion	Salt and pepper to taste
3 tablespoons oil	½ cup tomato paste
½ pound beef	1 bouillon cube
1 stalk celery	1 pound fettuccine
1 bay leaf	1 cup grated Parmesan cheese

Finely chop the onion, and sauté in the oil in a saucepan until golden. Add the beef, which you previously have cut into thin strips, and brown. Add the chopped celery, bay leaf, and salt and pepper. Stir over a high flame for 2 minutes, then add the tomato paste and the bouillon cube dissolved in 1½ cups of hot water. Stir and bring to a boil, then lower the flame and simmer covered for 60 minutes. About 10 minutes before the sauce is ready, cook the fettuccine in abundant boiling salted water for 6 minutes if fresh (8 minutes if dry). Drain and put on a serving dish with all the sauce, the meat, and the cheese. Toss until well mixed and serve immediately.
Serves 4.

RED FETTUCCINE WITH RAGÙ
(*Fettuccine Rosse Raguttate*)

Cooking time: 20 minutes

3 slices ham or bacon	6 tablespoons tomato paste
1 tablespoon oil	Salt and pepper to taste
¼ pound mortadella sausage	1 pound fettuccine
(or bologna)	4 tablespoons butter
2 bouillon cubes	1 cup grated Parmesan cheese

Cut the ham or bacon into julienne strips and brown in the oil in a saucepan. Cut the mortadella in the same manner and add, continuing to sauté slowly. Dissolve the bouillon cubes and the tomato paste in 1½ cups of hot water and add. Add salt and pepper to taste. Stir and simmer slowly for 15 minutes. In the meantime, cook the fettuccine in abundant boiling salted water for 6 minutes if fresh

(8 minutes if dry). Drain and put on a serving plate with the butter, all the sauce, and half the Parmesan. Mix well and serve with the rest of the cheese sprinkled on top. Serves 4.

FOUR FLAVORS FETTUCCINE
(*Fettuccine ai Quattro Gusti*)

Cooking time: 6 to 10 minutes

1 boiled chicken breast
½ cup chopped mortadella
  sausage (or bologna)
1 small black truffle
1 pound fettuccine

1 cup heavy cream
3 tablespoons butter
1 cup grated Parmesan cheese
Salt and pepper to taste
½ cup diced Gruyère cheese

Put a pot of salted water on the fire for cooking the fettuccine. Chop the cooked chicken breast, the mortadella, and the truffle. When the water comes to a boil, start cooking the fettuccine for 6 minutes if fresh (8 minutes if dry). In the meantime, put in a small saucepan ¼ cup of the boiling water in which the fettuccine are cooking, the cream, and the butter. Also add the grated Parmesan. Keep hot *without* allowing to come to a boil. Drain the cooked fettuccine and put in a serving bowl. Add the contents of the saucepan, salt and pepper, and mix. Cover with the chopped chicken, mortadella, and truffle. Sprinkle with the finely diced Gruyère. Serve immediately. Serves 4.

FETTUCCINE ALL'ALFREDO
(*Fettuccine all'Alfredo*)

This is the recipe that Alfredo has made famous all over the world (see introduction to Chapter II). Alfredo, when he gave me this recipe, told me that it is very important that the fettuccine be homemade, that the butter be absolutely fresh and of the best quality possible, and that the Parmesan cheese be true Parmesan, freshly grated.

Cooking time: 6 or 7 minutes

1 pound fettuccine
½ cup unsalted butter

1 cup freshly grated Parmesan
  cheese

Start cooking the fettuccine in abundant boiling salted water for 4 to 5 minutes. Put an oval serving dish in a hot oven to heat (it must be very hot when the fettuccine are put into it). Drain the cooked fettuccine, but not too much. The pasta should be slightly foamy. Turn onto the hot serving dish on which you have already put dabs of butter. Add the freshly grated cheese. Mix with a fork and spoon until all the ingredients are well blended. The result should be a rather creamy sauce. Serve immediately. Serves 4.

TAGLIATELLE WITH MEATLESS SAUCE
(*Tagliatelle di Magro*)

Cooking time: 10 minutes

1 pound tagliatelle	½ cup canned tuna (packed in olive oil)
4 tablespoons butter	
2 tablespoons oil	2 tablespoons chopped parsley
1 2-ounce can anchovies	Salt and pepper to taste

Prepare the tagliatelle as instructed in the recipe for Homemade Pasta (see Index). Put the butter and oil in a saucepan. Add the anchovies and sauté over a low flame, mashing well with a fork in order to reduce the anchovies to a creamy paste. Add the coarsely chopped tuna and stir for 1 minute. Add the parsley, salt and pepper, and 4 tablespoons of water. Simmer slowly. Cook the tagliatelle in boiling salted water for 6 minutes. Drain and put on serving dish. Add all the sauce and toss until well mixed. Serve immediately. Serves 4.

TAGLIATELLE UDINESE STYLE
(*Tagliatelle Udinese*)

Cooking time: 70 minutes

1 pound tagliatelle	Salt and pepper to taste
2 slices bacon	1 recipe Meat Ragù (see Index)
2 tablespoons butter	1 cup grated Parmesan cheese
¾ cup shelled peas	

Make the tagliatelle as instructed in the recipe for Homemade Pasta (see Index). Put the bacon cut into julienne strips in a saucepan with the butter and sauté. Add 1 cup of boiling water. Add the peas and cook over a high flame until tender. Add salt and pepper. Cook the tagliatelle in abundant boiling salted water for 6 minutes. Drain well and put on serving dish. Add the ragù, which you have prepared previously, and the grated Parmesan. Mix well and divide into 4 equal portions. Put a few spoonfuls of peas over each serving. Serves 4.

TAGLIATELLE ALLA CARBONARA
(*Tagliatelle alla Carbonara*)

Cooking time: 10 minutes

1 pound tagliatelle	4 egg yolks
4 slices bacon	1 cup grated Parmesan cheese
1 tablespoon oil	Salt and pepper to taste

Prepare the tagliatelle as instructed in the recipe for Homemade Pasta (see Index). Cut the bacon into julienne strips and put in a small saucepan with the oil. Sauté until well browned. Cook the tagliatelle in abundant boiling salted water for 6 minutes. Drain and put in a serving bowl. Add the bacon, including the fat. Mix. Add the egg yolks, which have been beaten with half the grated cheese and a generous pinch each of salt and pepper. Toss vigorously until very well mixed. Serve with the rest of the Parmesan sprinkled on top. Serves 4.

TAGLIATELLE WITH RAGÙ
(*Tagliatelle al Ragù*)

Cooking time: 80 minutes

1 clove garlic	1 carrot
6 rosemary needles (or ¼ teaspoon dried)	½ cup red wine
3 slices bacon	¼ cup tomato paste
Salt and pepper to taste	¾ pound peeled tomatoes (2 medium)
2½ pounds leg of lamb	1 bay leaf
2 tablespoons flour	3 basil leaves (or ¼ teaspoon dried)
4 tablespoons oil	
1 large onion	1 pound tagliatelle
2 stalks celery	1 cup grated Parmesan cheese

Chop the crushed clove of garlic, the rosemary, and the bacon so very finely they form a paste. Mix with salt and pepper. With a sharp-pointed knife, make several deep holes in the leg of lamb and insert a little of this paste in each hole. Rub with some of the flour and brown on all sides in hot oil in a large saucepan. While the meat is browning, add the coarsely chopped onion, the celery, and the carrot, and salt and pepper. Add the rest of the flour and the red wine. Allow half of the wine to evaporate, then add the tomato paste, the cut-up tomatoes, the bay leaf, the basil, and 1 cup of hot water. Stir and bring to a boil. Lower the flame and simmer slowly for 70 minutes. About 6 minutes before the sauce is ready, cook the tagliatelle in abundant boiling salted water. While they are cooking, remove the meat from the sauce and pass the sauce through a food mill or blend in a blender. Drain the cooked tagliatelle and put on a serving dish. Add three fourths of the sauce and half the grated cheese. Toss until well mixed. Serve with the rest of the cheese sprinkled on top. Slice the meat and serve as a second course with a little sauce spooned over each slice and accompanied by whatever vegetable you desire. Serves 6.

TAGLIATELLE WITH WHITE SAUCE
(*Tagliatelle alla Besciamella*)

This recipe comes from the beautiful restaurant Bianchi al Cenacolo Fiorentino, which is decorated in fourteenth-century Florentine antiques.

Cooking time: 30 minutes

1 pound tagliatelle	6 tablespoons butter
½ pound (or slightly less) fatty pork	4 tablespoons flour
	1 cup milk
1 tablespoon oil	1 egg
Salt and white pepper to taste	2 egg yolks
1 chicken bouillon cube	1⅓ cups grated Cheddar cheese

Prepare the tagliatelle as instructed in the recipe for Homemade Pasta (see Index). Finely chop the pork and brown in the oil in a small saucepan. Add salt and pepper to taste. When well browned add the bouillon cube dissolved in ⅔ cup hot water. Stir and simmer very slowly for 20 minutes. In the meantime, make a Béchamel (white) Sauce (see Index) with the butter, the flour, and the milk. Cook the white sauce over a very low flame for 10 minutes. Add salt and pepper. Cook the tagliatelle in abundant boiling salted water for 6 minutes. In the meantime, beat the egg and egg yolks together with a generous pinch of pepper. Add the ground pork and its sauce to the white sauce. Stir. Drain the cooked tagliatelle and put in a preheated serving bowl. Mix together with the white sauce and half the Cheddar. Add the beaten eggs and mix again. Serve with the rest of the Cheddar sprinkled on top. Serves 4.

TAGLIATELLE WITH SAUSAGES
(*Tagliatelle con Salcicce*)

Cooking time: 40 minutes

1 pound tagliatelle	1 cup white wine
¾ pound Italian pork sausages	1 pound ripe tomatoes (3
5 tablespoons oil	medium)
1 medium onion	1 bouillon cube
1 stalk celery	Salt and pepper to taste
1 clove garlic	1 cup grated Parmesan cheese
1½ tablespoons flour	
4 leaves fresh sage (or ¼	
teaspoon dried)	

Prepare the tagliatelle as instructed in the recipe for Homemade Pasta (see Index). Pierce skins of the sausages several times with a large needle. Brown in hot oil in a saucepan. Cut up the onion and sauté along with the sausages. When browned, add the celery and the unpeeled clove of garlic. Sauté for 2 minutes more. Add the flour and the sage and stir until the flour is well blended. Add the white wine. Allow half of it to evaporate over a high flame. Add the cut-up peeled tomatoes and the bouillon cube dissolved in ½ cup of hot water. Add salt and pepper to taste. Bring to a boil, then lower the flame and simmer slowly for 30 minutes, stirring from time to time. When the sauce is almost ready, cook the tagliatelle in abundant boiling salted water for 6 minutes. In the meantime, remove the sausages from the saucepan and put on a bread board. Pass the sauce through the fine blade of a food mill or blend in a blender. Drain the cooked tagliatelle and put on a serving dish. Pour on the sauce and half the cheese and mix well. Slice the sausages into wheels and arrange around the dish so as to form a frame for the pasta. Sprinkle with the rest of the cheese and serve. Serves 4.

TAGLIATELLE PARISIAN
(*Tagliatelle alla Parigina*)

Cooking time: 40 minutes

1 pound tagliatelle	4 tablespoons oil
⅓ cup seedless raisins	1 medium onion
½ pound turkey breast	½ cup white wine
Salt and pepper to taste	¼ cup tomato paste
1 egg	1 chicken bouillon cube
½ cup grated Gruyère cheese	4 tablespoons butter
4 tablespoons flour	1 cup grated Parmesan cheese

Prepare the tagliatelle as instructed in the recipe for Homemade Pasta (see Index). Put the raisins in a little warm water to soak for a few minutes. Remove from water, squeeze dry, and put through a meat chopper together with the turkey breast. Add the salt and pepper, egg, and 1 tablespoon of the grated Gruyère. Pass everything through the meat grinder again. Make little meat balls the size of a medium-size olive. Roll in flour and brown in a saucepan in the hot oil, turning often in order to brown evenly. Remove from the oil with a slotted spoon and set aside. Finely chop the onion and sauté in the same oil. Add what little flour is left and pour in the white wine. When the wine is half evaporated, add the tomato paste, salt and pepper, and the bouillon cube dissolved in 1 cup of hot water. Stir. Return the meat balls to the saucepan and continue to cook for 25 minutes over a low flame. When the sauce is almost ready, cook the tagliatelle in abundant boiling salted water for 6 minutes. Drain and put in a serving bowl together with dabs of butter and half of the grated cheeses. Mix well and serve with the rest of the cheese sprinkled on top. Arrange the meat balls so that they frame the tagliatelle on the platter. Serves 4.

DELICATE TAGLIATELLE
(*Tagliatelle Delicate*)

Cooking time: 40 minutes

1 pound tagliatelle	1 chicken bouillon cube
1 medium onion	½ cup chopped mortadella
½ pound chicken breast	sausage (or bologna)
4 tablespoons oil	3 tablespoons chopped, pitted
2 tablespoons flour	green olives
Salt and pepper to taste	4 tablespoons butter
¼ cup tomato paste	1 cup grated Cheddar cheese

Prepare the tagliatelle as instructed in the recipe for Homemade Pasta (see Index). Cut the onion and the chicken breasts into long thin strips and sauté together in the oil in a saucepan for 2 minutes over high heat. Add the flour, salt and pepper. Stir and lower the flame. Add the tomato paste and the bouillon cube dissolved in 1 cup of hot water. Stir and add the chopped mortadella and the chopped olives. Stir again and simmer for 30 minutes. If the water evaporates, add ½ cup more. When the sauce is almost ready, cook the tagliatelle in abundant boiling salted water for 6 minutes. In the meantime, pass the sauce through a food mill or blend in a blender. Drain the cooked tagliatelle and put on a platter. Add all the sauce and the butter in dabs. Also add half the grated cheese. Mix well. Serve with the rest of the cheese sprinkled on top.
Serves 4.

TAGLIATELLE WITH BRANDY
(*Tagliatelle al Brandy*)

Cooking time: 30 minutes

1 pound tagliatelle	¼ cup heavy cream
6 tablespoons butter	¼ teaspoon cayenne pepper
4 tablespoons flour	⅓ cup brandy
1½ cups milk	Salt and white pepper to taste
2 egg yolks	1½ cups grated Gruyère cheese

Prepare the tagliatelle as instructed in the recipe for Homemade Pasta (see Index). Make a very thin Béchamel (white) Sauce:

melt the butter in a small saucepan over very low heat. Add the flour
and mix. Gradually add the hot milk, stirring constantly. Cook over
a very low fire—or in a double boiler—for 10 minutes. Cook the
tagliatelle in abundant boiling salted water for 6 minutes. In the
meantime, in a small bowl, beat the egg yolks together with the
cream and the cayenne. Remove the white sauce from the fire and
add brandy, salt and pepper. Stir. Drain the cooked tagliatelle and
put on a serving dish. Add the white sauce and half the grated
Gruyère. Mix well. Add the egg-cream mixture. Toss vigorously and
serve with the rest of the cheese sprinkled on top. Serves 4.

TAGLIATELLE NEAPOLITAN
(*Tagliatelle alla Napoletana*)

Cooking time: 30 minutes

1 pound tagliatelle	2 tablespoons chopped parsley
1 medium onion	Salt and pepper to taste
5 tablespoons oil	2 tablespoons butter
1½ pounds peeled tomatoes	1 cup grated Parmesan or
(5 medium)	pecorino cheese
1 clove garlic	
4 leaves basil (or ¼ teaspoon dried)	

Prepare the tagliatelle as instructed in the recipe for Homemade
Pasta (see Index). Finely chop the onion and sauté in the oil in a
saucepan over low heat. Peel the tomatoes. Chop very finely together the crushed clove of garlic, the basil leaves, and the parsley.
Work salt and pepper and the butter into this chopped mixture with
a spatula, forming a paste. When the onions are golden, add this
paste and continue to sauté for 1 minute over moderate heat. Cut
up the tomatoes and add together with all their juice. Add salt and
pepper to taste. Bring to a boil over high heat, then lower heat and
simmer for 25 minutes. When the sauce is almost ready, cook the
tagliatelle in abundant boiling salted water for 6 minutes. Drain
and put on a serving dish. Pour on all the sauce and half the
grated cheese. Mix well and serve with the rest of the cheese sprinkled on top. Serves 4.

TAGLIATELLE ROYALE
(*Tagliatelle Reali*)

King Vittorio Emmanuel II of Sardinia (1820–78) loved pasta so much that he asked his cooks to prepare and serve this favorite dish of his the first Sunday of every month.

Cooking time: 60 minutes

1 medium onion	1 bay leaf
2 tablespoons oil	⅓ cup white wine
¼ pound veal	3 tablespoons tomato paste
¼ pound fatty pork	1 bouillon cube
¼ pound turkey breast	¼ cup shelled peas
½ stalk celery	1 pound tagliatelle
1 carrot	1 cup grated Cheddar cheese
Salt and pepper to taste	½ cup heavy cream

Finely chop the onion and sauté in the oil in a saucepan. Pass the meats through the fine blade of a meat grinder together with the celery and the carrot. When the onion begins to color, add the ground meat mixture, salt and pepper, and bay leaf, and brown well over high heat, stirring often. Add the white wine and allow half to evaporate. Dilute the tomato paste and the bouillon cube in 1½ cups of hot water and add. Stir and bring to a boil, then lower the heat and simmer covered for 40 minutes. Cook the peas in rapidly boiling water over high heat until tender. Six minutes before the sauce is ready, cook the tagliatelle in abundant boiling salted water. Drain and put on a serving dish. Pour on all the sauce and half the grated cheese. Mix well. Add the cream and mix again. Serve with the rest of the cheese and the drained cooked peas sprinkled on top. Serves 4.

GOURMET'S TAGLIATELLE
(*Tagliatelle del Buongustaio*)

Cooking time: 40 minutes

1 pound tagliatelle	Salt and pepper to taste
¼ cup seedless raisins	2 tablespoons flour
½ pound veal	⅓ cup white wine
1 carrot	1 chicken bouillon cube
1 stalk celery	2 slices ham
1 medium onion	4 tablespoons butter
4 tablespoons oil	1 cup grated Parmesan cheese

Prepare the tagliatelle as instructed in the recipe for Homemade Pasta (see Index). Put the raisins to soak in a cup of warm water. Grind the veal, the carrot, and the celery together in a meat chopper. Finely chop the onion and sauté in the oil in a saucepan over high heat. When it begins to color, add the meat mixture, salt and pepper. Brown for 4 minutes. Add the flour and stir. Add the wine. Dilute the bouillon cube in 1 cup of hot water and pour into the saucepan. Stir and bring to a boil again. Lower the heat and simmer slowly for 30 minutes. Cut the ham into julienne strips. Remove the raisins from the water and chop. Add the ham and the raisins to the sauce and continue to simmer. Cook the tagliatelle in abundant boiling salted water for 6 minutes. While they are cooking, add the butter to the sauce and stir. Taste for salt. Drain the cooked tagliatelle and put on a serving dish. Pour on all the sauce. Mix with half the Parmesan. Serve with the rest of the cheese sprinkled on top. Serves 4.

GABRIELE'S TAGLIATELLE
(*Tagliatelle di Gabriele*)

Cooking time: 50 minutes

1 pound tagliatelle	6 tablespoons butter
1 medium onion	4 tablespoons flour
3 tablespoons oil	¼ cup milk
3 basil leaves (or ¼ teaspoon dried)	1 chicken bouillon cube
1 stalk celery	Salt and pepper to taste
1 pound ripe tomatoes (3 medium)	1 cup grated Parmesan cheese

Prepare the tagliatelle as instructed in the recipe for Homemade Pasta (see Index). Slice the onion and sauté in the oil in a saucepan. When almost golden, add the cut-up basil, celery, and tomatoes. Boil for 15 minutes. In the meantime, prepare a Béchamel (white) Sauce (see Index) with the butter, flour, and milk. Dissolve the bouillon cube in ½ cup of hot water and add to the tomato sauce. Add salt and pepper. Simmer slowly for 10 minutes. Cook the tagliatelle in boiling salted water for 6 minutes. While they are cooking, pass the tomato sauce through the fine blade of a food mill or blend in a blender. Return to the saucepan. Add the white sauce and bring to a boil again. Drain the cooked tagliatelle and put on a preheated serving dish. Add all the sauce and half the Parmesan. Toss and serve with the rest of the cheese sprinkled on top. Serves 4.

TAGLIATELLE COUNTRY STYLE
(*Tagliatelle alla Paesana*)

Cooking time: 50 minutes

1 pound tagliatelle	2 basil leaves (or ⅛ teaspoon
½ pound Italian sausages	dried)
4 tablespoons oil	3 leaves fresh sage (or ¼
1 medium onion	teaspoon dried)
1 clove garlic	1 bouillon cube
1 stalk celery	¼ cup shelled green peas
Salt and pepper to taste	1 3-ounce can sliced mushrooms
⅓ cup white wine	1 cup grated pecorino cheese
1 pound ripe tomatoes (3	(or any sharp cheese)
medium)	

Prepare the tagliatelle as instructed in the recipe for Homemade Pasta (see Index). Pierce the skins of the sausages with a large pin or needle. Put in a saucepan together with the oil and the coarsely chopped onion and sauté. Add the unpeeled clove of garlic and the coarsely chopped celery. When all is nicely browned, add the salt and pepper and white wine. Cut up the tomatoes and add, together with the basil and sage. Dissolve the bouillon cube in ½ cup of hot water and add. Bring to a boil again over high heat, then lower the heat and simmer for 30 minutes. In the meantime, cook the peas in boiling water over a high flame in order to keep them green. Remove the sausages from the saucepan and pass the sauce through a food mill or blend in a blender. Return the sauce to the saucepan, add the drained mushrooms, and bring to a boil. Simmer for 10 minutes more. Slice the sausages into wheels and add together with the peas. Cook the tagliatelle in abundant boiling salted water for 6 minutes. Drain and put on serving dish with all the sauce and half the grated cheese. Mix and serve with the rest of the cheese sprinkled on top. Serves 4.

TAGLIATELLE PIEDMONT
(Tagliatelle alla Piemontese)

Cooking time: 90 minutes
½ recipe Ragù Piedmont
1 pound tagliatelle
4 tablespoons butter
1 cup grated Parmesan cheese
Salt and white pepper to taste

Prepare the Ragù alla Piemontese as instructed (see Index). Half a recipe is sufficient to prepare this dish. Make the tagliatelle as instructed in Homemade Pasta (see Index). Cook in abundant boiling salted water for 6 minutes. Drain and put on serving dish. Add the ragù, the butter in dabs, and half the grated Parmesan mixed with a generous pinch each of salt and white pepper. Mix well and serve with the rest of the cheese sprinkled on top.
Serves 4.

GREEN TAGLIATELLE BOLOGNESE
(Tagliatelle verdi alla Bolognese)

Cooking time: 70 minutes
1 pound green tagliatelle
2 slices bacon
3 tablespoons oil
1 medium onion
1 stalk celery
1 carrot
Generous ¼ pound baby beef, ground
Salt and pepper to taste
1 bay leaf
1 teaspoon flour
½ cup red wine
3 tablespoons tomato paste
1 bouillon cube
1 cup grated Parmesan cheese

Prepare the green tagliatelle as instructed in the recipe for Homemade Pasta (see Index). Cut the bacon into very thin strips and brown in the oil in a saucepan. Add the finely chopped onion and sauté along with the finely chopped celery and carrot. Add the meat and brown well for 10 minutes. Add salt and pepper and the bay leaf. Add the flour and stir until blended. Add the wine and allow to evaporate for 1 minute, stirring constantly. Add the tomato paste and bouillon cube diluted in 1½ cups of hot water. Simmer for 50 minutes. When the sauce is almost ready, cook the tagliatelle in boiling salted water for 6 minutes. Drain and put on a serving dish. Add the sauce and the grated cheese and mix very well. Serve immediately. Serves 4.

TAGLIOLINI, LOMBARD STYLE
(*Tagliolini alla Lombarda*)

Cooking time: 20 minutes

5 slices bacon	Salt and pepper to taste
1 small onion	¾ pound tagliolini
2 tablespoons oil	4 tablespoons butter
2 tablespoons flour	1¼ cups grated Parmesan
Generous pinch saffron	cheese
1 chicken bouillon cube	

Cut the bacon and the onion into strips as thin as the tagliolini. Sauté both in the oil in a saucepan until golden in color. Add the flour and stir for 1 minute. Dissolve the saffron in 1 cup of hot water in which you have already dissolved the bouillon cube and pour into the saucepan. Add salt and pepper. Simmer over low heat for 15 minutes. Cook the tagliolini in abundant boiling salted water for 6 minutes. Drain and put in a serving bowl. Add dabs of butter and all the sauce with half the grated cheese. Toss until well mixed. Serve with the rest of the cheese sprinkled on top. Serves 4.

TAGLIOLINI WITH POACHED EGGS
(*Tagliolini alle Uova in Camicia*)

Cooking time: 40 minutes

¾ pound tagliolini

1 medium onion

3 tablespoons oil

1½ cups chopped deboned
chicken

Salt and pepper to taste

1 pound ripe tomatoes (3
medium)

2 basil leaves (or ⅛ teaspoon
dried)

1 chicken bouillon cube

4 eggs

2 tablespoons vinegar

4 tablespoons butter

¾ cup grated Cheddar cheese

Commercially made tagliolini (egg noodles) may be used, but if you can, make your own. Finely chop the onion and sauté in the oil in a saucepan. Coarsely chop the chicken meat and brown until golden. Add salt and pepper. Add the cut-up tomatoes, the basil leaves, and the bouillon cube dissolved in ½ cup of hot water. Bring to a boil over high heat, then lower the flame to moderate and cook for 35 minutes. In the meantime, poach the eggs by breaking them carefully into a saucepan half full of boiling water and 2 tablespoons of vinegar. Cook for 3 minutes and remove with a slotted spoon. Set aside for use later. Cook the tagliolini in boiling salted water for 6 minutes. While they are cooking, put the sauce through the medium blade of a food mill or blend in a blender. Return the blended sauce to the saucepan and bring to a simmer. Drain the cooked tagliolini, add the sauce, butter, and half the grated cheese and toss until well mixed. Divide the pasta into 4 portions. Dust each portion with cheese and top each with a poached egg. Serves 4.

HOUSEWIFE'S TAGLIOLINI
(*Tagliolini della Massaia*)

Cooking time: 30 minutes

5 tablespoons dried mushrooms	1 bouillon cube
(or 1 4-ounce can chopped)	½ cup tomato paste
½ pound Italian pork sausages	1 tablespoon chopped parsley
1 clove garlic	Salt to taste
2 tablespoons oil	¾ pound tagliolini
2 tablespoons flour	6 tablespoons butter
Pepper	1 cup grated Parmesan cheese
½ cup white wine	

Put the dried mushrooms in a cup of warm water to soak. Remove the skin from the sausages and break them into pieces. Crush the clove of garlic and chop very finely. Sauté the sausage and garlic in the oil in a saucepan over moderate heat for 5 minutes. Add the flour and a pinch of pepper. Stir for 1 minute. Add the white wine and stir. Remove the mushrooms from the water (reserve ½ for later) and squeeze as dry as possible. Chop finely and add. Dissolve the bouillon cube in half the mushroom water. Also add the tomato paste and ½ cup of hot water to this water, stir, and add to the saucepan. Add the parsley and taste for salt. Cook over moderately low heat for 20 minutes. Cook the tagliolini in boiling salted water for 6 minutes, drain, and put in a serving bowl. Add the butter in dabs and all the sauce. Toss until well mixed. Sprinkle the Parmesan on top and serve immediately. Serves 4.

TAGLIOLINI CAVOUR
(*Tagliolini alla Cavour*)

Many streets and parks in Rome are named after Camillo Benso di Cavour, Minister of Agriculture and Commerce in 1850, for recognition of his service to his country. Like the streets and parks, this recipe was also named after him but for a different reason. Cavour was a large man weighing two hundred and sixty pounds and was known to be a great eater and lover of pasta. This recipe is said to have been invented for him.

Cooking time: 30 minutes

½ pound chicken breasts	Salt and white pepper to taste
2 tablespoons oil	6 tablespoons butter
3 tablespoons Marsala wine	4 tablespoons flour
¼ cup white wine	1 cup milk
2 tablespoons tomato paste	¾ pound tagliolini
1 chicken bouillon cube	1 cup grated Dutch cheese

Cut the chicken breasts into very fine julienne strips and brown in the oil in a saucepan over high heat for 2 minutes. Add the Marsala and allow half of it to evaporate. Add the white wine and while it is evaporating dilute the tomato paste and the bouillon cube in 1 cup of hot water and add to the saucepan. Add salt and pepper. Cook over moderate heat for 20 minutes. In the meantime, in a small saucepan make a Béchamel (white) Sauce (see Index) with the butter, flour, milk, salt and white pepper. Cook for 5 minutes. Six minutes before the sauce is ready, cook the tagliolini in boiling salted water for 6 minutes. Drain and put in a preheated serving bowl together with all the sauce and the meat. Toss until well mixed. Add the white sauce and half the grated cheese and mix well. Serve with the rest of the cheese sprinkled on top.
Serves 4.

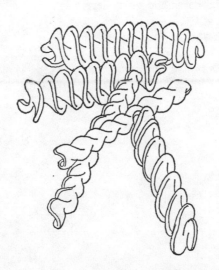

APPETIZING TAGLIOLINI
(*Tagliolini Appetitosi*)

Cooking time: 25 minutes

¼ pound pork
¼ pound veal
1 small onion
2 tablespoons oil
2 tablespoons flour
½ cup white wine
½ pound ripe tomatoes (2 medium)

1 chicken bouillon cube
Salt and pepper to taste
¾ pound tagliolini
4 tablespoons butter
1 cup grated Parmesan cheese
¼ cup cream

Finely chop the 2 meats and the onion and brown in the oil in a saucepan. Add the flour and stir for 1 minute. Be sure that the meat is well disintegrated and that no large pieces are formed. Add the white wine. Pass the tomatoes through the fine blade of a food mill and add. Dissolve the bouillon cube in 1 cup of hot water and add. Add salt and pepper. Cover the saucepan and cook for 20 minutes more over a low flame. Cook the tagliolini in abundant boiling salted water for 6 minutes. Drain and put in a serving bowl together with the butter. Mix. Add the contents of the saucepan and half the grated Parmesan. Mix again. Pour on the cream and mix. Dust with the rest of the Parmesan and serve. Serves 4.

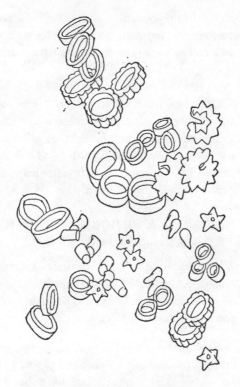

CHAPTER VIII
Soups and Minestrone

In Italy there are three different ways of preparing soups. Each, moreover, has a different name, as we shall soon see. The most common type of Italian soup is *minestrone*. It is always prepared with some type of pasta—macaroni, ditali, farfallette, bucatini, or any other type of pasta suitable for soups. Sometimes, too, the Italians put dried vegetables in this soup; for example, the most popular minestrone is Macaroni and Horse Bean Soup. One of the main ingredients of this minestrone is *fave,* or horse beans, just as the name indicates. Minestrone is a winter soup and is known to be a favorite in Northern Italy. In this chapter you will find recipes for minestrone to make practically a whole dinner in one dish.

The second type of soup is *minestra.* It is a light soup made from a small variety of fresh vegetables and pasta, and sometimes with one dried vegetable, cheese, fish, or meat. This is a comparatively inexpensive dish and is usually served before the main dish or as a light supper.

The third type of soup is the *zuppa,* a very copious dish. It is made from a mixture of fresh and dried vegetables and pasta. The difference between zuppa and the two other soups is that zuppa is neither heavy like minestrone nor as light as minestra, and zuppa is considered to be a more sophisticated dish, whereas minestrone is known as a peasants' soup. Zuppa is extremely nourishing and is particularly recommended for children.

MACARONI AND HORSE BEAN SOUP
(*Zuppa di Maccheroni e Fave*)

This recipe is typical of the north of Italy. I first ate it at the restaurant Sasso di Dante in Milan. I enjoyed it so much that I asked the chef if I could have his recipe for my book, and now I pass it on to you with pleasure.

Cooking time: 50 minutes

½ pound fave (horse beans)	Salt and pepper to taste
1 large onion	1 bouillon cube
5 tablespoons oil	1 clove garlic
2 stalks celery	2 tablespoons chopped parsley
2 tablespoons tomato paste	½ pound macaroni
2 bay leaves	⅔ cup grated Cheddar cheese

Boil the fave for 20 minutes in salted water. Sauté the coarsely chopped onion in the oil in a saucepan until golden. Add the sliced celery, the tomato paste, the bay leaves, and salt and pepper. Stir for a minute or so. Dissolve the bouillon cube in 4 cups of hot water and add. Cook over moderate heat for 30 minutes, stirring from time to time. When the fave are almost cooked, remove them from the water and remove the tough skins. (By making an incision on the side of each fave with a paring knife, you will find that the skin is easily removed.) Set aside the fave pulp for use later. When, after 30 minutes, the sauce is ready, pass it through the fine blade of a food mill or blend in a blender. Return to the saucepan. Add the fave pulp and cook for 10 minutes more. In the meantime, on a bread board, crush the garlic to a pulp and chop very finely together with the parsley and a pinch of pepper. Add to the saucepan. When the 10 minutes are up, add the macaroni broken into 1-inch lengths and cook over moderate heat for 10 minutes, stirring often. Taste for salt. Before serving add the grated cheese, stir, and serve. Serves 4.

LENTIL SOUP WITH DITALINI
(*Minestra di Lenticchie con Ditalini*)

Cooking time: 60 minutes

½ pound (or slightly less) lentils
1 bay leaf
2 leaves fresh sage (or ⅛ teaspoon dried)
2 tablespoons oil
3 slices bacon
1 clove garlic
3 stalks celery
1 medium onion
2 tablespoons tomato paste
Salt and pepper to taste
¼ pound ditalini
Grated Parmesan cheese (optional)

Cook the lentils in 3 quarts of water together with the bay leaf and the sage. Be careful not to allow the water to boil too rapidly or the lentils will break. In another saucepan put the oil and sauté the bacon, which has been cut into very thin julienne strips. Add the crushed clove of garlic, the chopped celery and onion, and continue to sauté slowly. Dilute the tomato paste in ½ cup of hot water and add to the saucepan. Add salt and pepper. Cook for 20 minutes. When the lentils are cooked, add this sauce to the pot of lentils. Taste for salt and add water if necessary. Bring to a boil again and add the pasta. Cook for 10 minutes more. Remove the bay leaf and sage. Serve with grated Parmesan if desired. Serves 4.

SOUP PARMESAN
(*Minestra Parmigiana*)

Cooking time: 2 hours if dried beans are used,
           50 minutes if beans are cooked

2 small potatoes	2 medium onions
2 carrots	2 whole cloves
2 white turnips	Salt and pepper to taste
2 stalks celery	1½ cups uncooked farfallette
¼ pound beans	6 tablespoons butter
2 basil leaves (or ⅛ teaspoon dried)	1 cup grated Parmesan cheese

In a saucepan put the potatoes, carrots, turnips, celery, beans, basil, and onions (in which you have stuck the cloves), salt and pepper. Add 3 quarts of water and bring to a boil. Lower heat and simmer for 2 hours (if dried beans are used; 50 minutes if cooked). Put the entire contents of the saucepan through a food mill or blend in a blender and return to the heat. When this liquid comes to a boil again, add the pasta and cook for 10 minutes more. Just before serving stir in the butter and the Parmesan. Serves 4.
NOTE: If in America (U.S.) farfallette does not exist, use farfalle.

SOUP WITH CHICKEN LIVERS
(*Minestra di Fegatini di Pollo*)

Cooking time: 20 minutes

1½ cups chopped chicken livers	Salt to taste
4 bouillon cubes	1 cup grated Parmesan cheese
¼ pound stelline	

Clean the chicken livers and cut up into small pieces. Put them in a small pan of boiling water for a minute or so. Drain. In another saucepan, bring 3 quarts of water to a boil. Add the bouillon cubes and the chicken livers. When it comes to a boil again, add the stelline. Cook for approximately 15 minutes. Taste for salt. Serve with the grated Parmesan sprinkled generously on top. Serves 4.

SOUP AUX FINES HERBES WITH SMALL PENNE
(Minestra alle Erbe Fini con Pennine)

Cooking time: 30 minutes

2 medium potatoes	¼ pound small penne
2 stalks celery, heart and leaves	Salt and pepper to taste
2 tablespoons chopped parsley	6 tablespoons butter
2 basil leaves, chopped (or	1 cup grated Parmesan cheese
⅛ teaspoon dried)	

In a saucepan cook the cut-up potatoes in 8 cups of salted water together with the celery leaves. Cook for 15 minutes, then put the entire contents of the saucepan through a food mill or blend in a blender. Put the puréed potatoes back in the saucepan and return to the fire. Add the finely chopped celery stalks, the parsley, and the basil. When the mixture comes to a boil, add the small penne and cook for 10 minutes. Taste for salt and add a generous pinch of pepper. When the penne are cooked, add the butter and Parmesan, stir, and serve. Serves 4.

PASTA AND FISH SOUP, SICILIAN STYLE
(Minestra di Pasta e Pesce alla Siciliana)

I particularly like this soup because it reminds me of bouillabaisse, the famous French soup that is the pride of Marseille.

Cooking time: 40 minutes

2 cloves garlic	½ pound fish (sea bass or
3 tablespoons oil	similar)
2 small ripe tomatoes	¼ pound spaghettini
Salt and pepper to taste	Pinch of saffron

Sauté the finely chopped garlic in the oil in a saucepan over low heat. Add the cut-up peeled tomatoes, from which you have removed the seeds. Stir until disintegrated. Add salt and pepper. Add the fish and 1 cup of water. Cook slowly for 25 minutes. Remove the fish from the saucepan carefully. Clean it by removing the skin and its bones. Break it into pieces. Add to the saucepan 8 cups of water and bring it to a boil. Add the fish and the spaghettini broken into

2-inch lengths. Cook for 15 minutes more. Taste for salt and add the saffron diluted in 1 tablespoon of hot water. Stir and serve. Serves 4.

CHEESE SOUP
(*Minestra al Formaggio*)

An excellent, easy-to-make soup . . .

Cooking time: 8 minutes

¼ pound stelline	Pepper to taste
3 eggs	1 cup grated Parmesan cheese
6 tablespoons butter	⅔ cup grated Gruyère cheese

Cook the stelline (little stars) in 8 cups of boiling salted water for 8 minutes. In the meantime, in a large bowl put the eggs, melted butter, pepper, and the grated cheeses. Beat together until a blended mixture results. Add the stelline to this mixture a ladleful at a time, stirring continuously until all of the pasta has been added. Serve immediately. Serves 4.

VERMICELLI SOUP
(*Minestra di Vermicelli*)

Cooking time: 10 minutes

4 bouillon cubes	1 cup grated Parmesan cheese
¼ pound vermicelli	

Bring 8 cups of water to a boil. Add the bouillon cubes and the vermicelli broken into 1½-inch lengths. Cook for 10 minutes. Serve with the grated Parmesan sprinkled generously on top. Serves 4.

BEAN SOUP WITH MACARONI
(*Maccheroncini con i Fagioli*)

Cooking time: 90 minutes if dried beans are used,
             30 minutes if cooked beans are used

1 pound navy beans	2 stalks celery
3 slices bacon	2 small ripe tomatoes
2 tablespoons oil	Salt and pepper to taste
1 small onion	1 tablespoon chopped parsley
1 clove garlic	¼ pound maccheroncini

Put the beans in a pot of cold water and cook for 60 minutes. Chop the bacon and brown it in the oil in a small saucepan. Add the finely chopped onion and garlic and sauté for 5 minutes over low heat. Add the chopped celery and chopped tomatoes. Stir for 5 minutes. Add salt and pepper. Cook slowly. When the beans are cooked, add the sauce you have prepared. Also add the parsley. Taste for salt. Add the maccheroncini broken into 1½-inch lengths, and cook for 10 minutes more. This dish may also be served cold. Serves 4.

SOUP WITH FARFALLETTE AND PEAS
(*Minestra di Farfallette con Piselli*)

Cooking time: 35 minutes

1 cup fresh shelled peas	Salt and white pepper to taste
1 medium onion	¼ pound farfallette
2 tablespoons oil	4 tablespoons butter
1 chicken bouillon cube	⅔ cup grated Parmesan cheese
1 tablespoon flour	

Cook the peas in 4 cups of boiling water for 20 minutes over high heat. In the meantime, sauté the finely chopped onion in the oil in a saucepan over low heat. Dissolve the bouillon cube in 4 cups of hot water. Add the flour to the onion in the saucepan and stir until blended. Add the broth a little at a time, stirring continuously. When all the broth has been added, pour in the entire contents of the other saucepan with the peas. Add salt and pepper. Bring to a boil again and add the pasta. Boil for 10 minutes more and remove from heat. Add the butter and Parmesan, stir, and serve. Serves 4.

ENDIVE SOUP WITH CONCHIGLIETTE
(*Minestra di Endivia con Conchigliette*)

Cooking time: 30 minutes

1 medium onion	Salt and pepper to taste
3 tablespoons oil	¼ pound conchigliette (shells)
2 small ripe tomatoes	3 basil leaves (or ¼ teaspoon
1 bouillon cube	dried)
1 large potato	2 tablespoons butter
1 pound endive	1 cup grated Parmesan cheese

Sauté the thinly sliced onion in the oil in a saucepan until almost golden. Add the chopped tomatoes and stir for 2 minutes. Pour in 8 cups of water in which you have dissolved the bouillon cube. Add the peeled whole potato and bring to a boil. Add the endive, which has been carefully washed and cut into 1-inch lengths. Add salt and pepper. Boil for 20 minutes, then add the small shells and continue cooking for 10 minutes. By this time the potato is done. Remove it from the pot and mash it with a fork. Return to the pot and stir for a minute or two. Chop the basil very finely and mix it with the softened butter, ⅓ cup of the Parmesan, and a pinch of pepper. Add to the pot. Taste for salt, stir, and serve. Sprinkle with remaining Parmesan. Serves 4.

SOUP PAVESE STYLE
(*Minestra alla Pavese*)

This recipe comes from Lombardy, a region in the north of Italy, situated at the foot of the Alps.

Cooking time: 10 minutes

4 bouillon cubes	1 small tomato, chopped and
4 slices bread	sautéed in 1 teaspoon of
4 tablespoons butter	butter
4 eggs	1 cup grated Parmesan cheese

Make a broth with the bouillon cubes and 2 quarts of water. In the meantime, fry the slices of bread in the butter in a skillet. Put a slice of bread in each of 4 soup dishes. When the broth has come to a boil, add the eggs one at a time. When the eggs begin to cook, carefully lift them out of the pot with a ladle and put one in each plate, over each slice of bread, which has been spread with a little bit of the chopped tomato and sprinkled with Parmesan. Fill the plates with broth and sprinkle generously with Parmesan.
Serves 4.

SOUP WITH DITALINI, POTATOES, AND CELERY
(*Minestra di Ditalini con Patate e Sedano*)

Cooking time: 30 minutes

1 medium onion	4 basil leaves (or ¼ teaspoon
3 tablespoons oil	dried)
3 small ripe tomatoes	4 tablespoons butter
4 stalks celery	Salt and white pepper to taste
2½ cups diced potatoes	1 cup grated Parmesan cheese
1 bouillon cube	¼ pound ditalini
1 tablespoon chopped parsley	

Sauté the finely chopped onion in the oil in a saucepan until golden. Add the chopped tomatoes and stir for a few minutes. Slice the celery, including the leaves (make sure the celery is very tender). Add the celery and potatoes to the saucepan. Add 2 quarts of boiling water and the bouillon cube. Stir well, bring to a boil again, and cook for 20 minutes. Combine the very finely chopped parsley and basil with the softened butter, a pinch each of salt and white pepper, and ¼ cup Parmesan, forming a smooth paste. Add to the saucepan. Add the ditalini and cook for 10 minutes over moderate heat, stirring often. Serve with the remaining Parmesan sprinkled on top. Serves 4.

GARDENER'S HEARTY SOUP
(*Zuppa dell'Ortolano*)

During the summer my wife and I used to go every weekend to Sabaudia, a small village on the coast 50 miles from Rome. This is where we met the little old lady who gave us this hearty soup recipe, which she made from her own garden-fresh vegetables.

Cooking time: 30 minutes

1 large onion	1 medium zucchini
1 small leek	1 medium potato
4 tablespoons oil	½ cup shelled green peas
3 small ripe tomatoes	½ cup alphabet pasta
1 bouillon cube	4 basil leaves (or ¼ teaspoon
2 carrots	dried)
2 stalks celery	Salt and pepper to taste
¼ pound green beans	1 cup grated Parmesan cheese

Sauté the finely chopped onion and leek in the oil in a saucepan until golden. Add the cut-up tomatoes and stir for 2 minutes. Add 2 quarts of water in which the bouillon cube has been dissolved. Bring to a boil. In the meantime, cut the carrots, celery, green beans, zucchini, and potato into julienne strips. Add to the saucepan together with the peas. Allow to boil over moderate heat for 25 minutes. Then add the pasta and cook for 5 more minutes. Be careful not to boil too rapidly, but at the same time it should not boil too slowly. Finely chop the basil and add. Season with salt and pepper. Dust with Parmesan and serve. If desired, this soup may be poured over slices of bread fried in butter. Serves 4.

SOUP WITH BROCCOLI AND BUCATINI
(*Zuppa di Bucatini con Broccoli*)

Cooking time: 40 minutes

½ pound broccoli

4 tablespoons oil

2 cloves garlic

1 tablespoon anchovy fillets
  (half of 2-ounce can)

2 small ripe tomatoes

Salt and pepper to taste

¼ pound bucatini

Cut the broccoli into small pieces and put in a saucepan with 2 quarts of lukewarm water with 3 tablespoons of salt. Set aside for use later. Sauté in the oil in another saucepan the very finely chopped garlic. Add the anchovies before the garlic begins to color and continue to sauté, crushing them with a wooden spoon so that they disintegrate. Add the chopped tomatoes and stir for 3 minutes. Add 2 quarts of water and bring to a boil. Add the broccoli, which you have removed from the salted water. Cook for 30 minutes over moderate heat. Add salt and pepper if needed. Add the bucatini broken into 1½-inch lengths. Cook for 10 minutes. May be served hot or cold. Serves 4.

SOUP JULIENNE
(*Zuppa Giulienne*)

Cooking time: 30 minutes

1 medium onion	¼ pound green beans
1 small leek	½ cup shelled green peas
3 tablespoons oil	Salt and white pepper to taste
1 bouillon cube	2 basil leaves (or ⅛ teaspoon
2 carrots	dried)
2 stalks celery	2 tablespoons butter
2 stalks Swiss chard	1 cup grated Parmesan cheese
2 potatoes	¼ teaspoon saffron
1 turnip	½ cup alphabet pasta

Cut the onion and leek into thin julienne strips and sauté in the oil in a saucepan. Do not allow to color. Dissolve the bouillon cube in 2 quarts of water and add to the saucepan. When the water comes to a boil, add the carrots, celery, and Swiss chard, which have been cut into 2-inch julienne strips. Do not allow the water to boil too rapidly. Add the potatoes, turnip, and beans, also cut into thin julienne strips, and the peas. Add salt and pepper. Cook for 25 minutes over moderate heat. Chop the basil very finely and combine it with the softened butter and half the Parmesan, forming a smooth paste. Add to the saucepan and stir. Dissolve the saffron in 2 tablespoons of hot water and add to the soup together with alphabet pasta. Simmer for 5 minutes more, then remove from fire and serve with the rest of the Parmesan sprinkled on top. Serves 4.

VERMICELLI SOUP WITH BASIL
(*Zuppa di Vermicelli al Basilico*)

Cooking time: 20 minutes

1 medium onion	Salt and pepper to taste
4 tablespoons oil	¼ pound vermicelli
1 stalk celery	6 basil leaves (or ¼ teaspoon
2 small ripe tomatoes	dried)
2 potatoes	2 tablespoons butter
1 cup cooked navy beans	⅔ cup grated Parmesan cheese

Sauté the thinly sliced onion in the oil in a saucepan large enough to contain soup for 4 persons. When the onion is almost golden, add the chopped celery and chopped tomatoes. Cook over low heat for 3 minutes, then add 2 quarts of water. Dice the potatoes and add together with the beans, salt and pepper. Cook for 10 minutes. Add the vermicelli broken into 1½-inch lengths and cook for 7 minutes more. While the vermicelli are cooking, finely chop the basil and combine it with the softened butter, a pinch of pepper, and the Parmesan. Add this mixture 2 minutes before the vermicelli are cooked. Remove pot from fire and cover. Allow to rest for 2 minutes before serving. Serves 4.

TOMATO PURÉE AND VERMICELLI SOUP
(*Zuppa di Purè di Pomodoro ai Vermicelli*)

Cooking time: 30 minutes

1 large onion	1 whole clove
½ pound butter	1 bay leaf
2 medium-size ripe tomatoes	Salt and pepper to taste
2 tablespoons chopped parsley	2 bouillon cubes
½ stalk celery	2 tablespoons flour
2 basil leaves (or ⅛ teaspoon dried)	¼ pound vermicelli
	1 cup grated Gruyère cheese

Cut the onion into julienne strips and sauté in 3 tablespoons of the butter in a saucepan until almost golden. Add the cut-up tomatoes, parsley, celery, basil, whole clove, bay leaf, salt and pepper. Cover the saucepan and cook for 20 minutes. In the meantime, dissolve the bouillon cubes in 3 cups of hot water. In another saucepan melt 5 tablespoons of the butter and add the flour, stirring continuously with a wooden spoon or, better still, a wire whisk. Gradually add the broth you have made, stirring constantly. A delicate cream should be the result. Pass the contents of the other saucepan through the fine blade of a food mill, making sure to remove the whole clove first. Combine with the creamy sauce you have made, taste for salt, and bring to a boil again. Add the vermicelli broken into 1½-inch lengths and continue to cook for 10 minutes. Add the grated Gruyère and serve immediately.
Serves 4.

MINESTRONE ITALIAN STYLE
(Minestrone all'Italiana)

Cooking time: 30 minutes

1 medium onion
1 small leek
2 tablespoons oil
3 slices bacon
Salt
2 small ripe tomatoes
1½ stalks celery
1 large carrot
¾ cup chopped cabbage
1 small potato

1 small zucchini
¾ cup cooked navy beans
¼ pound bucatini
½ small clove garlic
3 basil leaves (or ¼ teaspoon
   dried)
Pepper
½ cup grated pecorino cheese
   (or any sharp cheese)

Chop together the onion and the leek. Sauté in oil in a saucepan together with the chopped bacon. When golden, add salt and the cut-up tomatoes. Stir for 2 minutes. Pour in 8 cups of water and bring to a boil. In the meantime, coarsely chop the celery, carrot, cabbage, potatoe, and zucchini, and add to saucepan together with the beans. Add salt to taste. Boil for 20 minutes more. Add the bucatini broken into 1½-inch lengths and cook for 10 minutes more. While the pasta is cooking, chop together the crushed garlic and the basil. Mix with a generous pinch of pepper and the grated cheese. Add to the minestrone when the pasta is cooked. Stir and serve.
Serves 4.

MINESTRONE OF PASTA AND BEANS, VENETIAN STYLE
(Minestrone di Pasta e Fagioli alla Veneziana)

Cooking time: 60 minutes

½ pound navy beans
1 clove garlic
2 slices bacon
1 onion
4 tablespoons oil
3 stalks celery
3 fresh sage leaves (or ¼
   teaspoon dried)

2 small ripe tomatoes
Salt and pepper to taste
½ pound small ditali
⅔ cup grated pecorino cheese
   (or any sharp cheese)

Cook the beans in 5 cups of unsalted water for 50 minutes. While they are cooking crush the clove of garlic with the flat side of the blade of a knife. Cut the thinly sliced bacon into thin strips. Chop together *very* finely the crushed garlic and the bacon. Thinly slice the onion and sauté in the oil in a saucepan until golden. Add the garlic-bacon mixture and stir. Add the finely chopped celery, whole sage leaves, and the tomatoes cut in small pieces. Add salt and pepper. Pour in ½ cup water and cook over moderate heat for 30 minutes. When the beans are cooked, add them with all their water to the saucepan. Stir and bring to a boil again. Taste for salt. Add the small ditali and cook for 10 minutes over moderate heat. Stir often. When cooked, add a generous pinch of pepper and the grated pecorino and serve. Serves 4.

MINESTRONE NEAPOLITAN
(*Minestrone alla Napoletana*)

This recipe was given to me by the Neapolitan restaurant Starita.

Cooking time: 50 minutes

1 medium onion	Salt and pepper to taste
4 tablespoons butter	2 slices bacon
2 tablespoons oil	½ clove garlic
1 leek	2 basil leaves (or ⅛ teaspoon
1 large carrot	dried)
1 small zucchini	1 cup grated Parmesan cheese
2 stalks celery	¼ pound alphabet pasta
¼ pound navy beans (1 cup) freshly shelled	

Sauté the chopped onion in 2 tablespoons of the butter and 1 tablespoon of the oil in a saucepan until almost golden. Add the chopped leek and sauté for 1 minute more. Pour in 8 cups of water. Add the chopped carrot, zucchini, celery, and the shelled beans. Add salt and pepper. Stir and cook for 40 minutes over moderate heat. In a small skillet brown the finely diced bacon in 1 tablespoon of the oil. Crush the half clove of garlic and chop *very* finely together with the basil. Add to the remaining 2 tablespoons of butter 1 pinch of pepper and the grated cheese, working the mixture with a small spatula until a smooth paste results. Add the pasta to the

minestrone. When it is cooked, add the bacon with the oil and the paste you have made. Stir and cover the saucepan. Remove from the heat and allow to rest for 2 minutes before serving.
Serves 4.

MINESTRONE WITH SQUASH
(*Minestrone alla Zucca*)

Cooking time: 50 minutes

2 slices bacon	1 bay leaf
4 tablespoons oil	2 small ripe tomatoes
1 medium onion	Salt and pepper to taste
1 clove garlic	1 bouillon cube
2 stalks celery	½ pound yellow squash
3 leaves fresh sage (or ¼	½ pound bucatini
teaspoon dried)	⅔ cup grated Cheddar cheese

Cut the bacon into very thin julienne strips and brown in the oil in a saucepan together with the finely sliced onion and the unpeeled clove of garlic. When brown, add the sliced celery, the sage, and the bay leaf. Stir. Add the cut-up tomatoes, salt and pepper. Stir for 2 minutes. Dissolve the bouillon cube in 1 cup of hot water and pour into saucepan. Cook over moderate heat for 20 minutes. Pass the entire contents of the saucepan through the fine blade of a food mill or blend in a blender. Return to the saucepan, add 3 cups of hot water, and bring to a boil over high heat. Add the squash, which you have previously diced after having peeled it and removed all its filaments. When the minestrone comes to a boil again, lower the heat to moderate and cook for 30 minutes more. Ten minutes before the minestrone is ready, add the bucatini broken into 1-inch lengths. Cook for 10 minutes. Add a generous pinch of pepper and the grated cheese and serve. Serves 4.

MINESTRONE WITH BACON
(*Minestrone al Bacon*)

Cooking time: 40 minutes

4 slices bacon	¼ pound cabbage
3 tablespoons oil	1 bouillon cube
1 large onion	Salt and pepper to taste
1 small ripe tomato	1 small clove garlic
5 carrots	3 basil leaves (or ¼ teaspoon
2 stalks celery	dried)
2 medium potatoes	½ cup grated Parmesan cheese
¼ pound endive	½ pound bucatini

Cut the sliced bacon into spaghetti-like strips and sauté in the oil in a fairly large saucepan until brown. With a slotted spoon remove the bacon from the oil and drain on paper toweling. Sauté the thinly sliced onion in the oil left in the saucepan. When golden, add the chopped tomato and stir. Add the coarsely chopped carrots and celery and cook for 5 minutes, adding very little water if necessary. Add the diced potatoes, the thinly sliced endive and cabbage, and 3 cups of hot water in which the bouillon cube has been dissolved. Bring to a boil and add salt and pepper. Cook for 25 minutes. Crush the clove of garlic and chop it very finely together with the basil. Mix with a pinch of pepper and 2 teaspoons of the grated cheese and set aside for use later. Ten minutes before the minestrone is ready, add the bucatini cut into 1-inch lengths. Also add the chopped basil-garlic mixture. Stir often, tasting for salt and adding liquid if necessary. Cook for 10 minutes. Add the browned bacon and the grated Parmesan and serve. Serves 4.

MINESTRONE PUGLIA STYLE
(*Minestrone alla Pugliese*)

Cooking time: 50 minutes

1 large onion	Salt and pepper to taste
4 tablespoons oil	3 basil leaves (or ¼ teaspoon
2 stalks celery	dried)
2 ripe small tomatoes	4 tablespoons butter
1 bouillon cube	⅔ cup grated pecorino or
½ pound potatoes	Parmesan cheese
¼ pound cabbage	½ pound farfallette
½ cup shelled green peas	

Sauté the finely chopped onion in the oil in a saucepan until almost golden. Add the chopped celery and stir for a few minutes. Add the cut-up tomatoes and stir continuously for 3 minutes. Pour in the bouillon cube dissolved in 3 cups of hot water. Bring to a boil. Dice the potatoes and add. Also add the thinly sliced cabbage and the peas, salt and pepper. Cook over moderate heat for 30 minutes. In the meantime, finely chop the basil and mix it with the softened butter, a pinch of pepper, and 2 teaspoons of the grated cheese, working it with a small spatula until a smooth paste results. When the minestrone is almost ready, taste for salt and add the farfallette. Cook for 7 minutes, stirring often. Add the paste you have made and stir again. Add the remaining grated cheese and serve.
Serves 4.

SOUP WITH SMALL PENNE
(*Penne Piccole in Minestra*)

A lot of housewives don't like to cook cabbage because of the smell it releases during cooking. In this recipe you will not have to worry about that because the smell of the cabbage mixed with the perfumes of the other vegetables is unnoticeable. But, here's a great tip for those who do not know how to prevent cabbage from smelling during cooking: add two slices of bread to the cooking water.

Cooking time: 40 minutes

3 slices bacon
2 tablespoons oil
1 large onion
1 large carrot
2 stalks celery
¼ pound white cabbage

1 medium potato
Salt and pepper to taste
Generous ¼ pound small penne
2 tablespoons chopped parsley
1 cup grated Parmesan cheese

Brown the chopped bacon in the oil in a large saucepan. Add the thinly sliced onion and sauté until golden—about 5 minutes. Add 10 cups of water. Thinly slice the carrot, celery, cabbage, and potato and add. Add salt and pepper. Cook for 30 minutes. Now add the small penne and cook for 10 minutes more. Add the chopped parsley and the grated cheese. Stir and serve. Serves 4.

CREAM OF TOMATO SOUP WITH CROUTONS
(*Crema di Pomodoro con Crostini di Pane*)

Cooking time: 40 minutes

2 cups milk
2 pounds tomatoes (6 or 7 medium)
½ cup butter
1 medium onion
2 bay leaves

Salt and white pepper to taste
8 tablespoons potato flour
½ cup of alphabet pasta
4 slices bread
1 cup grated Gruyère cheese

First of all bring the milk to a full boil and allow to cool until it is tepid. Wash the tomatoes, cut them up, and put in a saucepan together with 5 tablespoons of the butter, the sliced onion, the bay leaves, and 1 cup of water. Also add salt and white pepper. Boil for 30 minutes. Put through a food mill and return to the saucepan. Add the potato flour to the lukewarm milk, stirring until smooth. Add to the tomato mixture, stirring continuously. Cook over low heat for 10 minutes. Add ½ cup of alphabet pasta 5 minutes before the mixture is finished cooking. Cut the bread into small dice and fry in a skillet with the rest of the butter. Pour the soup over the croutons, which you have placed in each dish, sprinkle with the grated cheese, and serve. Serves 4.

Index

294 INDEX